PUBLISHED BY THE

AMERICAN TRACT SOCIETY,

150 NASSAU-STREET, NEW YORK.

CONTENTS.

THE

EFFECTS OF ARDENT SPIRITS

UPON

THE HUMAN BODY AND MIND.

BY BENJAMIN RUSH, M. D.

By ardent spirits, I mean those liquors only which are obtained by distillation from fermented substances of any kind. To their effects upon the bodies and minds of men, the following inquiry shall be exclusively confined.

The effects of ardent spirits divide themselves into such as are of a prompt, and such as are of a chronic nature. The former discover themselves in drunkenness; and the latter in a numerous train of diseases and vices of the body and mind.

I. I shall begin by briefly describing their prompt or immediate effects in a fit of drunkenness.

This odious disease—for by that name it should be called—appears with more or less of the following symptoms, and most commonly in the order in which I shall enumerate them.

1. Unusual garrulity.
2. Unusual silence.
3. Captiousness, and a disposition to quarrel.
4. Uncommon good-humor, and an insipid simpering, or laugh.
5. Profane swearing and cursing.
6. A disclosure of their own or other people's secrets.
7. A rude disposition to tell those persons in company whom they know, their faults.
8. Certain immodest actions. I am sorry to say this sign of the first stage of drunkenness sometimes appears in women, who, when sober, are uniformly remarkable for chaste and decent manners.
9. A clipping of words.
10. Fighting; a black eye, or a swelled nose, often mark this grade of drunkenness.

11. Certain extravagant acts which indicate a temporary fit of madness. These are singing, hallooing, roaring, imitating the noises of brute animals, jumping, tearing off clothes, dancing naked, breaking glasses and china, and dashing other articles of household furniture upon the ground or floor. After a while the paroxysm of drunkenness is completely formed. The face now becomes flushed, the eyes project, and are somewhat watery, winking is less frequent than is natural; the under lip is protruded—the head inclines a little to one shoulder—the jaw falls—belchings and hiccough take place—the limbs totter—the whole body staggers. The unfortunate subject of this history next falls on his seat—he looks around him with a vacant countenance, and mutters inarticulate sounds to himself—he attempts to rise and walk: in this attempt he falls upon his side, from which he gradually turns upon his back: he now closes his eyes and falls into a profound sleep, frequently attended with snoring, and profuse sweats, and sometimes with such a relaxation of the muscles which confine the bladder and the lower bowels, as to produce a symptom which delicacy forbids me to mention. In this condition he often lies from ten, twelve, and twenty-four hours, to two, three, four, and five days, an object of pity and disgust to his family and friends. His recovery from this fit of intoxication is marked with several peculiar appearances. He opens his eyes and closes them again—he gapes and stretches his limbs—he then coughs and pukes—his voice is hoarse—he rises with difficulty, and staggers to a chair—his eyes resemble balls of fire—his hands tremble—he loathes the sight of food—he calls for a glass of spirits to compose his stomach—now and then he emits a deep-fetched sigh, or groan, from a transient twinge of conscience; but he more frequently scolds, and curses every thing around him. In this stage of languor and stupidity he remains for two or three days, before he is able to resume his former habits of business and conversation.

Pythagoras, we are told, maintained that the souls of men after death expiated the crimes committed by them in this world, by animating certain brute animals; and that the souls of those animals, in their turns, entered into men, and carried with them all their peculiar qualities and vices. This doctrine of one of the wisest and best of the Greek philosophers, was probably intended only to convey a lively idea of the changes which are induced in the body and mind of man by a fit of drunkenness. In folly, it causes him to resemble a calf—in stupidity, an ass—in roaring, a mad bull—in quarrelling and fighting, a dog—in cruelty, a tiger—in fetor, a skunk—in filthiness, a hog—and in obscenity, a he-goat.

It belongs to the history of drunkenness to remark, that its paroxysms occur, like the paroxysms of many diseases, at certain periods, and after longer or shorter intervals. They often begin with annual, and gradually increase in their frequency, until they appear in quarterly, monthly, weekly, and quotidian or daily periods. Finally, they afford scarcely any marks of remission, either during the day or the night. There was a citizen of Philadelphia, many years ago, in whom drunkenness appeared in this protracted form. In speaking of him to one of his neighbors, I said, "Does he not *sometimes* get drunk?" "You mean," said his neighbor, "is he not *sometimes* sober?"

It is further remarkable, that drunkenness resembles certain hereditary, family, and contagious diseases. I have once known it to descend from a father to four out of five of his children. I have seen three, and once four brothers, who were born of sober ancestors, affected by it; and I have heard of its speading through a whole family composed of members not originally related to each other. These facts are important, and should not be overlooked by parents, in deciding upon the matrimonial connections of their children.

II. Let us next attend to the chronic effects of ardent spirits upon the body and mind. In the body they dispose to every form of acute disease; they moreover *excite* fevers in persons predisposed to them from other causes. This has been remarked in all the yellow-fevers which have visited the cities of the United States. Hard-drinkers seldom escape, and rarely recover from them. The following diseases are the usual consequences of the habitual use of ardent spirits:

1. A decay of appetite, sickness at stomach, and a puking of bile, or a discharge of a frothy and viscid phlegm, by hawking, in the morning.

2. Obstructions of the liver. The fable of Prometheus, on whose liver a vulture was said to prey constantly, as a punishment for his stealing fire from heaven, was intended to illustrate the painful effects of ardent spirits upon that organ of the body.

3. Jaundice, and dropsy of the belly and limbs, and finally of every cavity in the body. A swelling in the feet and legs is so characteristic a mark of habits of intemperance, that the merchants in Charleston, I have been told, cease to trust the planters of South Carolina as soon as they perceive it. They very naturally conclude industry and virtue to be extinct in that man, in whom that symptom of disease has been produced by the intemperate use of distilled spirits.

4. Hoarseness, and a husky cough, which often terminate in consumption, and sometimes in an acute and fatal disease of the lungs.

5. Diabetes, that is, a frequent and weakening discharge of pale or sweetish urine.

6. Redness, and eruptions on different parts of the body. They generally begin on the nose, and after gradually extending all over the face, sometimes descend to the limbs in the form of leprosy. They have been called "rum-buds," when they appear in the face. In persons who have occasionally survived these effects of ardent spirits on the skin, the face after a while becomes bloated, and its redness is succeeded by a death-like paleness. Thus, the same fire which produces a red color in iron, when urged to a more intense degree, produces what has been called a white-heat.

7. A fetid breath, composed of every thing that is offensive in putrid animal matter.

8. Frequent and disgusting belchings. Dr. Haller relates the case of a notorious drunkard having been suddenly destroyed, in consequence of the vapor discharged from his stomach by belching, accidentally taking fire by coming in contact with the flame of a candle.

9. Epilepsy.

10. Gout, in all its various forms of swelled limbs, colic, palsy, and apoplexy.

11. Lastly, madness. The late Dr. Waters, while he acted as house-pupil and apothecary of the Pennsylvania

hospital, assured me, that in one-third of the patients confined by this terrible disease, it had been induced by ardent spirits.

Most of the diseases which have been enumerated are of a mortal nature. They are more certainly induced, and terminate more speedily in death, when spirits are taken in such quantities, and at such times, as to produce frequent intoxication; but it may serve to remove an error with which some intemperate people console themselves, to remark, that ardent spirits often bring on fatal diseases without producing drunkenness. I have known many persons destroyed by them who were never completely intoxicated during the whole course of their lives. The solitary instances of longevity which are now and then met with in hard-drinkers, no more disprove the deadly effects of ardent spirits, than the solitary instances of recoveries from apparent death by drowning, prove that there is no danger to life from a human body lying an hour or two under water.

The body, after its death from the use of distilled spirits, exhibits, by dissection, certain appearances which are of a peculiar nature. The fibres of the stomach and bowels are contracted—abscesses, gangrene, and schirri are found in the viscera. The bronchial vessels are contracted—the bloodvessels and tendons in many parts of the body are more or less ossified, and even the hair of the head possesses a crispness which renders it less valuable to wig-makers than the hair of sober people.

Not less destructive are the effects of ardent spirits upon the human mind. They impair the memory, debilitate the understanding, and pervert the moral faculties. It was probably from observing these effects of intemperance in drinking upon the mind, that a law was formerly passed in Spain which excluded drunkards from being witnesses in a court of justice. But the demoralizing effects of distilled spirits do not stop here. They produce not only falsehood, but fraud, theft, uncleanliness, and murder. Like the demoniac mentioned in the New Testament, their name is "Legion," for they convey into the soul a host of vices and crimes.

A more affecting spectacle cannot be exhibited than a person into whom this infernal spirit, generated by habits of intemperance, has entered: it is more or less affecting, according to the station the person fills in a family, or in society, who is possessed by it. Is he a husband? How deep the anguish which rends the bosom of his wife! Is she a wife? Who can measure the shame and aversion which she excites in her husband? Is he the father, or is she the mother of a family of children? See their averted looks from their parent, and their blushing looks at each other. Is he a magistrate? or has he been chosen to fill a high and respectable station in the councils of his country? What humiliating fears of corruption in the administration of the laws, and of the subversion of public order and happiness, appear in the countenances of all who see him. Is he a minister of the gospel? Here language fails me. If angels weep, it is at such a sight.

In pointing out the evils produced by ardent spirits, let us not pass by their effects upon the estates of the persons who are addicted to them. Are they inhabitants of cities? Behold their houses stripped gradually of their furniture, and pawned, or sold by a constable, to pay tavern debts. See their names upon record in the dockets of every court, and whole pages of newspapers filled with advertisements of their estates for public sale. Are they inhabitants of country places? Behold their houses with shattered windows—their barns with leaky roofs—their gardens overrun with weeds—their fields with broken fences—their hogs without yokes—their sheep without wool—their cattle and horses without fat—and their children, filthy and half-clad, without manners, principles, and morals. This picture of agricultural wretchedness is seldom of long duration. The farms and property thus neglected and depreciated, are seized and sold for the benefit of a group of creditors. The children that were born with the prospect of inheriting them, are bound out to service in the neighborhood; while their parents, the unworthy authors of their misfortunes, ramble into new and distant settlements, alternately fed on their way by the hand of charity, or a little casual labor.

Thus we see poverty and misery, crimes and infamy, diseases and death, are all the natural and usual consequences of the intemperate use of ardent spirits.

I have classed death among the consequences of hard drinking. But it is not death from the immediate hand of the Deity, nor from any of the instruments of it which were created by him: it is death from *suicide*. Yes, thou poor degraded creature who art daily lifting the poisoned bowl to thy lips, cease to avoid the unhallowed ground in which the self-murderer is interred, and wonder no longer that the sun should shine, and the rain fall, and the grass look green upon his grave. *Thou* art perpetrating gradually, by the use of ardent spirits, what he has effected suddenly by opium or a halter. Considering how many circumstances from surprise, or derangement, may palliate his guilt, or that, unlike yours, it was not preceded and accompanied by any other crime, it is probable his condemnation will be less than yours at the day of judgment.

I shall now take notice of the occasions and circumstances which are supposed to render the use of ardent spirits necessary, and endeavor to show that the arguments in favor of their use in such cases are founded in error, and that in each of them ardent spirits, instead of affording strength to the body, increase the evils they are intended to relieve.

1. They are said to be necessary in very cold weather. This is far from being true, for the temporary warmth they produce is always succeeded by a greater disposition in the body to be affected by cold. Warm dresses, a plentiful meal just before exposure to the cold, and eating occasionally a little gingerbread, or any other cordial food, is a much more durable method of preserving the heat of the body in cold weather.

2. They are said to be necessary in very warm weather. Experience proves that they increase, instead of lessening the effects of heat upon the body, and thereby dispose to diseases of all kinds. Even in the warm climate of the West Indies, Dr. Bell asserts this to be true. "Rum," says this author, "whether used habitually, moderately, or in excessive quantities, in the West Indies, always diminishes the strength of the body, and renders men more susceptible of disease, and unfit for any service in which vigor or activity is required."* As well might we throw oil into a house, the roof of which was on fire, in order to

* See his "Inquiry into the Causes which Produce, and the Means of Preventing Diseases among British Officers, Soldiers, and others, in the West Indies."

prevent the flames from extending to its inside, as pour ardent spirits into the stomach to lessen the effects of a hot sun upon the skin.

3. Nor do ardent spirits lessen the effects of hard labor upon the body. Look at the horse, with every muscle of his body swelled from morning till night in the plough, or a team; does he make signs for a draught of toddy, or a glass of spirits, to enable him to cleave the ground, or to climb a hill? No; he requires nothing but cool water and substantial food. There is no nourishment in ardent spirits. The strength they produce in labor is of a transient nature, and is always followed by a sense of weakness nd fatigue.

DANGER FROM ARDENT SPIRITS.

Every man is in danger of becoming a drunkard who is in the habit of drinking ardent spirits—1. When he is warm. 2. When he is cold. 3. When he is wet. 4. When he is dry. 5. When he is dull. 6. When he is lively. 7. When he travels. 8. When he is at home. 9. When he is in company. 10. When he is alone. 11. When he is at work. 12. When he is idle. 13. Before meals. 14. After meals. 15. When he gets up. 16. When he goes to bed. 17. On holidays. 18. On public occasions. 19. On any day; or, 20. On any occasion.

PUBLISHED BY THE AMERICAN TRACT SOCIETY.

ON THE

TRAFFIC IN ARDENT SPIRIT.

ARDENT spirit is composed of alcohol and water, in nearly equal proportions. Alcohol is composed of hydrogen, carbon, and oxygen, in the proportion of about fourteen, fifty-two, and thirty-four parts to the hundred. It is, in its nature, as manifested by its effects, a *poison*. When taken in any quantity it disturbs healthy action in the human system, and in large doses suddenly destroys life. It resembles opium in its nature, and arsenic in its effects. And though when mixed with water, as in ardent spirit, its evils are somewhat modified, they are by no means prevented. Ardent spirit is an enemy to the human constitution, and cannot be used as a drink without injury. Its ultimate tendency invariably is, to produce weakness, not strength; sickness, not health; death, not life.

Consequently, to use it is an immorality. It is a violation of the will of God, and a sin in magnitude equal to all the evils, temporal and eternal, which flow from it. Nor can the furnishing of ardent spirit for the use of others be accounted a less sin, inasmuch as this tends to produce evils greater than for an individual merely to drink it. And if a man knows, or has the opportunity of knowing, the nature and effects of the traffic in this article, and yet continues to be engaged in it, he may justly be regarded as an immoral man; and for the following reasons, viz.

Ardent spirit, as a drink, is *not needful*. All men lived without it, and all the business of the world was conducted without it, for thousands of years. It is not three hundred years since it began to be generally used as a drink in Great Britain, nor one hundred years since it became common in America. Of course it is not needful.

It is *not useful*. Those who do not use it are, other things being equal, in all respects better than those who do. Nor does the fact that persons have used it with more or less frequency, in a greater or smaller quantity, for a longer or shorter time, render it either needful, or useful, or harmless, or right for them to continue to use it. More than a million of persons in this country, and multitudes in other countries, who once did use it, and thought it needful, have, within five years, ceased to use it, and they have found that they are in all respects better without it. And this number is so great, of all ages, and conditions, and employments, as to render it certain, should the experiment be fairly made, that this would be the case with all. Of course, ardent spirit, as a drink, is not useful.

It is *hurtful*. Its whole influence is injurious to the body and the mind for this world and the world to come.

1. It forms an *unnecessary, artificial, and very dangerous appetite*; which, by gratification, like the desire for sinning, in the man who sins, tends continually to increase. No man can form this appetite without increasing his danger of dying a drunkard, and exerting an influence which tends to perpetuate drunkenness, and all its abominations, to the end of the world. Its very formation, therefore, is a violation of the will of God. It is, in its nature, an immorality, and springs from an inordinate desire of a kind or degree of bodily enjoyment—animal gratification, which God has shown to be inconsistent with his glory, and the highest

good of man. It shows that the person who forms it is not satisfied with the proper gratification of those appetites and passions which God has given him, or with that kind and degree of bodily enjoyment which infinite wisdom and goodness have prescribed as the utmost that can be possessed consistently with a person's highest happiness and usefulness, the glory of his Maker, and the good of the universe. That person covets more animal enjoyment; to obtain it he forms a new appetite, and in doing this he rebels against God.

That desire for increased animal enjoyment from which rebellion springs is sin, and all the evils which follow in its train are only so many voices by which Jehovah declares "the way of transgressors is hard." The person who has formed an appetite for ardent spirit, and feels uneasy if he does not gratify it, has violated the divine arrangement, disregarded the divine will, and if he understands the nature of what he has done, and approves of it, and continues in it, it will ruin him. He will show that there is one thing in which he will not have God to reign over him. And should he keep the whole law, and yet continue knowingly, habitually, wilfully, and perseveringly to offend in that one point, he will perish. Then, and then only, according to the Bible, can any man be saved, when he has respect to all the known will of God, and is disposed to be governed by it. He must carry out into practice, with regard to the body and the soul, "Not my will, but thine be done." His grand object must be, to know the will of God, and when he knows it, to be governed by it, and with regard to all things. This, the man who is not contented with that portion of animal enjoyment which the proper gratification of the appetites and passions which God has given him will afford, but forms an appetite for ardent spirit, or continues to gratify it after it is formed, does not do. In this respect, if he understands the nature and effects of his actions, he prefers his own will to the known will of God, and is ripening to hear, from the lips of his Judge, "Those mine enemies, that would not that I should *reign* over them, bring them hither and slay them before me." And the men who traffic in this article, or furnish it as a drink for others, are tempting them to sin, and thus uniting their influence with that of the devil for ever to ruin them. This is an aggravated immorality, and the men who continue to do it are immoral men.

2. The use of ardent spirit, to which the traffic is accessory, causes a great and wicked *waste of property*. All that the users pay for this article is to them lost, and worse than lost. Should the whole which they use sink into the earth, or mingle with the ocean, it would be better for them, and better for the community, than for them to drink it. All which it takes to support the paupers, and prosecute the crimes which ardent spirit occasions, is, to those who pay the money, utterly lost. All the diminution of profitable labor which it occasions, through improvidence, idleness, dissipation, intemperance, sickness, insanity, and premature deaths, is to the community so much utterly lost. And these items, as has often been shown, amount in the United States to more than $100,000,000 a year. To this enormous and wicked waste of property, those who traffic in the article are knowingly accessory.

A portion of what is thus lost by others, they obtain themselves; but without rendering to others any valuable equivalent. This renders their business palpably unjust; as really so as if they should obtain that money by gambling; and it is as really immoral. It is also unjust in another respect: it burdens the community with taxes both for the support of pauperism, and for the prosecution of crimes, and without rendering to that community any adequate compensation. These taxes, as shown by facts, are four times as great as they would be if there were no sellers of ardent spirit. All the profits, with the exception perhaps of a mere pittance which he pays for license, the seller puts into his own pocket, while the burdens are thrown upon the community. This is palpably unjust, and utterly immoral. Of 1,969 paupers in different almshouses in the United States, 1,790, according to the testimony of the overseers of the poor, were made such by spirituous liquor. And of 1,764 criminals in different prisons, more than 1,300 were either intemperate men, or were under the power of intoxicating liquor when the crimes for which they were imprisoned were committed. And of 44 murders, according to the testimony of those who prosecuted or conducted the defence of the murderers, or witnessed their trials, 43 were committed by intemperate men, or upon intemperate men, or those who at the time of the murder were under the power of strong drink.

The Hon. Felix Grundy, United States senator from Tennessee, after thirty years' extensive practice as a lawyer, gives it as his opinion that four-fifths of all the crimes committed in the United States can be traced to intemperance. A similar proportion is stated, from the highest authority, to result from the same cause in Great Britain. And when it is considered that more than 200 murders are committed, and more than 100,000 crimes are prosecuted in the United States in a year, and that such a vast proportion of them are occasioned by ardent spirit, can a doubt remain on the mind of any sober man, that the men who know these facts, and yet continue to traffic in this article, are among the chief causes of crime, and ought to be viewed and treated as immoral men? It is as really immoral for a man, by doing wrong, to excite others to commit crimes, as to commit them himself; and as really unjust wrongfully to take another's property with his consent, as without it. And though it might not be desirable to have such a law, yet no law in the statute-book is more righteous than one which should require that those who make paupers should support them, and those who excite others to commit crimes, should pay the cost of their prosecution, and should, with those who commit them, bear all the evils. And so long as this is not the case they will be guilty, according to the divine law, of defrauding, as well as tempting and corrupting their fellow-men. And though such crimes cannot be prosecuted, and justice be awarded in human courts, their perpetrators will be held to answer, and will meet with full and awful retribution at the divine tribunal. And when judgment is laid to the line, and righteousness to the plummet, they will appear as they really are, criminals, and will be viewed and treated as such for ever.

There is another view in which the traffic in ardent spirit is manifestly highly immoral. It exposes the children of those who use it, in an eminent degree, to dissipation and crime. Of 690 children prosecuted and imprisoned for crimes, more than 400 were from intemperate families. Thus the venders of this liquor exert an influence which tends strongly to ruin not only those who use it, but their children; to render them far more liable to idleness, profligacy, and ruin, than the children of those who do not use it; and through them to extend these evils to others, and to perpetuate them to future generations. This is a sin of which all who traffic in ardent spirit are guilty. Often the deepest pang which a dying parent feels for his children, is lest, through the instrumentality of such men, they should be ruined. And is it not horrible wickedness for them, by exposing for sale one of the chief causes of this ruin, to tempt them in the way to death? If he who takes money from others without an equivalent, or wickedly destroys property, is an immoral man, what is he who destroys character, who corrupts children and youth, and exerts an influence to extend and perpetuate immorality and crime through future generations? This every vender of ardent spirit does; and if he continues in this business with a knowledge of the subject, it marks him as an habitual and persevering violater of the will of God.

3. Ardent spirit *impairs*, and often *destroys reason*. Of 781 maniacs in different insane hospitals, 392, according to the testimony of their own friends, were rendered maniacs by strong drink. And the physicians who had the care of them gave it as their opinion, that this was the case with many of the others. Those who have had extensive experience, and the best opportunities for observation with regard to this malady, have stated, that probably from one-half to three-fourths of the cases of insanity, in many places, are occasioned in the same way. Ardent spirit is a poison so diffusive and subtile that it is found, by actual experiment, to penetrate even the brain.

Dr. Kirk, of Scotland, dissected a man a few hours after death who died in a fit of intoxication; and from the lateral ventricles of the brain he took a fluid distinctly visible to the smell as whiskey; and when he applied a candle to it in a spoon, it took fire and burnt blue; "the lambent blue flame," he says, "characteristic of the poison, playing on the surface of the spoon for some seconds."

It produces also, in the children of those who use it freely, a predisposition to intemperance, insanity, and various diseases of both body and mind, which, if the cause is continued, becomes hereditary, and is transmitted from generation to generation; occasioning a diminution of size, strength, and energy, a feebleness of vision, a feebleness and imbecility of purpose, an obtuseness of intellect, a depravation of moral taste, a premature old age, and a general deterioration of the whole character. This is the case in every country, and in every age.

Instances are known where the first children of a family, who were born when their parents were temperate, have been healthy, intelligent, and active; while the last children, who were born after the parents had become intemperate, were dwarfish and idiotic. A medical gentleman writes, "I have no doubt that a disposition to nervous diseases of a peculiar character is transmitted by drunken parents." Another gentleman states that, in two families within his knowledge, the different stages of intemperance in the parents seemed to be marked by a corresponding deterioration in the bodies and minds of the children. In one case, the eldest of the family is respectable, industrious, and accumulates property; the next is inferior, disposed to be industrious, but spends all he can earn in strong drink. The third is dwarfish in body and mind, and, to use his own language, "a poor, miserable remnant of a man."

In another family of daughters, the first is a smart, active girl, with an intelligent, well-balanced mind; the others are afflicted with different degrees of mental weakness and imbecility, and the youngest is an idiot. Another medical gentleman states, that the first child of a family, who was born when the habits of the mother were good, was healthy and promising; while the four last children, who were born after the mother had become addicted to the habit of using opium, appeared to be stupid; and all, at about the same age, sickened and died of a disease apparently occasioned by the habits of the mother.

Another gentleman mentions a case more common, and more appalling still. A respectable and influential man early in life adopted the habit of using a little ardent spirit daily, because, as he thought, it did him good. He and his six children, three sons and three daughters, are now in the drunkard's grave, and the only surviving child is rapidly following in the same way, to the same dismal end.

The best authorities attribute one-half the madness, three-fourths of the pauperism, and four-fifths of the crimes and wretchedness in Great Britain to the use of strong drink.

4. Ardent spirit increases the number, frequency, and violence of *diseases*, and tends to bring those who use it to a premature grave. In Portsmouth, New Hampshire, of about 7,500 people, twenty-one persons were killed by it in

a year. In Salem, Massachusetts, of 181 deaths, twenty were occasioned in the same way. Of ninety-one adults who died in New Haven, Connecticut, in one year, thirty-two, according to the testimony of the Medical Association, were occasioned, directly or indirectly, by strong drink, and a similar proportion had been occasioned by it in previous years. In New Brunswick, New Jersey, of sixty-seven adult deaths in one year, more than one-third were caused by intoxicating liquor. In Philadelphia, of 4,292 deaths, 700 were, in the opinion of the College of Physicians and Surgeons, caused in the same way. The physicians of Annapolis, Maryland, state that, of thirty-two persons, male and female, who died in 1828, above eighteen years of age, ten, or nearly one-third, died of diseases occasioned by intemperance; that eighteen were males, and that of these, nine, or one-half, died of intemperance. They also say, "When we recollect that even the temperate use, as it is called, of ardent spirits, lays the foundation of a numerous train of incurable maladies, we feel justified in expressing the belief, that were the use of distilled liquors entirely discontinued, the number of deaths among the male adults would be diminished at least one-half."

Says an eminent physician, "Since our people generally have given up the use of spirit, they have not had more than half as much sickness as they had before; and I have no doubt, should all the people of the United States cease to use it, that nearly half the sickness of the country would cease." Says another, after forty years' extensive practice, "Half the men every year who die of fevers might recover, had they not been in the habit of using ardent spirit. Many a man, down for weeks with a fever, had he not used ardent spirit, would not have been confined to his house a day. He might have felt a slight headache, but a little fasting would have removed the difficulty, and the man been well. And many a man who was never intoxicated, when visited with a fever, might be raised up as well as not, were it not for that state of the system which daily moderate drinking occasions, who now, in spite of all that can be done, sinks down and dies."

Nor are we to admit for a moment the popular reasoning, as applicable here, "that the abuse of a thing is no argument against its use;" for, in the language of the late Secretary of the College of Physicians and Surgeons of Philadelphia, Samuel Emlen, M. D., "All use of ardent spirits," *i. e.* as a drink, "is an abuse. They are mischievous under all circumstances." Their tendency, says Dr. Frank, when used even moderately, is to induce disease, premature old age, and death. And Dr. Trotter states, that no cause of disease has so wide a range, or so large a share, as the use of spirituous liquors.

Dr. Harris states, that the *moderate* use of spirituous liquors has destroyed many who were never drunk; and Dr. Kirk gives it as his opinion, that men who were never considered intemperate, by daily drinking have often shortened life more than twenty years; and that the respectable use of this poison kills more men than even drunkenness. Dr. Wilson gives it as his opinion, that the use of spirit in large cities causes more diseases than confined air, unwholesome exhalations, and the combined influence of all other evils.

Dr. Cheyne, of Dublin, Ireland, after thirty years' practice and observation, gives it as his opinion, that should ten young men begin at twenty-one years of age to use but one glass of two ounces a day, and never increase the quantity, nine out of ten would shorten life more than ten years. But should moderate drinkers shorten life only five years, and drunkards only ten, and should there be but four moderate drinkers to one drunkard, it would in thirty years cut off in the United States 32,400,000 years of human life. An aged physician in Maryland states, that when the fever breaks out there, the men who do not use ardent spirit are not half as likely as other men to have it; and that if they do have it, they are ten times as likely to recover. In the island of Key West, on the coast of Florida, after a great mortality, it was found that every person who had died had been in the habit of using ardent spirit. The quantity used was afterwards diminished more than nine-tenths, and the inhabitants became remarkably healthy.

A gentleman of great respectability from the south, states, that those who fall victims to southern climes, are almost invariably addicted to the free use of ardent spirit. Dr. Mosely, after a long residence in the West Indies, declares, "that persons who drink nothing but cold water, or make it their principal drink, are but little affected by tropical climates; that they undergo the greatest fatigue without inconvenience, and are not so subject as others to dangerous diseases;" and Dr. Bell, "that rum, when used even moderately, always diminishes the strength, and renders men more susceptible of disease; and that we might as well throw oil into a house, the roof of which is on fire, in order to prevent the flames from extending to the inside, as to pour ardent spirits into the stomach to prevent the effect of a hot sun upon the skin."

Of seventy-seven persons found dead in different regions of country, sixty-seven, according to the coroners' inquests, were occasioned by strong drink. Nine-tenths of those who die suddenly after the drinking of cold water, have been habitually addicted to the free use of ardent spirit; and that draught of cold water, that effort, or fatigue, or exposure to the sun, or disease, which a man who uses no ardent spirit will bear without inconvenience or danger, will often kill those who use it. Their liability to sickness and to death is often increased tenfold. And to all these evils, those who continue to traffic in it, after all the light which God in his providence has thrown upon the subject, are knowingly accessory. Whether they deal in it by whole sale or retail, by the cargo or the glass, they are, in their influence, drunkard-makers. So are also those who furnish the materials; those who advertise the liquors, and thus promote their circulation; those who lease their tenements to be employed as dram-shops, or stores for the sale of ardent spirit; and those also who purchase their groceries of spirit dealers rather than of others, for the purpose of saving to the amount which the sale of ardent spirit enables such men, without loss, to undersell their neighbors. These are all accessory to the making of drunkards, and as such will be held to answer at the divine tribunal. So are those men who employ their shipping in transporting the liquors, or are in any way knowingly aiding and abetting in perpetuating their use as a drink in the community.

It is estimated that four-fifths of those who were swept away by the late direful visitation of CHOLERA, were such as had been addicted to the use of intoxicating drink. Dr. Bronson, of Albany, who spent some time in Canada, and whose professional character and standing give great weight to his opinions, says, "Intemperance of any species, but particularly intemperance in the use of *distilled liquors*, has been a more productive cause of cholera than any other, and indeed than all others." And can men, for the sake of money, make it a business knowingly and perseveringly to furnish the most productive cause of cholera, and not be guilty of *blood*—not manifest a recklessness of character which will brand the mark of vice and infamy on their foreheads? "Drunkards and tipplers," he adds, "have been searched out with such unerring certainty as to show that the arrows of death have not been dealt out with indiscrimination. An indescribable terror has spread through the ranks of this class of beings. They see the bolts of destruction aimed at their heads, and every one calls himself a victim. There seems to be a natural affinity between cholera and ardent spirit." What, then, in days of exposure to this malady, is so great a nuisance as the places which furnish this poison? Says Dr. Rhinelander, who, with Dr. De Kay, was deputed from New York to visit Canada, "We may be asked who are the victims of this disease? I answer, the intemperate it invariably cuts off." In Montreal, after 1,200 had been attacked, a Montreal paper states, that "not a drunkard who has been attacked has recovered of the disease, and almost all the victims have been at least *moderate* drinkers." In Paris, the 30,000 victims were, with few exceptions, those who freely used intoxicating liquors. Nine-tenths of those who died of the cholera in Poland were of the same class.

In St. Petersburgh and Moscow, the average number of deaths in the bills of mortality, during the prevalence of the cholera, when the people ceased to drink brandy, was no greater than when they used it during the usual months of health—showing that brandy, and attendant dissipation, killed as many people in the same time as even the cholera itself, that pestilence which has spread sackcloth over the nations. And shall the men who know this, and yet continue to furnish it for all who can be induced to buy, escape the execration of being the destroyers of their race? Of more than 1,000 deaths in Montreal, it is stated that only two were members of Temperance societies. It was also stated, that as far as was known no members of Temperance societies in Ireland, Scotland, or England, had yet fallen victims to that dreadful disease.

From Montreal, Dr. Bronson writes, "Cholera has stood up here, as it has done everywhere, the advocate of Temperance. It has pleaded most eloquently, and with tremendous effect. The disease has searched out the haunt of the drunkard, and has seldom left it without bearing away its victim. Even *moderate* drinkers have been but little better off. Ardent spirits, in any shape, and in all quantities, have been *highly* detrimental. Some temperate men resorted to them during the prevalence of the malady as a preventive, or to remove the feeling of uneasiness about the stomach, or for the purpose of drowning their apprehensions, but they did it at their peril."

Says the London Morning Herald, after stating that the cholera fastens its deadly grasp upon this class of men, "The same preference for the intemperate and uncleanly has characterized the cholera *everywhere*. Intemperance is a qualification which it never overlooks. Often has it passed harmless over a wide population of temperate country people, and poured down, as an overflowing scourge, upon the drunkards of some distant town." Says another English publication, "All experience, both in Great Britain and elsewhere, has proved that those who have been addicted to drinking spirituous liquors, and indulging in irregular habits, have been the greatest sufferers from cholera. In some towns the drunkards are all dead." Rammohun Fingee, the famous Indian doctor, says, with regard to India, that people who do not take opium, or spirits, do not take this disorder even when they are with those who have it. Monsieur Huber, who saw 2,160 persons perish in twenty-five days in one town in Russia, says, "It is a most remarkable circumstance, that persons given to drinking have been swept away like flies. In Tiflis, containing 20,000 inhabitants, every drunkard has fallen—all are dead, not one remains."

Dr. Sewall, of Washington city, in a letter from New York, states, that of 204 cases of cholera in the Park hospital, there were only six temperate persons, and that those had recovered; while 122 of the others, when he wrote, had died; and that the facts were similar in all the other hospitals.

In Albany, a careful examination was made by respectable gentlemen into the cases of those who died of the cholera in that city in 1832, over sixteen years of age. The result was examined in detail by nine physicians, members of the medical staff attached to the board of health in that city—all who belong to it, except two, who were at that time absent—and published at their request under the signature of the Chancellor of the State, and the five distinguished gentlemen who compose the Executive Committee of the New York State Temperance Society, and is as follows: number of deaths, 366; viz. intemperate, 140; free drinkers, 55; moderate drinkers, mostly habitual, 131; strictly temperate, who drank no ardent spirits, 5; members of Temperance societies, 2; and when it is recollected that of more than 5,000 members of Temperance societies in the city of Albany, only two, not one in 2,500, fell by this disease, while it cut off more than one in fifty of the inhabitants of that city, we cannot but feel that men who furnish ardent spirit as a drink for their fellow-men, are manifestly inviting the ravages, and preparing the victims of this fatal malady, and of numerous other mortal diseases; and when inquisition is made for blood, and the effects of their employment are examined for the purpose of rendering to them according to their work, they will be found, should they continue, to be guilty of knowingly destroying their fellow-men.

What right have men, by selling ardent spirit, to increase the danger, extend the ravages, and augment and perpetuate the malignancy of the cholera, and multiply upon the community numerous other mortal diseases? Who cannot see that it is a foul, deep, and fatal injury inflicted on society? that it is in a high degree cruel and unjust? that it scatters the population of our cities, renders our business stagnant, and exposes our sons and our daughters to premature and sudden death? So manifestly is this the case, that the board of health of the city of Washington, on the approach of the cholera, declared the vending of ardent spirit, *in any quantity*, to be a *nuisance;* and, as such, ordered that it be discontinued for the space of ninety days. This was done in self-defence, to save the community from the sickness and death which the vending of spirit is adapted to occasion Nor is this tendency to occasion disease and death confined to the time when the cholera is raging.

By the statement of the physicians in Annapolis, Maryland, it appears that the average number of deaths by intemperance for several years, has been one to every 329 inhabitants; which would make in the United States 40,000 in a year. And it is the opinion of physicians, that as many more die of diseases which are induced, or aggravated, and rendered mortal by the use of ardent spirit. And to those results, all who make it, sell it, or use it, are accessory.

It is a principle in law, that the perpetrator of crime, and the accessory to it, are both guilty, and deserving of punishment. Men have been brought to the gallows on this principle. It applies to the law of God. And as the drunkard cannot go to heaven, can drunkard-makers? Are they not, when tried by the principles of the Bible, in view of the developments of Providence, manifestly immoral men? men who, for the sake of money, will knowingly be instrumental in corrupting the character, increasing the diseases, and destroying the lives of their fellow-men?

"But," says one, "I never sell to drunkards; I sell only to sober men." And is that any better? Is it a less evil to the community to make drunkards of sober men than it is to kill drunkards? Ask that widowed mother who did her the greatest evil: the man who only killed her drunken husband, or the man who made a drunkard of her only son? Ask those orphan children who did them the greatest injury: the man who made their once sober, kind, and affectionate father a drunkard, and thus blasted all their hopes, and turned their home, sweet home, into the emblem of hell; or the man who, after they had suffered for years the anguish, the indescribable anguish of the drunkard's children, and seen their heart-broken mother in danger of an untimely grave, only killed their drunken father, and thus caused in their habitation a great calm? Which of these two men brought upon them the greatest evil? Can you doubt? You, then, do nothing but make drunkards of sober men, or expose them to become such. Suppose that all the evils which you may be instrumental in bringing upon other children, were to come upon your own, and that *you* were to bear all the anguish which you may occasion; would you have any doubt that the man who would knowingly continue to be accessory to the bringing of these evils upon you, must be a notoriously wicked man?

5. Ardent spirit destroys the *soul.*

Facts in great numbers are now before the public, which show conclusively that the use of ardent spirit tends strongly to hinder the moral and spiritual illumination and purification of men; and thus to prevent their salvation, and bring upon them the horrors of the second death.

A disease more dreadful than the cholera, or any other that kills the body merely, is raging, and is universal, threatening the endless death of the soul. A remedy is provided all-sufficient, and infinitely efficacious; but the use of ardent spirit aggravates the disease, and with millions and millions prevents the application of the remedy and its effect.

It appears from the fifth report of the American Temperance Society, that more than four times as many, in proportion to the number, over wide regions of country, during the preceding year, have apparently embraced the gospel, and experienced its saving power, from among those who had renounced the use of ardent spirit, as from those who continued to use it.

The committee of the New York State Temperance Society, in view of the peculiar and unprecedented attention to religion which followed the adoption of the plan of abstinence from the use of strong drink, remark, that when this course is taken, the greatest enemy to the work of the Holy Spirit on the minds and hearts of men, appears to be more than half conquered.

In three hundred towns, six-tenths of those who two years ago belonged to Temperance societies, but were not hopefully pious, have since become so; and eight-tenths of those who have within that time become hopefully pious, who did not belong to Temperance societies, have since joined them. In numerous places, where only a minority of the people abstained from the use of ardent spirit, nine-tenths of those who have of late professed the religion of Christ, have been from that minority. This is occasioned in various ways. The use of ardent spirit keeps many away from the house of God, and thus prevents them from coming under the sound of the gospel. And many who do come, it causes to continue stupid, worldly-minded, and unholy. A single glass a day is enough to keep multitudes of men, under the full blaze of the gospel, from ever experiencing its illuminating and purifying power. Even if they come to the light, and it shines upon them, it shines upon darkness, and the darkness does not comprehend it; while multitudes who thus do evil will not come to the light, lest their deeds should be reproved. There is a total contrariety between the effect produced by the Holy Spirit, and the effect of spirituous liquor upon the minds and hearts of men. The latter tends directly and powerfully to counteract the former. It tends to make men feel in a manner which Jesus Christ hates, rich spiritually, increased in goods, and in need of nothing; while it tends for ever to prevent them from feeling, as sinners must feel, to buy of him gold tried in the fire, that they may be rich. Those who use it, therefore, are taking the direct course to destroy their own souls; and those who furnish it, are taking the course to destroy the souls of their fellow-men.

In one town, more than twenty times as many, in proportion to the number, professed the religion of Christ during the past year, of those who did not use ardent spirit, as of those who did; and in another town more than thirty times as many. In other towns, in which from one-third to two-thirds of the people did not use it, and from twenty to forty made a profession of religion, they were all from the same class. What, then, are those men doing who furnish it, but taking the course which is adapted to keep men stupid in sin till they sink into the agonies of the second death? And is not this an immorality of a high and aggravated description? and one which ought to mark every man who understands its nature and effects, and yet continues to live in it, as a notoriously immoral man? What though he does not live in other immoralities—is not this enough? Suppose he should manufacture poisonous miasma, and cause the cholera in our dwellings; sell, knowingly, the cause of disease, and increase more than one-fifth over wide regions of country the number of adult deaths, would he not be a murderer? "I know," says the learned Judge Cranch, "that the cup" which contains ardent spirit "is poisoned; I know that it may cause death, that it may cause more than death, that it may lead to crime, to sin, to the tortures of everlasting remorse. Am I not, then, a murderer? worse than a murderer? as much worse as the soul is better than the body? If ardent spirits were nothing worse than a deadly poison—if they did not excite and inflame all the evil passions—if they did not dim that heavenly light which the Almighty has implanted in our bosoms to guide us through the obscure passages of our pilgrimage—if they did not quench the Holy Spirit in our hearts, they would be comparatively harmless. It is their moral effect—it is the ruin of the *soul* which they produce, that renders them so dreadful. The difference between death by simple poison, and death by habitual intoxication, may extend to the whole difference between ever lasting happiness and eternal death."

And, say the New York State Society, at the head of which is the Chancellor of the State, "Disguise that business as they will, it is still, in its true character, the business of destroying the bodies and souls of men. The vender and the maker of spirits, in the whole range of them, from the pettiest grocer to the most extensive distiller, are fairly chargeable, not only with *supplying* the appetite for spirits, but with *creating* that unnatural appetite; not only with supplying the drunkard with the fuel of his vices, but with *making* the drunkard.

"In reference to the taxes with which the making and vending of spirits loads the community, how unfair towards others is the occupation of the maker and vender of them! A town, for instance, contains one hundred drunkards. The profit of making these drunkards is enjoyed by some half a dozen persons; but the burden of these drunkards rests upon the whole town. We do not suggest that there should be such a law, but we ask whether there would be one law in the whole statute-book more *righteous* than that which should require those who have the profit of making our drunkards to be burdened with the support of them."

Multitudes who once cherished the fond anticipation of happiness in this life and that to come, there is reason to believe, are now wailing beyond the reach of hope, through the influence of ardent spirit; and multitudes more, if men continue to furnish it as a drink, especially sober men, will go down to weep and wail with them to endless ages.

"But," says one, "the traffic in ardent spirit is a lawful business; it is approbated by law, and is therefore right." But the keeping of gambling houses is, in some cases, approbated by human law. Is that therefore right? The keeping of brothels is, in some cases, approbated by law. Is that therefore right? Is it human law that is the standard of morality and religion? May not a man be a notoriously wicked man, and yet not violate human law? The question is, Is it right? Does it accord with the divine law? Does it tend in its effects to bring glory to God in the highest, and to promote the best good of mankind? If not, the word of God forbids it; and if a man who has the means of understanding its nature and effects continues to follow it, he does it at the peril of his soul.

"But," says another, "if I should not sell it, I could not sell so many other things." If you could not, then you are forbidden by the word of God to sell so many other things. And if you continue to make money by that which tends to destroy your fellow-men, you incur the displeasure of Jehovah. "But if I should not sell it, I must change my business." Then you are required by the Lord to change your business. A voice from the throne of his excellent glory cries, "Turn ye, turn ye from this evil way; for why will ye die?"

"If I should turn from it, I could not support my family." This is not true; at least, no one has a right to say that it is true till he has tried it, and done his whole duty by ceasing to do evil and learning to do well, trusting in God, and has found that his family is not supported. Jehovah declares, that such as seek the Lord, and are governed by his will, shall not want any good thing. And till men have made the experiment of obeying him in all things, and found that they cannot support their families, they have no right to say that it is necessary for them to sell ardent spirit. And if they do say this, it is a libel on the divine character and government. There is no truth in it. He who feeds the sparrow and clothes the lily, will, if they do right, provide for them and their families; and there is no shadow of necessity, in order to obtain support, for them to carry on a business which destroys their fellow-men.

"But others will do it, if I do not." Others will send out their vessels, steal the black man, and sell him and his children into perpetual bondage, if you do not. Others will steal, rob, and commit murder, if you do not; and why may not you do it, and have a portion of the profit, as well as they? Because, if you do, you will be a thief, a robber, and a murderer, like them. You will here be partaker of their guilt, and hereafter of their plagues. Every friend, therefore, to you, to your Maker, or the eternal interests of men, will, if acquainted with this subject, say to you, As you value the favor of God, and would escape his righteous and eternal indignation, renounce this work of death; for he that soweth death, shall also reap death.

"But our fathers imported, manufactured, and sold ardent spirit, and were they not good men? Have not they gone to heaven?" Men who professed to be good once had a multiplicity of wives, and have not some of them too gone to heaven? Men who professed to be good once were engaged in the slave-trade, and have not some of them gone to heaven? But can men who understand the will of God with regard to these subjects, continue to do such things now, and yet go to heaven? The principle which applies in this case, and which makes the difference between those who did such things once, and those who continue to do them now, is that to which Jesus Christ referred when he said, "If I had not come and spoken to them, they had not had sin; but now they have no cloak for their sin." The days of that darkness and ignorance which God may have winked at have gone by, and he now commandeth all men to whom his will is made known to repent. Your fathers, when they were engaged in selling ardent spirit, did not know that all men, under all circumstances, would be better without it. They did not know that it caused three-quarters of the pauperism and crime in the land—that it deprived many of reason—greatly increased the number and severity of diseases, and brought down such multitudes to an untimely grave. The facts had not then been collected and published. They did not know that it tended so fatally to obstruct the progress of the Gospel, and ruin, for eternity, the souls of men. You do know it, or have the means of knowing it. You cannot sin with as little guilt as did your fathers. The facts, which are the voice of God in his providence, and manifest his will, are now before the world. By them he has come and spoken to you. And if you continue, under these circumstances, to violate his will, you will have no cloak, no covering, no excuse for your sin. And though sentence against this evil work is not executed at once, judgment, if you continue, will not linger, nor will damnation slumber.

The accessory and the principal, in the commission of crime, are both guilty. Both by human laws are condemned. The principle applies to the law of God; and not only drunkards, but drunkard-makers—not only murderers, but those who excite others to commit murder, and furnish them with the known cause of their evil deeds, will, if they understand what they do, and continue thus to rebel against God, be shut out of heaven.

Among the Jews, if a man had a beast that went out and killed a man, the beast, said Jehovah, shall be slain, and his flesh shall not be eaten. The owner must lose the whole of him as a testimony to the sacredness of human life, and a warning to all not to do any thing, or connive at any thing that tended to destroy it. But the owner, if he did not know that the beast was dangerous, and liable to kill, was not otherwise to be punished. But if he did know, if it had been testified to the owner that the beast was dangerous, and liable to kill, and he did not keep him in, but let him go out, and he killed a man, then, by the direction of Jehovah, the beast and the owner were both to be put to death. The owner, under these circumstances, was held responsible, and justly too, for the injury which his beast might do. Though men are not required or permitted now to execute this law, as they were when God was the Magistrate, yet the reason of the law remains. It is founded in justice, and is eternal. To the pauperism, crime, sickness, insanity, and death temporal and eternal, which ardent spirit occasions, those who knowingly furnish the materials, those who manufacture, and those who sell it, are all accessory, and as such will be held responsible at the divine tribunal. There was a time when the owners did not know the dangerous and destructive qualities of this article—when the facts had not been developed and published, nor the minds of men turned to the subject; when they did not know that it caused such a vast portion of the vice and wretchedness of the community, and such wide-spreading desolation to the temporal and eternal interests of men; and although it then destroyed thousands, for both worlds, the guilt of the men who sold it was comparatively small. But now they sin against light, pouring down upon them with unutterable brightness; and if they know what they do, and in full view of its consequences continue that work of death—not only let the poison go out, but furnish it, and send it out to all who are disposed to purchase—it had been better for them, and better for many others, if they had never been born. For, briefly to sum up what we have said,

1. It is the selling of that, without the use of which nearly all the business of this world was conducted, till within less than three hundred years, and which of course is not *needful.*

2. It is the selling of that which was not generally used by the people of this country for more than a hundred years after the country was settled, and which by hundreds of thousands, and some in all kinds of lawful business, is not used now. Once they did use it, and thought it needful or useful. But by experiment, the best evidence in the world, they have found that they were mistaken, and that they are in all respects better without it. And the cases are so numerous as to make it *certain*, that should the experiment be

fairly made, this would be the case with all. Of course it is not *useful.*

3. It is the selling of that which is a real, a subtile and very destructive *poison* a poison which, by men in health, cannot be taken without deranging healthy action, and inducing more or less disease, both of body and mind; which is, when taken in any quantity, positively *hurtful;* and which is of course forbidden by the word of God.

4. It is the selling of that which tends to form an unnatural, and a very dangerous and destructive appetite; which, by gratification, like the desire of sinning in the man who sins, tends continually to increase, and which thus exposes all who form it to come to a *premature grave.*

5. It is the selling of that which causes a great portion of all the pauperism in our land; and thus, for the benefit of a few—those who sell—brings an enormous tax on the whole community. Is this fair? Is it just? Is it not exposing our children and youth to become drunkards? And is it not inflicting great evils on society?

6. It is the selling of that which excites to a great portion of all the crimes that are committed, and which is thus shown to be in its effects hostile to the moral government of God, and to the social, civil, and religious interests of men; at war with their highest good, both for this life and the life to come.

7. It is the selling of that, the sale and use of which, if continued, will form intemperate appetites, which, if formed, will be gratified, and thus will perpetuate intemperance and all its abominations to the end of the world.

8. It is the selling of that which makes wives widows, and children orphans; which leads husbands often to murder their wives, and wives to murder their husbands; parents to murder their children, and children to murder their parents; and which prepares multitudes for the prison, for the gallows, and for hell.

9. It is the selling of that which greatly increases the amount and severity of sickness; which in many cases destroys reason; which causes a great portion of all the sudden deaths, and brings down multitudes who were never intoxicated, and never condemned to suffer the penalty of the civil law, to an untimely grave.

10. It is the selling of that which tends to lessen the health, the reason, and the usefulness, to diminish the comfort, and shorten the lives of all who habitually use it.

11. It is the selling of that which darkens the understanding, sears the conscience, pollutes the affections, and debases all the powers of man.

12. It is the selling of that which weakens the power of motives to do right, and increases the power of motives to do wrong, and is thus shown to be in its effects hostile to the moral government of God, as well as to the temporal and eternal interests of men; which excites men to rebel against him, and to injure and destroy one another. And no man can sell it without exerting an influence which tends to hinder the reign of the Lord Jesus Christ over the minds and hearts of men, and to lead them to persevere in iniquity, till, notwithstanding all the kindness of Jehovah, their case shall become hopeless.

Suppose a man, when about to commence the traffic in ardent spirit, should write in great capitals on his sign-board, to be seen and read of all men, what he will do, viz., that so many of the inhabitants of this town or city, he will, for the sake of getting their money, make paupers, and send them to the almshouse, and thus oblige the whole community to support them and their families; that so many others he will excite to the commission of crimes, and thus increase the expenses, and endanger the peace and welfare of the community; that so many he will send to the jail, and so many more to the state prison, and so many to the gallows;

that so many he will visit with sore and distressing diseases; and in so many cases diseases which would have been comparatively harmless, he will by his poison render fatal; that in so many cases he will deprive persons of reason, and in so many cases will cause sudden death; that so many wives he will make widows, and so many children he will make orphans, and that in so many cases he will cause the children to grow up in ignorance, vice, and crime, and after being nuisances on earth, will bring them to a premature grave; that in so many cases he will prevent the efficacy of the Gospel, grieve away the Holy Ghost, and ruin for eternity the souls of men. And suppose he could, and should give some faint conception of what it is to lose the soul, and of the overwhelming guilt and coming wretchedness of him who is knowingly instrumental in producing this ruin; and suppose he should put at the bottom of the sign this question, viz., What, you may ask, can be my object in acting so much like a devil incarnate, and bringing such accumulated wretchedness upon a comparatively happy people? and under it should put the true answer, MONEY; and go on to say, I have a family to support; I want money, and must have it; this is my business, I was brought up to it; and if I should not follow it I must change my business, or I could not support my family. And as all faces begin to gather blackness at the approaching ruin, and all hearts to boil with indignation at its author, suppose he should add for their consolation, "If I do not bring this destruction upon you, somebody else will." What would they think of him? what would all the world think of him? what *ought* they to think of him? And is it any worse for a man to tell the people beforehand honestly what he will do, if they buy and use his poison, than it is to go on and do it? And what if they are not aware of the mischief which he is doing them, and he can accomplish it through their own perverted and voluntary agency? Is it not equally abominable, if *he knows* it, and does not cease from producing it?

And if there are churches whose members are doing such things, and those churches are not blessed with the presence and favor of the Holy Ghost, they need not be at any loss for the reason. And if they should *never* again, while they continue in this state, be blessed with the reviving influence of God's Spirit, they need not be at any loss for the reason. Their own members are exerting a strong and fatal influence against it; and that too after Divine Providence has shown them what they are doing. And in many such cases there is awful guilt with regard to this thing resting upon the whole church. Though they have known for years what these men were doing; have seen the misery, heard the oaths, witnessed the crimes, and known the wretchedness and deaths which they have occasioned, and perhaps have spoken of it, and deplored it among one another; many of them have never spoken on this subject to the persons themselves. They have seen them scattering firebrands, arrows, and death temporal and eternal, and yet have never so much as warned them on the subject, and never besought them to give up their work of death.

An individual lately conversed with one of his professed Christian brethren who was engaged in this traffic, and told him not only that he was ruining for both worlds many of his fellow-men, but that his Christian brethren viewed his business as inconsistent with his profession, and tending to counteract all efforts for the salvation of men; and the man, after frankly acknowledging that it was wrong, said that this was the first time that any of them had conversed with him on the subject. This may be the case with other churches; and while it is, the whole church is conniving at the evil, and the whole church is guilty. Every brother, in such a case, is bound, on his own account, to converse with him who is thus aiding the powers of darkness, and opposing the kingdom of Jesus Christ, and try to persuade him to cease from this destructive business.

The whole church is bound to make efforts, and use all proper means to accomplish this result. And before half the individual members have done their duty on this subject, they may expect, if the offending brother has, and manifests the spirit of Christ, that he will cease to be an offence to his brethren, and a stumbling-block to the world, over which such multitudes fall to the pit of woe. And till the church, the whole church, do their duty on this subject, they cannot be freed from the guilt of conniving at the evil. And no wonder if the Lord leaves them to be as the mountains of Gilboa, on which there was neither rain or dew. And should the church receive from the world those who make it a business to carry on this notoriously immoral traffic, they will greatly increase their guilt, and ripen for the awful displeasure of God. And unless members of the church shall cease to teach, by their business, the fatal error that it is right for men to buy and use ardent spirit as a drink, the evil will never be eradicated, intemperance will never cease, and the day of millennial glory never come.

Each individual who names the name of Christ is called upon, by the providence of God, to act on this subject openly and decidedly for him, and in such a manner as is adapted to banish intemperance and all its abominations from the earth, and to cause temperance and all its attendant benefits universally to prevail. And if ministers of the Gospel and members of Christian churches do not connive at the sin of furnishing this poison as a drink for their fellow-men; and men who, in opposition to truth and duty, continue to be engaged in this destructive employment, are viewed and treated as wicked men; the work which the Lord hath commenced and carried forward with a rapidity, and to an extent hitherto unexampled in the history of the world, will continue to move onward till not a name, nor a trace, nor a shadow of a drunkard, or a drunkard-maker, shall be found on the globe.

PROFESSED CHRISTIAN—In the manufacture or sale of ardent spirit as a drink, you do not, and you cannot honor God; but you do, and, so long as you continue it, you will greatly dishonor Him. You exert an influence which tends directly and strongly to ruin, for both worlds, your fellow-men. Should you take a quantity of that poisonous liquid into your closet, present it before the Lord, confess to him its nature and effects, spread out before him what it has done and what it will do, and attempt to ask him to bless you in extending its influence; it would, unless your conscience is already seared as with a hot iron, appear to you like blasphemy. You could no more do it than you could take the instruments of gambling and attempt to ask God to bless you in extending them through the community. And why not, if it is a lawful business? Why not ask God to increase it, and make you an instrument in extending it over the country, and perpetuating it to all future generations? Even the worldly and profane man, when he hears about professing Christians offering prayer to God that he would bless them in the manufacture or sale of ardent spirit, involuntarily shrinks back and says, "That is too bad." He can see that it is an abomination. And if it is too bad for a professed Christian to pray about it, is it not too bad for him to practise it? If you continue, under all the light which God in his providence has furnished with regard to its hurtful nature and destructive effects, to furnish ardent spirit as a drink for your fellow-men, you will run the fearful hazard of losing your soul, and you will exert an influence which powerfully tends to destroy the souls of your fellow-men. Every time you furnish it you are rendering it less likely that they will be illuminated, sanctified, and saved, and more likely that they will continue in sin and go down to the chambers of death.

It is always worse for a church-member to do an immoral act, and teach an immoral sentiment, than for an immoral man, because it does greater mischief. And this is understood, and often adverted to by the immoral themselves. Even drunkards are now stating it to their fellow-drunkards, that church-members are not better than they. And to prove it, are quoting the fact, that although they are not drunkards, and perhaps do not get drunk, they, for the sake of money, carry on the business of making drunkards. And are not the men and their business of the same character? "The deacon," says a drunkard, "will not use ardent spirit himself: he says, 'It is poison!' But for six cents he will sell it to me. And though he will not furnish it to his own children, for he says, 'It will ruin them!' yet he will furnish it to mine. And there is my neighbor, who was once as sober as the deacon himself, but he had a pretty farm, which the deacon wanted, and for the sake of getting it he has made him a drunkard. And his wife, as good a woman as ever lived, has died of a broken heart, because her children would follow their father." No, you cannot convince even a drunkard, that the man who is selling him that which he knows is killing him, is any better than the drunkard himself. Nor can you convince a sober man, that he who, for the sake of money, will, with his eyes open, make drunkards of sober men, is any less guilty than the drunkards he makes.

Is this writing upon their employment "Holiness unto the Lord," without which no one, from the Bible, can expect to be prepared for the holy joys of heaven? As ardent spirit is a poison which, when used even moderately, tends to harden the heart, to sear the conscience, to blind the understanding, to pollute the affections, to weaken and derange and debase the whole man, and to lessen the prospect of his eternal life, it is the indispensable duty of each person to renounce it. And he cannot refuse to do this without becoming, if acquainted with this subject, knowingly accessory to the temporal and eternal ruin of his fellow-men. And what will it profit him to gain even the whole world by that which ruins the soul?

My friend, you are soon to die, and in eternity to witness the influence, the whole influence, which you exert while on earth, and you are to witness its consequence in joy or sorrow to endless being. Imagine yourself now, where you soon will be, *on your death-bed*. And imagine that you have a full view of the property which you have caused to be wasted, or which you have gained without furnishing any valuable equivalent; of the health which you have destroyed, and the characters which you have demoralized; of the wives that you have made widows, and the children that you have made orphans; of all the lives that you have shortened, and all the souls that you have destroyed. O! imagine that these are the only "rod and staff" which you have to comfort you as you go down the valley of the shadow of death, and that they will all meet you in full array at the judgment and testify against you. What will it profit you, though you have gained more money than you otherwise would, when you have left it all far behind in that world which is destined to fire, and the day of perdition of ungodly men? What will it profit, when you are enveloped in the influence which you have exerted, and are experiencing its consequences to endless ages; finding for ever that as a man soweth so must he reap, and that if he has sowed death he must reap *death?* Do not any longer assist in destroying men, nor expose yourself and your children to be destroyed. Do good, and good only, to all as you have opportunity, and good shall come unto you.

THE

REWARDS OF DRUNKENNESS.

If you wish to be always thirsty, be a Drunkard; for the oftener and more you drink, the oftener and more thirsty you will be.

If you seek to prevent your friends raising you in the world, be a Drunkard; for that will defeat all their efforts.

If you would effectually counteract your own attempts to do well, be a Drunkard; and you will not be disappointed.

If you wish to repel the endeavors of the whole human race to raise you to character, credit, and prosperity, be a Drunkard; and you will most assuredly triumph.

If you are determined to be poor, be a Drunkard; and you will soon be ragged and pennyless.

If you would wish to starve your family, be a Drunkard; for that will consume the means of their support.

If you would be imposed on by knaves, be a Drunkard; for that will make their task easy.

If you would wish to be robbed, be a Drunkard; which will enable the thief to do it with more safety.

If you would wish to blunt your senses, be a Drunkard; and you will soon be more stupid than an ass.

If you would become a fool, be a Drunkard; and you will soon lose your understanding.

If you wish to unfit yourself for rational intercourse, be a Drunkard; for that will accomplish your purpose.

If you are resolved to kill yourself, be a Drunkard; that being a sure mode of destruction.

If you would expose both your folly and secrets, be a Drunkard; and they will soon be made known.

If you think you are too strong, be a Drunkard; and you will soon be subdued by so powerful an enemy.

If you would get rid of your money without knowing how, be a Drunkard; and it will vanish insensibly.

If you would have no resource when past labor but a workhouse, be a Drunkard; and you will be unable to provide any.

If you are determined to expel all comfort from your house, be a Drunkard; and you will soon do it effectually.

If you would be always under strong suspicion, be a Drunkard; for little as you think it, all agree that those who steal from themselves and families will rob others.

If you would be reduced to the necessity of shunning your creditors, be a Drunkard; and you will soon have reason to prefer the by-paths to the public streets.

If you would be a dead weight on the community, and "cumber the ground," be a Drunkard; for that will render you useless, helpless, burdensome, and expensive.

If you would be a nuisance, be a Drunkard; for the approach of a Drunkard is like that of a dunghill.

If you would be hated by your family and friends, be a Drunkard; and you will soon be more than disagreeable.

If you would be a pest to society, be a Drunkard; and you will be avoided as infectious.

If you do not wish to have your faults reformed, continue to be a Drunkard, and you will not care for good advice.

If you would smash windows, break the peace, get your bones broken, tumble under carts and horses, and be locked up in watch-houses, be a Drunkard; and it will be strange if you do not succeed.

If you wish all your prospects in life to be clouded, be a Drunkard; and they will soon be dark enough.

If you would destroy your body, be a Drunkard; as drunkenness is the mother of disease.

If you mean to ruin your soul, be a Drunkard; that you may be excluded from heaven.

Finally, if you are determined to be utterly destroyed, in estate, body, and soul, be a Drunkard; and you will soon know that it is impossible to adopt a more effectual means to accomplish your—END.

"All the crimes on earth," says Lord Bacon, "do not destroy so many of the *human race*, nor alienate so much *property*, as *drunkenness*."

Drunkenness expels reason—drowns the memory—defaces beauty—diminishes strength—inflames the blood—causes internal, external, and incurable wounds—is a witch to the senses, a devil to the soul, a thief to the purse—the beggar's companion, the wife's woe, and children's sorrow—makes a strong man weak, and a wise man a fool. He is worse than a beast, and is a self-murderer, who drinks to others' good health, and robs himself of his own. He is worse than a beast, for no animal will designedly intoxicate itself; but a drunkard swallows his liquor, well knowing the condition to which it will reduce him, and that these draughts will deprive him of the use of his reason, and render him worse than a beast. By the effects of liquor his evil passions and tempers are freed from restraint; and, while in a state of intoxication, he commits actions, which, when sober, he would have shuddered to have thought of. Many an evil deed has been done, many a MURDER has been committed, when those who did these things were intoxicated.

Tremble, then, if ever you taste the intoxicating draught. Reflect, before you put the cup to your lips. Remember that you are forming a habit which will lead on to the commission of every crime to which the propensities of your nature, rendered violent by indulgence, can urge you. Before you are aware, you may find yourself awaking from a fit of intoxication, guilty of offences against the laws of your country which will draw down just vengeance upon your head; abhorring yourself, and an abhorrence in the sight of heaven.

Drunkenness, persisted in, will assuredly *destroy your soul*, and consign you to everlasting misery. Hear what the *word* of *God* declares.

"Awake, ye drunkards, and weep." Joel 1 : 5.

"Who hath woe? who hath sorrow? who hath contention? who hath wounds without cause? They that tarry long at the wine, they that go to seek mixed wine. Look not thou upon the wine; at the last it biteth like a serpent, and stingeth like an adder." Prov. 23 : 29–32.

"Woe unto them that rise up in the morning, that they may follow strong drink; that continue until night, till wine inflame them." Isa. 5 : 11.

"Woe unto them that are mighty to drink wine, and men of strength to mingle strong drink." Isa. 5 : 22.

"The works of the flesh are manifest, which are these: uncleanness, murders, drunkenness, revellings, and such like; of the which I tell you, that they which do such things shall not inherit the kingdom of God." Gal. 5 : 19, 21.

These are awful declarations, and they will certainly be fulfilled upon him who continues to delight in drunkenness; he cannot enjoy the love of God, he will not be received into heaven.

Separate yourself, then, utterly from this ensnaring sin. "Touch not; taste not; handle not." In ENTIRE ABSTINENCE is your only safety. This persevered in, you shall never fall. Wherever and however the temptation is presented, "avoid it—turn from it, and pass away." Turn also from every sin. "Commit your way unto the Lord," and he will "direct your paths." A glorious provision is made for your salvation, through the atoning blood of Christ. "God so loved the world, that he gave his only-begotten Son, that whosoever believeth in him should not perish, but have everlasting life." John 3 : 16. Commit your soul and your all to him. He will guide you through life, enable you to vanquish every foe, and crown you with victory in heaven.

PUBLISHED BY THE AMERICAN TRACT SOCIETY.

THE

WELL-CONDUCTED FARM.

Mr. B——, a respectable farmer in Massachusetts, came, a number of years ago, into the possession of a farm of about six hundred acres. On this farm he employed eight or ten men. These men were in the habit, and had been for years, of taking each a portion of ardent spirit, when they labored, every day. They had grown up in the practice of taking it, and the idea was fixed in their minds that they *could* not do without. It was the common opinion in the place, that, for laboring men, who had to work hard, some ardent spirit was *necessary*. Mr. B—— for a time followed the common practice, and furnished his men with a portion of spirit *daily*. But after much attentive observation and mature reflection, he became deeply impressed with the conviction that the practice was not only useless, but hurtful. He became convinced that it tends to lead men to intemperance; to undermine their constitutions; and to sow the seeds of death, temporal and eternal. And he felt that he could not be justified in continuing to cultivate his farm by means of a practice which was ruining the bodies and souls of his fellow-men. He therefore called his men together, and told them, in a kind and faithful manner, what were his convictions. He told them that he was perfectly satisfied that the practice of taking ardent spirits was not only needless, but hurtful—that it tended to weaken and destroy both the body and mind; and that he could not, consistently with his duty, be instrumental in continuing a practice which he had no doubt tended to destroy them both for this world and the world to come. He therefore, from that time, should furnish them with no ardent spirits.

One of them said that he could not work without it; and if he did not furnish them with it, he would not stay with him. "Very well," said Mr. B——; "hand me your bill, and be off." The man replied, that he presumed all the others would leave him. "Very well," said Mr. B——; "tell them, any of them who choose to leave—all of them, if they choose to go—to hand in their bills, and they shall have their money to-night. If they stay, however, they shall have nourishing food and drink, at any time, and in any abundance which they wish; and at the close of the year each one shall have twelve dollars, that is, one dollar a month, in addition to his wages. But I shall furnish no spirits of any kind, neither shall I have it taken by men in my employment. I had rather my farm would grow up to weeds, than be cultivated by means of so pernicious a practice as that of taking ardent spirits." However, none of the men left, except that one. And when he saw that all the others concluded to stay, he came back, and said, that as the others had concluded to stay, and do without rum, he believed that he could, and he should be glad to stay, too, if Mr. B—— had no objection. But he told him, No, he did not wish him to stay; he would make of him an example, and he must go. So he departed. The rest went to work, and he furnished them with no spirits from that time through the season. Yet his work, he said, was done "with less trouble, in a better manner, and in better season, than ever before." Some of his men, however, he found, when they went abroad, did take ardent spirits. They sometimes procured it at the tavern, or a store; and in some instances took it secretly, while on his farm. The evil, therefore, although greatly lessened, was not entirely done away.

When he came to hire men again, he let it be known that he did not wish to hire any man who was not willing to abstain entirely, and at all times, from the use of ardent spirits. His neighbors told him that he could not hire men on those conditions; that men could not be found who would do without rum, especially in haying and harvesting. Well, he said, then he would not hire them at all. His farm should grow up to weeds. As to cultivating it by the help of rum, he would not. By allowing men in his employment, and for whose conduct he was in a measure responsible, to take ardent spirits, he should be lending his influence to continue a practice, or he should at least be conniving at a practice, which was "destroying more lives, making more mothers widows, and children orphans, than famine, pestilence, and sword: a practice which was destroying by thousands, and tens of thousands, not only the bodies, but the *souls* of men, rendering them, and their children after them, wretched for this world, and the world to come. "No," said he, "I will clear my hands of this enormous guilt. I will not by practice encourage, or by silence, or having men in my employment who take ardent spirits, connive at this deadly evil." However, he found no difficulty in hiring men, and of the best kind. And when his neighbors saw, that by giving one dollar a month more than others, he could hire as many men as he pleased, they gave up that objection. But they said, it was bad policy; for the men would not do so much work, and he would, in the end, be a loser. But he told them that, although they might not at first do quite so much, he presumed that they would in the end do more. But if they should not, only let them do, said he, what they easily can, and I shall be satisfied. My Maker does not require of me any more than I can do without rum, (for he used no ardent spirits himself) and I shall require no more of them. His men went to work. And his business prospered exceedingly. His men were remarkably uniform in their temper and deportment; still, and peaceable.

He found them every day alike, and he could always safely trust them. What he expected to have done, he found *was* done, in good season, and in the best manner. His men never made so few mistakes, had so few disputes among themselves; they never injured and destroyed so few tools, found so little fault with their manner of living, or were, on the whole, so pleasant to one another, and to their employer. The men appeared, more than ever before, like brethren of the same family, satisfied with their business, contented, and happy.

At the close of the year, one of them came to Mr. B——, and, with tears in his eyes, said, "Sir, I thought that you were very hard, in keeping us from drinking rum. I had always been accustomed to it, and I thought that I could not do without it. And for the first three months," said he, "it was hard, very hard. I had such a *caving in* here"—putting his hands up to his side—"I had such a *desperate caving in* here, that I thought I should die. But, as you gave us good wages, and good pay, and the rest resolved to stand it without rum, I thought I would.

"And now," said he, "I am well and happy. I work with ease, sleep sweetly, and when I get up in the morning, instead of having, as I used to, my mouth and throat" —to use his own words—"so *full of cobwebs*, as to be *spitting cotton wool* all the time, my mouth and throat are clear as a whistle. I feel active, have a good appetite, and can eat any thing.

"Formerly, when I worked hard, I was at night tired, and could not sleep. When I got up in the morning I was so sore and stiff, so filled up in my throat, and my appetite was so gone, that I could do nothing till I had taken a glass of rum and molasses. I then stood it till breakfast. But my breakfast did not relish, and what I took did not seem to nourish me. Soon after I got to work I was *so hollow and so tired*, that I felt *desperate ugly* till 11 o'clock. Then I took a *new vamper*. And by the strength of that I got on till dinner. Then I must have a little more to give me an appetite. At three o'clock in the afternoon I must have recourse"—these were his words—"*to the hair of the same dog*, to keep up my sinking spirits. And thus I got along till night. Then I must have a little to sharpen appetite for supper. And after supper I could not sleep, till I had taken *another nightcap*.

"Thus I continued," said he, "year after year, undermining a constitution which was naturally very robust; and growing worse and worse, until I came under your wise and excellent regulations. And now," said he, "I am cured. I *am cured*. I can now do more labor than when I took spirits, without *half* the fatigue, and take nothing stronger than pure cold water. If a man would give me the same wages that you do, and a dollar a day in addition, to return to the practice of drinking rum, I would laugh at him." All this was the free, spontaneous effusion of his own mind, in view of the great change wrought in his feelings by leaving off *entirely* the use of ardent spirits.

Another of the workmen came to Mr. B—— and said, that he had found it very hard to do without rum at first; but he could now freely say, that he never enjoyed so good health, or felt so well, as he did then. He said that in cold weather in the winter, and after chopping all day in the woods, especially if exposed to rains, or if his feet were wet, he had for a long time been accustomed to a very bad rheumatism, and at night to a dreadful headache. He took spirits temperately, and he supposed it was necessary to guard him against these evils. Still he suffered them; and he found nothing that would prevent them. But since he had left off entirely the use of spirits, he had had no rheumatism, and been entirely free from the headache.

Another of the workmen said he thought at first that he could do very well without spirits three quarters of the year; but that, in haying and harvesting, he should want a little. But he had found that a dish of bread and milk, or some other nourishing food, at 11 o'clock, answered his purpose at all times just as well as grog, and he thought a little better. And as he was now entirely free from the habit of taking spirits, he would not on any account be placed in a situation where he should be tempted to renew it.

Such were the feelings of men who had always been accustomed to the practice of taking spirits, till they came into Mr. B——'s employment, and who afterwards had not taken a drop. They had tried both sides, and had found, by experience, that the practice of taking ardent spirits is utterly useless; nay, that it is positively hurtful. It was their united testimony, that they enjoyed better health, were more happy, could do more work, and with less fatigue, than when they took spirits.

They said, to be sure, that they found it hard to do without it at first. And so would a man who had been in the habit of taking laudanum, or any poison, that was not fatal, but was stimulating and pleasant to the taste, however destructive it might be in the end to his constitution. But after they had freed themselves from the habit of taking spirits, they found no inconvenience; but were in all respects better than they were before. And they acknowledged that they were exceedingly indebted to him, who, by his wise regulations, had been the means of improving their condition. The following were some of the advantages to *them*.

1. They had a better appetite, partook of their food with a keener relish, and it was more nourishing to them than before.

2. They possessed much greater vigor and activity, both of body and mind.

3. They performed the same labor with much greater ease; and were in a great measure free from that lassitude and fatigue to which they were before accustomed.

4. They had greater wages, and they laid up a much greater portion of what they had. Before, numbers used to spend a great portion of their wages in scenes of amusement and dissipation. Now, they have no inclination to frequent such scenes. The consequence is, they lay up more money. They are, also, more serious in their deportment, spend more of their leisure time in useful reading, much oftener peruse the Scriptures, and attend public worship; and they are more attentive to all the means of grace. In a word, they are more likely to become useful and happy in this life, and to be prepared for lasting blessedness in the life to come.

5. Their example will be more likely to be useful to those around them; and that for both worlds.

The following are some of the advantages to *their employer*.

1. The men, he says, in the course of the year, do more work, in a better manner, and at a much less expense of tools.

2. He can now with much greater ease have a place for every thing, and every thing in its place.

3. When a stone has fallen from the wall it is now laid up, as the men are passing by, without his mentioning it. The gates are locked, and the bars put up; so that the cattle do not, as before, get in and destroy the crops.

4. His summer work is done in such season, that earth, loam, etc., is carted into the yard in the fall, instead of being carted in in the spring, as before. The consequence is, when carried out it is richer, and renders the farm more productive.

5. His barns, in winter, are kept clean, and less fodder

is wasted. The cattle and horses are daily curried, and appear in better order.

6. When his men go into the forests, instead, as before, of cutting down the nearest, thriftiest, and largest trees, they cut those that are decayed, crooked, and not likely to grow any better; pick up those that are blown down, and thus leave the forests in a better state.

7. The men are more uniform, still, and peaceable; are less trouble in the house, and more contented with their manner of living.

8. At morning and evening prayer, they are more ready than before to attend, and in season; appearing to esteem it not only a duty, but a privilege and a pleasure to be present, and unite with the family in the daily worship of God.

9. On the Sabbath, instead of wishing, as before, to stay at home, or to spend the day in roving about the fields, rivers, and forests, they choose statedly and punctually to attend public worship. In a word, their whole deportment, both at home and abread, is improved, and to a greater extent than any, without witnessing it, can well imagine.

All these and many more advantages resulted from their abstaining *entirely, and at all times,* from the use of ardent spirits.

Nor were the benefits confined to them and their employer. Some of his *neighbors,* witnessing the complete success of his system, have themselves adopted it. When Mr. B—— went into that part of the country, many of the farmers in his neighborhood were in debt. Their farms were mortgaged, some for $300, some for $500, and some for $1000, or more. They complained much of *hard times,* especially for farmers.

Mr. B—— told them that so long as they continued to drink rum, they must expect hard times; for it was no profit, but a great expense, and in more ways than they imagined. They came to him to borrow money to save their farms from attachment. But he told them, No. It will do men who continue to drink rum no good to have money. Nay, it will be to them an evil. The sooner their property is gone, and they have nothing with which to buy rum, the better. For then they will do less mischief than if they have money, and continue to drink rum. But, said he, if you will leave off the use of spirits, and not take a drop for three months, I will lend you money, and you may keep it, by paying the interest, as long as you continue to take no ardent spirits. But when I learn that you begin to take it, I shall call for the money. Some went away in disgust. Others said, As Mr. B—— can do without rum, why cannot we? and if we can, it will be a great saving of expense. They made the experiment, and found that they could, without the least inconvenience, do without it. After a few months, they made known to Mr. B—— the result; and he helped them to as much money as they needed. They continued to do without spirits, and they had none used by men in their employment. Their business began to prosper, and their prospects to brighten. Their debts are now paid, and their farms free from all incumbrance. The times with them have altered, and they are now thriving, respectable, and useful members of the community.

Others, who a few years ago were in no worse a condition than they, but who continued the practice of drinking spirits, have lost their farms; lost their reputation; lost their health, and eventually their lives; and there is reason to fear, their souls. By the temperate but habitual use of spirits, they formed an *intemperate appetite*. This at first was occasionally, and then habitually indulged; and they were ruined for both worlds. The evil may extend to their children, and children's children.

But those who have entirely relinquished the use of spirits, until the desire for it is removed, have experienced a wonderful transformation in their feelings, their conduct, and their prospects. And the change is visible not only in them, but their families, and all their concerns. Their windows are not broken out as before; nor their gates and garden-fences falling down. The kitchen does not smoke as it used to do, because they keep it more *clean*, have drier and better wood, and lay it on the fire in a better manner. The wife does not scold as she once did, because she is well provided for, is treated kindly, and has encouragement to labor. The children are not now in rags, but are comfortably and decently clad; they are obedient, respectful, and mannerly; and appear to be growing up in the nurture and admonition of the Lord. In short, they appear almost like a new race of beings. And if they should never again adopt the practice of taking ardent spirits, there is vastly more reason than before, to hope that they will be led by the word and Spirit of God to such a course of conduct as will greatly increase their happiness and usefulness on earth, and be the means of preparing them, through grace, for the everlasting joys of heaven.

Should each individual in our country adopt the same course, the following are some of the advantages which would result from it.

1. They would enjoy better health, be able to perform more labor, and would live to a greater age.

2. The evils of intemperance would soon be done away: for all who are now intemperate, and continue so, will soon be dead, and no others will be found to succeed them.

3. There will be a saving every year of more than *thirty millions of dollars*, which are now expended for ardent spirits. There will be a saving of more than two-thirds of all the expense of supporting the poor, which, in Massachusetts alone, would amount to more than $600,000 annually. And there would be a saving of all that idleness and dissipation which intemperance occasions, and of the expense of more than two-thirds of all the criminal prosecutions in the land. In one of our large cities, in which there were one thousand prosecutions for crimes, more than eight hundred of them were found to have sprung from the use of ardent spirits.

4. There would be a saving of a vast portion of sickness; and of the lives probably of thirty thousand persons every year.

Let these four considerations be added together, and traced in their various bearings and consequences upon the temporal and eternal welfare of men; and then let each individual say, whether, in view of all the evils connected with the practice of taking ardent spirits, he can, in the sight of God, be justified in continuing the practice. That it is *not necessary*, has been fully proved. No one thinks it to be necessary, except those who use it. And *they* would not think so, if they were not in the habit of using it. Let any man *leave off entirely* the use of ardent spirits for only one year, and he will find by his own experience that it is not necessary or useful. The fathers of New England did not use it, nor did their children. They were never, as a body, in the practice of taking it. And yet they enjoyed better health, attained to a larger stature, and, with fewer comforts of life, performed more labor, endured more fatigue, and lived, upon an average, to a greater age than any generation of their descendants who have been in the practice of taking spirits. As it was not necessary for the fathers of New England, it is certain that it is not necessary for their descendants, or for any portion of our inhabitants. Hundreds of healthy, active, respectable, and useful men, who *now* do not use it, can testify that it is not necessary. And this will be the testimony of every one who will only relinquish entirely the use of it.

It is by the temperate and habitual use of ardent spirits, that *intemperate appetites* are formed. And the temperate use of it cannot be continued, without, in many cases, forming intemperate appetites; and after they are formed, multitudes will be destroyed by their gratification.

Natural appetites, such as are implanted in our constitution by the Author of nature, *do not by their gratification increase in their demands*. What satisfied them years ago, will satisfy them now. But *artificial appetites*, which are formed by the wicked practices of men, are *constantly increasing in their demands.* What satisfied them once, will *not* satisfy them now. And what satisfies them now, will not satisfy them in future. They are constantly crying, "*Give, give.*" And there is not a man, who is in the habitual use of ardent spirits, who is not in danger of dying a drunkard. Before he is aware, an intemperate appetite may be formed, the gratification of which may prove his temporal and eternal ruin. And if the practice should not come to this result with regard to himself, it may with regard to his children, and children's children. It may with regard to his neighbors, and their children. It may extend its baleful influences far and wide; and transmit them, with all their innumerable evils, from generation to generation.

Can, then, *temperate, sober men be clear from guilt,* in continuing a practice which is costing annually more than $30,000,000; increasing more than threefold the poor-rates, and the crimes of the country; undermining the health and constitution of its inhabitants; and cutting off annually thirty thousand lives!

There is tremendous guilt somewhere. And it is a truth which ought to press with overwhelming force upon the mind of every sober man, that a portion of this guilt rests upon *every one* who, with a knowledge of facts, continues the *totally unnecessary and awfully pernicious practice of taking ardent spirits.* Each individual ought, without delay, in view of eternity, to clear himself, and neither by precept nor example, ever again encourage or even connive at this deadly evil.

ADDRESS

ON

THE EFFECTS OF ARDENT SPIRITS.

BY JONATHAN KITTREDGE, ESQ.

FELLOW-CITIZENS—That intemperance, in our country, is a great and growing evil, all are ready to admit. When we look abroad, and examine into the state of society, we find the number of those who are in the constant and habitual practice of an excessive use of ardent spirits to be alarming. We see the effects that they produce among our friends and our neighbors, but the evil is so common, and it is so fashionable to drink, and I had almost said, to drink to excess, that the sight of it has lost half its terror, and we look upon an intemperate man without those feelings of disgust and abhorrence which his real situation and character are calculated to produce. This is the natural result of things. The mind becomes familiar with the contemplation, the eye accustomed to the sight; we pay but little attention to the object—he passes on—we laugh at the exhibition, and grow callous and indifferent to the guilt. Our pity is not excited, our hearts do not ache at the scenes of intoxication that are almost daily exhibited around us. But if for a moment we seriously reflect upon the real situation of the habitually intemperate; if we call to mind what they have been—what they now are; if we cast our eye to the future, and realize what, in a few years, they will be; if we go further, and examine into the state of their families, of their wives and their children, we shall discover a scene of misery and wretchedness that will not long suffer us to remain cold, and indifferent, and unfeeling.

This examination we can all make for ourselves. We can all call to mind the case of some individual, whom we have known for years, perhaps from his infancy, who is now a poor, miserable drunkard. In early life his hopes and prospects were as fair as ours. His family was respectable, and he received all those advantages which are necessary, and which were calculated to make him a useful and respectable member of society. Perhaps he was our schoolfellow, and our boyhood may have been passed in his company. We witnessed the first buddings of his mental powers, and know that he possessed an active, enterprising mind. He grew up into life with every prospect of usefulness. He entered into business, and, for a while, did well. His parents looked to him for support in old age, and he was capable of affording it. He accumulated property, and, in a few years, with ordinary prudence and industry, would have been independent. He married, and became the head of a family, and the father of children, and all was prosperous and happy around him. Had he continued as he began, he would now have been a comfort to his friends, and an honor to the community. But the scene quickly changed.

He grew fond of ardent spirits. He was seen at the store and the tavern. By degrees he became intemperate. He neglected his business, and his affairs went to gradual decay. He is now a drunkard, his property is wasted, his parents have died of broken hearts, his wife is pale and emaciated, his children ragged, and squalid, and ignorant. He is the tenant of some little cabin that poverty has erected to house him from the storm and the tempest. He is useless, and worse than useless: he is a pest to all around him. All the feelings of his nature are blunted; he has lost all shame; he procures his accustomed supply of the poison that consumes him; he staggers through mud and through filth to his hut; he meets a weeping wife and starving children; he abuses them, he tumbles into his straw, and he rolls and foams like a mad brute, till he is able to go again. He calls for more rum—he repeats the scene from time to time, and from day to day, till soon his nature faints, and he becomes sober in death.

Let us reflect, that this guilty, wretched creature had an immortal mind—he was like us, of the same flesh and blood—he was our brother, destined to the same eternity, created by, and accountable to, the same God; and will, at last, stand at the same judgment-bar; and who, amid such reflections, will not weep at his fate—whose eye can remain dry, and whose heart unmoved?

This is no picture of the imagination. It is a common and sober reality. It is what we see almost every day of our lives; and we live in the midst of such scenes and such events. With the addition or subtraction of a few circumstances, it is the case of every one of the common drunkards around us. They have not completed the drama—they are alive—but they are going to death with rapid strides, as their predecessors have already gone. Another company of immortal minds are coming on to fill their places, as they have filled others. The number is kept good, and increasing. Shops, as nurseries, are established in every town and neighborhood, and drunkards are raised up by the score. They are made—they are formed—for no man was ever born a drunkard—and, I may say, no man was ever born with a taste for ardent spirits. They are not the food which nature has provided. The infant may cry for its mother's milk, and for nourishing food, but none was ever heard to cry for ardent spirits. The taste is created, and in some instances may be created so young, that, perhaps, many cannot remember the time when they were not fond of them.

And here permit me to make a few remarks upon the *formation, or creation of this taste.* I will begin with the infant, and I may say that he is born into rum. At his birth, according to custom, a quantity of ardent spirits is provided; they are thought to be as necessary as any thing else. They are considered as indispensable as if the child could not be born without them. The father treats his friends and his household, and the mother partakes with the rest. The infant is fed with them, as if he could not know the good things he is heir to without a taste of ardent spirits. They are kept on hand, and often given to him as medicine, especially where the parents are fond of them themselves. By this practice, even in the cradle, his disrelish for ardent spirits is done away. He grows up, and during the first months or years of his existence, his taste and his appetite are formed. As he runs about, and begins to take notice of passing events, he sees his father and friends drink; he partakes, and grows fond of them. In most families, ardent spirits are introduced and used on every extraordinary occasion. Without mentioning many, that the knowledge and experience of every man can supply, I will instance only the case of visitors.

A gentleman's friends and acquaintance call on him. He is glad to see them, and fashion and custom make it necessary for him to invite them to the sideboard. This is all done in his best style, in his most easy and affable manner. The best set of drinking-vessels are brought forward, and make quite a display. The children of the family notice this; they are delighted with the sight and the exhibition; they are pleased with the manners, and gratified with the conversation of the visitors on the occasion. As soon as they go abroad, they associate the idea of drinking with all that is manly and genteel. They fall into the custom, and imitate the example that is set them. Circumstances and situations expose one to more temptations than the rest. Perhaps his resolution, or his moral principle, is not so strong; and in this way, one out of twenty-five of those who live to thirty years of age becomes intemperate. He becomes so, perhaps not from any uncommon predisposition to the vice, but is at first led on by fashion, and custom, and favorable circumstances, till at last he plunges headlong into the vortex of dissipation and ruin. Our natural disrelish for ardent spirits is first done away—a relish for them is then created. They next become occasional, next habitual drinks. The habit gains strength, till, at last, the daily drinker is swept away by the first adverse gale.

It is on this principle, and let the fact operate as a caution to those who need it, that many men of fair unblemished characters, who have made a temperate, but habitual use of ardent spirits in days of prosperity, have, on a change of fortune, become notorious drunkards; while those who have refrained in prosperity, have encountered all the storms of adversity unhurt. We frequently hear a man's intemperance attributed to a particular cause, as loss of friends, loss of property, disappointed love, or ambition; when, if the truth were known, it would be seen that such men had previously been addicted to the use of ardent spirits, perhaps not immoderately, and fly to them on such events as their solace and support. Intemperance requires an apprenticeship, as much as law or physic; and a man can no more become intemperate in a month, than he can become a lawyer or a physician in a month. Many wonder that certain intemperate men, of fine talents, noble hearts, and manly feelings, do not reform; but it is a greater wonder that any ever do. The evil genius of intemperance gradually preys upon the strength of both body and mind, till the victim, when he is caught, finds, that although he was a giant once, he is now a child. Its influence is seductive and insinuating, and men are often irretrievably lost before they are aware of it. Let them beware how they take the first step. It is by degrees that men become intemperate. No man ever became so all at once—it is an impossibility in the nature of things. It requires time to harden the heart, to do away shame, to blunt the moral principle, to deaden the intellectual faculties, and temper the body. The intemperance of the day is the natural and legitimate consequence of the customs of society—of genteel and respectable society. It is the common and ordinary use of ardent spirits, as practised in our towns and villages, that has already peopled them with drunkards, and which, unless checked, will fill them with drunkards. The degree of intemperance that prevails, and the quantity of ardent spirits used, in our most respectable towns, is almost incredible. Perhaps some facts on this subject will be interesting.

As it regards *the degree of intemperance that prevails*, it may be safely said, that one out of a hundred of the inhabitants of this part of the country is a common drunkard. By a common drunkard is meant one who is habitually intemperate, who is often intoxicated, and who is restrained from intoxication neither by principle nor shame. Of such there are from ten to twenty, and upward, in every inhabited township. There is another class who are intemperate, and many of them are occasional drunkards. This class is more numerous than the former, and one out of about forty of the inhabitants belongs to one or the other class. Is not this a horrid state of society? But any one can satisfy himself of the truth of the statement, by making the examination himself.

The quantity of ardent spirits yearly consumed in our towns, varies from six to ten thousand gallons. It will answer the argument I intend to draw from it, to state the annual quantity in this town to be six thousand gallons, although short of the truth. This would be three gallons to every inhabitant, or twenty-one gallons to every legal voter. The cost of this liquid, at the low price of fifty cents per gallon, will be three thousand dollars, which will pay all your town, county, and state taxes three years, and is as much as it costs you to support and maintain all your privileges, civil, religious, and literary. In one hundred years you would drink up all the town in ardent spirits; or it would cost just such a town as this, with all your farms, stock, and personal property, to furnish the inhabitants with ardent spirits, at the present rate of drinking, only one hundred years. But should the town continue to drink as they now do for fifty years, and in the mean time suffer the cost of the spirits to accumulate by simple interest only, the whole town, at the end of the term, could not pay their rum bills. It can be no consolation that all other towns would be alike insolvent.

But this is not all. Add to this sum the loss of time and the waste of property occasioned by it, independent of its cost, and it swells the amount to a monstrous size. Here you have an account of the cost of ardent spirits, calculated within bounds. At present there is a great complaint about the pressure of the times, and the complaint is doubtless well-founded. "Hard times" is in every body's mouth; but if you had for the last year only abstained from the use of ardent spirits, you would now have been independent and easy in your circumstances. Three thousand dollars, which you have paid for them, divided among you, would pay all the debts you are called upon to pay. I do not mean that no one wants more than his proportion of this sum, but there are some who want none of it, and who would circulate it, by loan or otherwise, among those who do want it, and it would relieve the whole town from the distress they are now in.

If this town had an income that would pay all its taxes, you would consider it a matter of great joy and congratulation. But if it had an income that would discharge all its taxes, and each man, instead of paying, should receive the amount he now pays, you would consider your situation highly prosperous and enviable. Discontinue the use of ardent spirits, and you have it. Use none, and your situation, as a town, will be as good, yea, far better than if you had an income of three thousand dollars yearly, to be divided among its inhabitants.

If we carry this calculation farther, we shall find, on the principle adopted, that there are in the state of New Hampshire 2,441 common drunkards, and 3,663 intemperate, or occasional drunkards—in the whole, 6,104; and that the state consumes 732,483 gallons of ardent spirits annually, which cost, at 50 cents a gallon, $366,241. In the United States, there would be 96,379 common, and 240,949 common and occasional drunkards; and the country would consume annually 28,913,887 gallons of ardent spirits, which cost, at 50 cents per gallon, $14,456,943—as much as it costs to support the whole system of our national government, with all that is laid out in improvements, roads, canals, pensions, etc., etc., and is more than one-half of the whole revenue of the Union for the last year. It must be remembered that this calculation embraces only the quantity and cost of the spirits, and is on the supposition that this town consumes only 6,000 gallons, at 50 cents per gallon, and is a fair criterion for the state and nation. As it regards this state, it would be safe nearly to double the quantity, and to treble the cost of the spirits; and as it regards the nation, it would be safe to double all my calculations. In the United States, the quantity of ardent spirits yearly consumed, may be fairly estimated at 60,000,000 gallons, the cost at $30,000,000, and the number of drunkards, of both kinds, at 480,000.

But we all know, and it is common to remark, that the cost of the article is comparatively nothing; that it hardly makes an item in the calculation of pernicious consequences resulting from the consumption of ardent spirits. Were we to embrace the usual concomitants, and estimate the value of time lost, the amount of property wasted, of disease produced, and of crime committed, where ardent spirits are the only cause, it would transcend our conceptions, and the imagination would be lost in the contemplation. The number of drunkards in the United States would make an army as large as that with which Bonaparte marched into Russia; and would be sufficient to defend the United States from the combined force of all Europe. Convert our drunkards into good soldiers, and one-tenth of them would redeem Greece from the Turks. Convert them into apostles, and they would Christianize the world. And what are they now? Strike them from existence, and who would feel the loss? Yes, strike them from existence, and the United States would be benefited by the blow.

But this is not half. I cannot tell you half the effects of ardent spirits. And yet ardent spirits are said to be useful and necessary. It is false! It is nothing but the apology that love of them renders for their use. There are only two cases in which, Dr. Rush says, they can be administered without injury, and those are cases of persons like to perish, and where substitutes may be applied of equal effect. What rational man would use them, for the sake of these two possible cases? As well might he introduce rattlesnakes among his children, because their oil is good in diseases with which they may possibly be afflicted.

The number of persons in the United States who are mentally deranged, I do not know; probably there are several thousands; and it is ascertained, that one-third of those confined in the insane hospitals of Philadelphia and New York, are rendered insane by the use of ardent spirits. Yes, one-third of the poor, miserable maniacs of our land, are made such by the use of that which, in the opinion of some, is a very useful and necessary article, and which they cannot do without. This article has deprived one-third of the crazy wretches of our land of their reason—of that which makes them men—of the very image of their God.

Out of the number of the intemperate in the United States, ten thousand die annually from the effects of ardent spirits. And what a death! To live a drunkard is enough; but to die so, and to be ushered into the presence of your angry Judge, only to hear the sentence, "Depart, thou drunkard!" Ah! language fails, and I leave it to your imagination to fill up the horrid picture.

This death happens in various ways. Some are killed instantly; some die a lingering, gradual death; some commit suicide in fits of intoxication; and some are actually burnt up.

I read of an intemperate man, a few years since, whose breath caught fire by coming in contact with a lighted candle, and he was consumed. At the time, I disbelieved the story, but my reading has since furnished me with well authenticated cases of a combustion of the human body from the use of ardent spirits. Trotter mentions ten such cases, and relates them at length. They are attended with all the proof we require to believe any event. They are attested by living witnesses, examined by learned men, and published in the journals of the day without contradiction. It would be unnecessary to relate the whole, but I will state one of them, and from this an idea can be formed of the rest. It is the case "of a woman eighty years of age, exceedingly meagre, who had drunk nothing but ardent spirits for several years. She was sitting in her elbow-chair, while her waiting-maid went out of the room for a few moments. On her return, seeing her mistress on fire, she immediately gave an alarm; and some people coming to her assistance, one of them endeavored to extinguish the flames with his hands, *but they adhered to them as if they had been dipped in brandy or oil on fire.* Water was brought and thrown on the body in abundance, *yet the fire appeared more violent, and was not extinguished till the whole body had been consumed.* The lady was in the same place in which she sat every day, there was no extraordinary fire, and she had not fallen."*

This, with nine other cases, related by the same author, was a consumption of the body produced by the use of ardent spirits. The horror of a drunkard's death beggars description. Need I point to yonder grave, just closed over the remains of one who went from the cup of excess to almost instant death? You all know it.

But this is not all. One half the poor you support by taxes and individual charity, are made poor by the use of ardent spirits. This has been demonstrated by actual inquiry and examination. In the city of New York, where there are more poor, and where more is done for them than

* Trotter on Drunkenness, pp. 78, 79.

in any other city of the United States, a committee appointed for the purpose, ascertained by facts, that more than one half of the city poor were reduced to poverty by intemperance. This is also the case throughout the Union. And here permit me to state a case, with which I am acquainted. I do it with a double object. I do it to show that the use of ardent spirits produces poverty and distress, and the disuse of them restores to wealth and comfort.

A gentleman in the city of New York, who carried on ship-building on an extensive scale, and employed a great number of hands daily, and paid them all in the same manner, and nearly to the same amount, was struck with the difference in their situations. A few, and only a few, were able, from their wages, to support their families; but these were out of debt, and independent in their circumstances. They always had money on hand, and frequently suffered their wages to lie in the hands of their employer. The rest were poor and harassed, the former easy and comfortable in their circumstances, and he resolved, if possible, to ascertain the cause of the difference. On inquiry and examination, he found that those of them who were above-board used no ardent spirits, while the others were in the constant and daily use of them. He satisfied himself that this use of ardent spirits was the only cause of the difference in their condition. He determined, if he could, to prevail upon them all to abstain altogether from their use. On a thorough and parental representation of the case to them, he succeeded, and they all agreed to make use of none for a year. At the end of the year they were all, to a man, out of debt, had supported their families in better condition, had done more work, destroyed fewer tools, and were hearty and robust, and enjoyed better health.

This fact speaks volumes, and needs no comment. Adopt the same practice in this town, and the result will be the same. "What, drink none?" Yes, I say, drink none—one gallon for this town is just four quarts too much. In addition to the miseries of debt and poverty which they entail upon a community, they are the parent of one half the diseases that prevail, and one half the crimes that are committed. It is ardent spirits that fill our poor-houses and our jails; it is ardent spirits that fill our penitentiaries, our mad-houses, and our state prisons; and it is ardent spirits that furnish victims for the gallows. They are the greatest curse that God ever inflicted on the world, and may well be called the seven vials of his wrath. They are more destructive in their consequences than war, plague, pestilence, or famine; yea, than all combined. They are slow in their march, but sure in their grasp. They seize not only the natural, but the moral man. They consign the body to the tomb, and the soul to hell.

While on earth, the victim of intemperance is as stupid as an ass, as ferocious as a tiger, as savage as a bear, as poisonous as the asp, as filthy as the swine, as fetid as a goat, and as malignant as a fiend. No matter what may be the original materials of the man; his figure may possess every grace of the sculptor; his mind may be imbued with every art and science; he may be fit to command at the head of armies, to sway a Roman senate, to wield the destinies of nations; his heart may be the seat of every virtue; but ardent spirits will strip him of the whole, and convert him into a demon. Need I tell how? Need I point out the change that ebriety produces in the moral and social affections? Need I present the sword red with a brother's blood? It was in a drunken revel that the infuriate Alexander slew his best friend and most beloved companion Clytus. And it was in a drunken revel that he proclaimed himself a god, and died.

"But have not ardent spirits one good quality, one redeeming virtue?" None. I say, none. There is nothing, not even the shadow of a virtue, to rescue them from universal and everlasting execration.

"But they are good as a medicine." No, not as a medicine. There is no physician, that does not love them, that needs them in his practice. There is no disease that they cure or relieve, that cannot be cured or relieved without them. They add to no man's health; they save no man's life.*

It is impossible to name a single good thing that they do. Give them to the divine; do they add to his piety, to his zeal, to his faithfulness, to his love of God or man? No; they destroy them all. Give them to the physician; do they increase his skill, his power to discriminate amid the symptoms of disease, his judgment to apply the appropriate remedies, his kind and affectionate solicitude? Nay, verily, they destroy them all. Give them to the legal advocate; do they increase his knowledge, his perception to discover the points of his case, his readiness to apply the evidence, his ability to persuade a court and jury? No; they destroy them all. Give them to the mechanic; do they assist his ingenuity, his judgment, or his taste? No;

* The writer is aware that spirits or alcohol are necessary in some preparations of the chemist and apothecary. But it is the use of them as drinks which he is combating, and which, he is assured by respectable physicians, are not only unnecessary, but hurtful, in sickness and in health. Were they to exist only in the apothecary's shop in the state of alcohol, it would be all that the world needs of them. Some physicians, nevertheless, may think them useful in two or three cases or conditions of the body; but it is apprehended, that if they should discontinue the use of them altogether, except in certain tinctures, etc., they would be as successful as they now are. They are often used where they would not be, if they were not the most common thing that could be found.

they destroy them all. Give them to the laborer; do they add to his strength? Do they enable him to bear fatigue, to endure heat and cold? Can he do more work, or do it better? No; they are the ruin of the whole. They reduce his strength, weaken his frame, make him more susceptible to heat and cold, disorganize his whole system, and unfit him for labor.

"But there are some men," say you, "who use ardent spirits, and who get along very well." Admitted. They endure it. So there are some men who get along very well with poor health and feeble constitutions. Are poor health and feeble constitutions, therefore, no evils? Is the prosperity of such to be attributed to them? As much as is that of the former to the use of ardent spirits. Was ever a man made rich by the use of ardent spirits? Never; but millions have been made beggars by it.

Yet some say, they *feel better* by drinking ardent spirits. Let us examine this excuse. It is nothing but an excuse, and he who loves rum and is ashamed to own it, says he feels better to drink it. Let us inquire how. Are they conducive to health? On this subject let the physician decide. One, as great as this country has produced, Dr. Rush, says that the habitual use of ardent spirits usually produces the following diseases: A loss of appetite, sickness at the stomach, obstruction of the liver, jaundice and dropsy, hoarseness and a husky cough, which often ends in consumption, diabetes, redness and eruptions of the skin, a fetid breath, frequent and disgusting belchings, epilepsy, gout, and madness. This is the train of diseases produced by the use of ardent spirits, and the usual, natural, and legitimate consequences of their use. And now, I ask, can that which, of its own nature, produces these diseases, make a man feel better? Reason might answer; and were she on her throne, uninfluenced and unbiassed by the love of ardent spirits, she would unequivocally answer, No. And we find that those who say they feel better to drink ardent spirits, are those who are in health, but love rum, and it gratifies their appetite, and this is what they mean by feeling better.

I will examine for a moment the effect, the immediate effect of ardent spirits upon the man. I will take a man in health, and give him a glass of ardent spirits. The effect is, to produce mental derangement and false notions and conceptions. But one glass will not have much effect. I will give him another, and, if he loves rum, he feels better; another, and he feels better; another, better yet. By this time he has got to feel pretty well; quite happy. He has no fear or shame. He can curse, and swear, and break things. "He is fit for treason, stratagems, and spoils." He fears no consequences, and can accomplish impossibilities. If he is a cripple, he fancies he can dance like a satyr; if he is slow and unwieldy, he can run like a hart; if he is weak and feeble in strength, he can lift like Samson, and fight like Hercules; if he is poor and pennyless, he is rich as Crœsus on his throne, and has money to lend. This is all a correct representation. It is what happens universally with the drunkard. I know one man who is intemperate, who is poor, and never known to have five dollars at a time, who, when he is intoxicated, has often, and does usually, offer to lend me a thousand dollars. Poor, miserable, and deluded man! But he feels well; he is one of those who feel better to drink. He is mentally deranged; his imagination is disordered. He fancies bliss, and felicity, and plenty, and abundance, which do not exist; and he awakes to misery, and poverty, and shame, and contempt. Yet this is the exact feeling of all those who feel better to drink spirits. He who drinks but a glass, has not the same degree, but precisely the same kind of feeling with the one I have described.

And this is all—this is all that rum does to make a man feel better. If his wife and children are starving, he feels it not. He feels better. If his affairs are going to ruin, or are already plunged into ruin, he is not sensible to his condition. If his house is on fire, he sings the maniac's song, and regards it not. He feels better.

Let him who likes this better feeling enjoy it. Enjoy it, did I say? No. Reclaim him, if possible. Convince him that he labors under a delusion. Restore him to truth, and to reason; banish the cup from his mouth, and change the brute into the man.

And now, need any more be said to persuade mankind to abandon the use of ardent spirits? the appalling facts, in relation to them, are known to all. Experience and observation teach us that they are the source of ruin, and misery, and squalid wretchedness, in a thousand shapes. They are the three-headed monster; they are the Gorgons with their thousand snakes; their name is Legion. And shall I yet find advocates for their use? Will this enlightened community yet say, they are useful and necessary? All those who have used them, and discontinued the use of them, say they are totally unnecessary and useless. We see that those who live without them enjoy more happiness and better health than those who use them—that they live longer lives. But oh, the folly, the stupidity, and the delusion of rum-drinkers!

But perhaps it may be said, that the effects and consequences that I have mentioned, result from the abuse, and not from the proper and moderate use of ardent spirits; and that on many occasions, in small quantities, they are useful. Let us examine the circumstances and occasions when they are said to be necessary; and perhaps I cannot do it better than in the words of another.

"They are said to be necessary in very *cold weather*.

This is far from being true; for the temporary heat they produce is always succeeded by a greater disposition in the body to be affected by cold. Warm dresses, a plentiful meal just before exposure to the cold, and eating occasionally a cracker or any other food, is a much more durable method of preserving the heat of the body in cold weather." In confirmation of this, the case of the vessel wrecked off the harbor of Newburyport, a few years since, may be adduced. On an intensely cold night, when all the men of that vessel were in danger of freezing to death, the master advised them to drink no ardent spirits. He told them, if they did, they must surely freeze. Some took his advice, while others, notwithstanding his most earnest entreaties, disregarded it. The result was, that of those who used the spirits, some lost their hands, some their feet, and some perished; while the rest survived unhurt.

"They are said to be necessary in very *warm weather*. Experience proves that they increase, instead of lessening the effects of heat upon the body, and thereby expose it to diseases of all kinds. Even in the warm climate of the West Indies, Dr. Bell asserts this to be true. Rum, says this author, whether used habitually, moderately, or in excessive quantities, always diminishes the strength of the body, and renders man more susceptible to disease, and unfit for any service in which vigor or activity is required. As well might we throw oil into a house, the roof of which was on fire, in order to prevent the flames from extending to its inside, as pour ardent spirits into the stomach, to lessen the effects of a hot sun upon the skin." And here permit me to add, that they are said to be necessary in cold weather to warm, and in warm weather to cool. The bare statement of the argument on these two points confounds itself.

"Nor do ardent spirits lessen the effects of *hard labor* upon the body. Look at the horse, with every muscle of his body swelled from morning till night, in a plough or a team. Does he make signs for a glass of spirits, to enable him to cleave the ground or climb a hill? No; he requires nothing but cold water and substantial food. There is no nourishment in ardent spirits. The strength they produce in labor is of a transient nature, and is always followed by a sense of weakness and fatigue."*

Some people, nevertheless, pretend that ardent spirits add to their strength, and increase their muscular powers; but this is all a delusion. They think they are strong when they are weak. Rum makes them boast, and that is all. The truth is, it weakens them in body, but strengthens them in imagination. Was not one reason why Samson was forbidden by the angel of God to drink either wine or strong drink, that he might thus increase and preserve his strength? When you hear a man telling how strong rum makes him, you may be sure he is weak, both in body and mind.

There is one other occasion for using ardent spirits, which it will be proper to examine. They are said to be necessary to keep off the *contagion* of disease, and are recommended to attendants upon the sick. But the united testimony of all physicians proves, that the intemperate are first attacked by epidemic disorders. This is almost universally the case in the southern states, and in the West Indies. Experience also proves that those attendants upon the sick, who refrain from the use of ardent spirits, escape, while those who use them are swept away. If facts could convince, the use of ardent spirits would be abolished. But the love of rum is stronger on the human mind than the truth of Heaven.

If, then, ardent spirits are not necessary in sickness; if they do not prevent the effects of heat and cold; if they do not add to our strength, and enable us to perform more

* Dr. Rush.

labor; when are they necessary? Why, people in health say, they want to drink them now and then—they do them good. What good? If they are well, why do they need them? For nothing but to gratify the taste, and to produce a feeling of intoxication and derangement, slight in its degree when moderately used, as they are by such people, but the character of the feeling is no less certain. It is the same feeling that induces the drunkard to drink. One man takes a glass to do him good, to make him feel better; another wants two; another three; another six; and by this time he is intoxicated, and he never feels well till he is so. He has the same feeling with the man who drinks a single glass, but more of it; and that man who, in health, drinks one glass to make him feel better, is just so much of a drunkard; one-sixth, if it takes six glasses to intoxicate him. He has one-sixth of the materials of a drunkard in his constitution.

But it is this *moderate use* of ardent spirits that produces all the excess. It is this which paves the way to downright and brutal intoxication. Abolish the ordinary and temperate use of ardent spirits, and there would not be a drunkard in the country. He who advises men not to drink to excess, may lop off the branches; he who advises them to drink only on certain occasions, may fell the trunk; but he who tells them not to drink at all, strikes and digs deep for the root of the hideous vice of intemperance; and this is the only course to pursue. It is this temperate use of ardent spirits that must be discontinued. They must be no longer necessary when friends call, when we go to the store to trade, to the tavern to transact business, when we travel the road on public days—in fact, they must cease to be fashionable and customary drinks. Do away the fashion and custom that attend their use, and change the tone of public feeling, so that it will be thought disgraceful to use them as they are now used by the most temperate and respectable men, and an end is for ever put to the prevalence of the beastly disease of intoxication. Let those who cannot be reclaimed from intemperance go to ruin, and the quicker the better, if you regard only the public good; but save the rest of our population; save yourselves; save your children! Raise not up an army of drunkards to supply their places. Purify your houses. They contain the plague of death; the poison that, in a few years, will render some of your little ones what the miserable wretches that you see staggering the streets are now. And who, I ask, would not do it? What father, who knew that one of his sons that he loves was, in a few years, to be what hundreds you can name are now, would hesitate, that he might save him, to banish intoxicating drinks from his premises for ever?

But if all will do it, he is saved; and he who contributes but a mite in this work of God, deserves the everlasting gratitude of the republic. If the names of a Brainerd, of a Swartz, of a Buchanan, have been rendered immortal by their efforts to convert the heathen to Christianity, the names of those men who shall succeed in converting Christians to temperance and sobriety, should be written in letters of ever-during gold, and appended by angels in the temple of the living God. The sum of their benevolence would be exceeded only by His, who came down from heaven for man's redemption. Then banish it; this is the only way to save your children. As long as you keep ardent spirits in your houses, as long as you drink it yourselves, as long as it is polite and genteel to sip the intoxicating bowl, so long society will remain just what it is now, and so long drunkards will spring from your loins, and so long drunkards will wear your names to future generations. And there is no other way given under heaven, whereby man can be saved from the vice of intemperance, but that of *total abstinence.*

And, if ardent spirits are the parent of all the poverty, and disease, and crime, and madness, that I have named, and if they produce no good, what rational man will use them? If he loves himself, he will not; if he loves his children, he will not; and as Hamilcar brought Hannibal to the altar, at eight years of age, and made him swear eternal hatred to the Romans, so every parent should bring his children to the altar, and make them swear, if I may so speak, eternal hatred to ardent spirits. He should teach them by precept and example. He should instil into his children a hatred of ardent spirits, as much as he does of falsehood and of theft. He should no more suffer his children to drink a little, than he does to lie a little, and to steal a little.

And what other security have you for your children, or for yourselves? Yes, for yourselves. I knew a man who, a few years ago, was as temperate as any of you; was as respectable as any of you, as learned as any of you, and as useful in life as any of you; I have heard him from the sacred desk again and again; but by the same use of ardent spirits that most men justify and advocate, under the mistaken notion that they were beneficial to him, he has at last fallen the victim of intemperance. And this is not a solitary example. I had almost said, it is a common example. I could easily add to the number.

And now, what security have you for yourselves? You have none but in the course I have recommended. If it is necessary for the intemperate man to write on every vessel containing ardent spirits, "Taste not, touch not, handle not," and to brand them as full of the very wrath of God, it is also necessary for the temperate man to do so, to save himself from intemperance.

But the difficulty on this subject is to convince men of their individual danger; that intemperance stands at their own doors, and is knocking for an entrance into their own houses; that they and their children are the victims that he seeks.

But if the places of the present generation of drunkards are to be supplied, whence will the victims come but from your own children? And who knows but that the infant the mother is now dandling upon her knee, and pressing to her bosom, however lovely he may appear, however respectable and elevated she is, will be selected to be one of that degraded, and squalid, and filthy class that, in her old age, will walk the streets as houseless, hopeless, and abandoned drunkards? You have no security, no assurance.

But we are apt to think that the wretches whom we see and have described were always so; that they were out of miserable and degraded families; and that they are walking in the road in which they were born. But this is not so. Among the number may be found a large proportion who were as lovely in their infancy, as promising in their youth, and as useful in early life, as your own children, and have become drunkards—I repeat it, and never let it be forgotten—*have become drunkards by the temperate, moderate, and habitual use of ardent spirits, just as you use them now.* Were it not for this use of ardent spirits, we should not now hear of drunken senators and drunken magistrates; of drunken lawyers and drunken doctors; churches would not now be mourning over drunken ministers and drunken members; parents would not be weeping over drunken children, wives over drunken husbands, husbands over drunken wives, and angels over a drunken world.

Then cease. No longer use that which is the source of infinite mischief, without one redeeming benefit; which has entailed upon you, upon your children, and upon society, woes unnumbered and unutterable. Banish it from your houses: it can be done. You have only to will, and it is effected. Use it not at home. Let it never be found to pollute your dwellings. Give it not to your friends or to your workmen. Touch it not yourselves, and suffer not your children to touch it; and let it be a part of your morning and evening prayer, that you and your children may be saved from intemperance, as much as from famine, from sickness, and from death.

Reader, have you perused this pamphlet; and are you still willing to drink, use, or sell this soul-destroying poison? If so—if you are willing to risk your own soul, disgrace your friends, and ruin your children by this fell destroyer, then go on; but remember, that to the drunkard is allotted the "blackness of darkness and despair for ever." But if not—if you feel the magnitude of the evil; if you are willing to do something to correct it, sit not down in hopeless silence, but arouse to action; "resist the devil, and he will flee from you;" not only banish it from your houses, but from your stores, your shops, your farms; give it not to your workmen; refuse to employ those who use it; invite, entreat, conjure your friends and neighbors to refrain wholly from the use of it; never forgetting that the day of final account is at hand; that what we do for Christ, and for the good of our fellow-men, must be done soon; and that those who sacrifice interest for the sake of conscience, and who are instrumental in turning men from their errors, shall not lose their reward.

This address was originally delivered before a large public meeting in Lyme, New Hampshire, Jan. 8, 1827.

APPEAL TO YOUTH.

A TRACT FOR THE TIMES.

BY REV. AUSTIN DICKINSON.

To arrest a great moral evil, and elevate the general standard of character in a community, the influence of the young is all-important. *They* can, if they please, put an end to the most demoralizing scourge that has ever invaded our country, and introduce a state of society far more pure and elevated than the world has yet seen.

Consider then, beloved youth, some of the numerous motives for abstaining from intoxicating liquor and other hurtful indulgences, and employing your time and faculties with a view to the highest improvement and usefulness.

The use of such liquor, as a beverage, *will do you no good*. It will not increase your property or credit: no merchant would deem a relish for it any recommendation for a clerk or partner in business. It will not invigorate your body or mind; for chemistry shows, that alcohol contains no more nutriment than fire or lightning. It will not increase the number of your respectable friends: no one, in his right mind, would esteem a brother or neighbor the more, or think his prospects the better, on account of his occasional use of intoxicating liquor. Nor will it in the least purify or elevate your affections, or help to fit you for the endearments of domestic life, or social intercourse; but on the contrary, Scripture and observation alike testify, that wine and its kindred indulgences "*take away the heart.*" Why, then, should a rational being, capable of the purest happiness, and capable of blessing others by an example of temperance, indulge in a beverage in no respect useful to those in health, but the occasion of countless miseries!

But strict temperance has a direct influence on *the health and vigor of both mind and body*. The most eminent physicians bear uniform testimony to its propitious effect.

And the Spirit of inspiration has recorded, *He that striveth for the mastery, is temperate in all things.* Many striking examples might be adduced. The mother of Samson, that prodigy of human strength, was instructed by an angel of God to preserve him from the slightest touch of "wine, or strong drink, or any unclean thing." And Luther, who burst the chains of half Europe, was as remarkable for temperance, as for great bodily and intellectual vigor. Sir Isaac Newton, also, while composing his Treatise on Light, a work requiring the greatest clearness of intellect, it is said, very scrupulously abstained from all stimulants. The immortal Edwards, too, repeatedly records his conviction and experience of the happy effect of strict temperance, both on mind and body. And recent reformations from moderate drinking have revealed numerous examples of renovated health and spirits in consequence of the change.

But not to multiply instances, let any youth, oppressed with heaviness of brain or dulness of intellect, judiciously try the experiment of *temperance in all things,* united with habitual activity, and he will be surprised at the happy effect.

Consider, again, that *in the purest state of morals, and the most elevated and refined circles, the use of intoxicating drink is now discountenanced, and regarded as unseemly.* Inspiration has declared, "It is not for kings to drink wine, nor for princes strong drink." And who would not regard any of the truly noble, as lowering themselves by disparaging this sentiment? What clerical association, or what convention of philanthropists, would now be found "mingling strong drink?" What select band of students, hoping soon to officiate honorably at the altar of God, before the bench of justice, or in the chamber of affliction, would now call for brandy or wine? What circle of refined females would not feel themselves about as much degraded by familiarity with such indulgences, as by smoking, or profane language? Or what parent, inquiring for an eligible boarding-school, would think of asking, whether his son or daughter might there have the aid of such stimulus, or the example of its use? If, then, intoxicating liquor is thus disparaged in the most moral and intelligent circles, why should it not be universally abjured by individuals? Why should not the young, especially, of both sexes, keep themselves unspotted, and worthy of the most elevated society?

Consider, moreover, that if the habit of drinking be indulged, *it may be difficult, if not impossible,* should you live, *to break off in more advanced life.* Thus, even in this day of reform, there are individuals, calling themselves respectable, so accustomed to drink, or traffic in the poison, that all the remonstrances of philanthropists and friends, the wailings of the lost, the authority of Heaven, and the anathema of public sentiment combined, cannot now restrain them. Let the youth, then, who turns with shame from such examples of inconsistency, beware of a habit so hardening to the conscience, so deadening to the soul.

But, to increase your contempt for the habit of drinking, think how it especially prevails *among the most degraded portions of the community.* Inquire through the city, or village, for those who are so polluted as to be shut out from all decent society—so inured to vice that they cannot be looked upon but with utter disgust; learn their history, and you invariably find that the insidious glass has been their companion, their solace, and their counsellor. And should not dark suspicion and decided reprobation be stamped upon that which is thus associated with the lowest debasement and crime?

Such drink, in its very nature, has a perverting and debasing tendency—leading to foul speeches, foolish contracts, and every sensual indulgence. Those under its influence will say and do, what, in other circumstances, they would abhor: they will slander, reveal secrets, throw away property, offend modesty, profane sacred things, indulge the vilest passions, and cover themselves and friends with infamy. Hence the solemn caution, "Look not thou on the wine, when it giveth its color in the cup: at the last it biteth like a serpent, and stingeth like an adder: thine eyes shall behold strange women, and thy heart utter perverse things." Those who, by gaming or intrigue, rob others of their property, and those who allure "the simple" to ruin, it is said, fully understand its perverting influence. "Is it not a little one?" say they; and so the unwise are "caused to fall, by little and little."

"She urged him still to *fill another cup;*
* * * and in the dark, still night,
When God's unsleeping eye alone can see,
He went to her adulterous bed. At morn

I looked, and saw him not among the youths;
I heard his father mourn, his mother weep;
For none returned that went with her. The dead
Were in her house; her guests in depths of hell:
She wove the winding-sheet of souls, and laid
Them in the urn of everlasting death."

Such is ever the tendency of the insidious cup. For the unerring word declares, "Wine is a mocker, strong drink is raging; and whosoever is deceived thereby *is not wise.*" "They are out of the way through strong drink; they err in vision, they stumble in judgment."

Indeed, the *whole spirit of the Bible,* as well as uncorrupted taste, is in direct hostility to this indulgence. Its language in regard to all such stimulants to evil is, *Touch not, taste not, handle not.* And to such as glory in being above danger, it says, with emphasis, "We, then, that are strong, ought to bear the infirmities of the weak, and *not to please ourselves.*"

He who hath declared, *Drunkards shall not inherit the kingdom of God,* cannot, surely, be expected to adopt, as heirs of his glory, any who, under all the light that has been shed on this subject, perseveringly resolve to sip the exhilarating glass for mere selfish pleasure, when they know that their example may probably lead others to endless ruin. Common sense, as well as humanity, revolts at the thought.

On the other hand, strict temperance is pleasing to the Most High. Hence, it is said of him who was honored to announce the Saviour's advent, "He shall be great in the sight of the Lord, and shall drink neither wine nor strong drink."

Moreover, the habit of strict temperance, being allied to other virtues, will secure for you the *respect and confidence of the best portions of the community,* as well as the approbation of God, and thus lead to your more extensive usefulness. The youth who promptly comes up to the pledge and practice of total abstinence, and persuades others to do so, gives evidence of decision and moral courage—gives evidence of an intellect predominating over selfish indulgence, and superior to the laugh of fools; and such is the man whom an intelligent community will delight to honor.

But you are to live, not merely for self-advancement, or happiness: consider, then, that *true patriotism and philanthropy rightfully demand* your cordial support of the Temperance cause. A thick, fiery vapor, coming up from the pit, has been overspreading our whole land and blighting half its glory. Thousands, through the noxious influence of this vapor, have yearly sunk to that pit, to weep and lament for ever. Thousands more are groping their miserable way thither, who, but for this pestilence, might be among our happiest citizens. Still greater numbers, of near connections, are in consequence, covered with shame. Ah, who can say, he has had no relative infected by this plague? But Providence, in great mercy, has revealed the only effectual course for exterminating the plague—*total abstinence from all that can intoxicate.* And the adoption of this course, instead of involving any real sacrifice, might be an annual saving to the nation of *many millions of dollars.* What youth, then, who loves his country, will not cheerfully coöperate with the most respected of every profession in encouraging this course? Who does not see its certain efficacy, and the grandeur of the result?

Were a foreign despot, with his armies, now invading our country, every youthful bosom would swell with indignation. And will you not combine to arrest the more cruel despot, Intemperance, whose vessels are daily entering our ports, whose magazines of death are planted at the corners of our streets, and whose manufactories are like "the worm that dieth not, and the fire that is not quenched?"

Were all who have, in the compass of a year, been found drunk in the land, assembled in one place, they would make a greater army than ever Bonaparte commanded. And yet, unless patriot hearts and hands interpose, myriads more, from generation to generation, coming on in the same track, will go down like these to the drunkard's grave.

Were all the thousands that annually descend to the drunkard's grave, cast out at once into an open field, their loathsome carcases would cover many acres of ground. And yet the *source* of all this pollution and death is moderate drinking.

Were the thousands of distilleries and breweries, still at work day and night in the land, placed in one city or county, they would blacken all the surrounding heavens with their smoke. And could all the oaths, obscenities, and blasphemies they occasion every hour, be uttered in one voice, it would be more terrific than "seven thunders."

And are those armies of drunkards, that liquid fire, those carcases of the slain, those ever-burning manufactories, and those blasphemies in the ear of Heaven, less appalling, less stirring to patriotism, because scattered throughout the land? Shall there be no burst of indignation against this monster of despotism and wickedness, because he has *insidiously* entered the country, instead of coming in by bold invasion? Shall he still deceive the nation, and pursue his ravages? Or shall he not, at once, be arrested, when it can be done without cost, and with infinite gain?

It must not be forgotten, that, in this country, every drunkard has equal power in the elective franchise with the most virtuous citizen. Nor must it be forgotten, that should the reform now cease, and intemperance again increase for the fifty years to come, in only the same ratio that it did for twenty years previous to the commencement of general reform in 1826, about one-third of our voters would be drunkards. What, then, would be the character of our beloved republic?

But should intemperance increase in that ratio for *eighty* years, a *majority* of our voters would be drunkards, and our population amount to several hundred millions. Who then could turn back the burning tide; or who could govern the maddening multitudes?

It is not a vain thing, then, that patriots have waked up to this subject. Their trumpet should now thrill through the land, and urge all the young to enlist, at once, on the side of virtue. These can, if they will, cause the river of abominations to be dried up.

But the subject of temperance has still another aspect, far more serious. It must be a solemn consideration to such as realize, in any measure, the worth of the soul and the necessity of its regeneration, that indulgence in the use of intoxicating drink, in this day of light, *may grieve the Holy Spirit,* whose presence alone can insure salvation. Indeed, to say nothing of the deadening influence of such liquor on the conscience, unless heaven and hell can mingle together, we cannot, surely, expect God to send *his* Spirit to coöperate *with that* which is peculiarly offensive to the most devoted and self-denying of his friends, and which Satan employs, more than any other agent, in fitting men for his service. For, "what communion hath light with darkness?"—"what concord hath Christ with Belial?" Beware, then, of the arch-deceiver, in this matter. "It is not a vain thing for you, because it is your life."

It is obvious that if such stimulants were wholly done away, *the Gospel would have far mightier sway*, and human nature generally assume a higher character. Pure moral stimulus would take the place of what is low, sensual, and selfish. Better health, better temper, higher intellect, and more generous benevolence would everywhere appear.

It is obvious, likewise, that Providence has great designs to be accomplished by the younger portions of this generation. Unto us are committed those oracles which declare, "Instead of thy fathers shall be thy children, whom thou mayest make princes in all the earth." And already do I see, in the silent kindling of unnumbered minds, in our Sabbath-schools and other institutions, the presage of unexampled good to the nations. Who, then, of the rising race, is so dead to generous feeling, so deaf to the voice of Providence, so blind to the beauty of moral excellence, that he will not now aspire to some course of worthy action? Let this motto, then, stand out like the sun in the firmament: HE THAT STRIVETH FOR THE MASTERY, IS TEMPERATE IN ALL THINGS.

One word in reference to making and observing a *pledge* for abstinence. As it respects yourself, it will show a resolute, independent mind, and be deciding the question once for all, and thus supersede the necessity of deciding it a thousand times, when the temptation is offered. It will, moreover, supersede the inconvenience of perpetual warfare with appetite and temptation. And as it respects others, of feebler minds, or stronger appetites, your *example* may be immeasurably important. Multitudes may thus be secured to a life of sobriety, who, but for this pledge, would never have had the requisite firmness. Your influence may thus extend on the right hand and on the left, and down to future ages; and by such united pledges and efforts, countless multitudes may be saved from a life of wretchedness, a death of infamy, and an eternity of woe.

But does any one still say, "I will unite in no pledge, because in no danger?" Suppose *you are safe;* have you then no *benevolence?* Are you utterly *selfish?* Think of the bosom now wrung with agony and shame, over a drunken husband, or father, or brother. And have you no *pity?* Think of the millions of hopes, for both worlds, suspended on the success of the temperance cause. And will you do nothing to speed its triumph?

Do you say, your influence is of no account? It was one "poor man" that saved a "little city," when a "great king besieged it." Another saved a "great city," when the anger of Jehovah was provoked against it. Small as your influence may be, you are accountable to God and your country; and your finger may touch some string that shall vibrate through the nation.

But are you conscious of possessing talent? Then rally the circle of your acquaintance, and enlist them in the sacred cause. And do you save a little by abstinence? Then *give* a little to extend the benign influence. What youth cannot, at least, circulate a few Tracts, and perhaps enlist as many individuals? And who can estimate the endless influence of those individuals, or their capacity for rising with you in celestial splendor?

But have you wealth, or power with the pen? Then speak by ten thousand tongues: send winged messengers through the city, the country, the town, the village, the harbor; and thus may you enjoy *now* the highest of all luxuries—the luxury of *doing good.* And, at the same time, trusting in HIM who came from the abodes of light, "to seek and save the lost," you may secure *durable riches* in that world, where, saith the Scripture, neither *covetous,* nor *drunkards,* nor extortioners, nor revilers, nor the *slothful,* nor mere *lovers of pleasure,* nor *any thing that defileth,* shall ever enter; but where THEY THAT BE WISE shall shine forth as the brightness of the firmament for ever and ever.

When these opposite characters and their changeless destinies are *seriously* weighed, none, surely, can hesitate which to prefer. But, "what thou doest, do quickly."

NOTE.—A premium of fifty dollars, offered by a friend, was awarded to the author of this Tract.

PUBLISHED BY THE AMERICAN TRACT SOCIETY.

ALARM TO DISTILLERS.

BY REV. BAXTER DICKINSON, D. D.

The art of turning the products of the earth into a fiery spirit was discovered by an *Arab*, about nine hundred years ago. The effects of this abuse of nature's gifts were soon viewed with alarm. Efforts were made, even by a heathen people, to arrest the evil; and it shows the mighty agency and cunning of Satan, that Christian nations should ever have been induced to adopt and encourage this deadliest of man's inventions. In the guilt of encouraging the destructive art, our own free country has largely participated. In the year 1815, as appears from well-authenticated statistics, our number of distilleries had risen to nearly *forty thousand;* and, until within a few years past, the progress of intemperance threatened all that was fair and glorious in our prospects. The reformation recently commenced is one of the grandest movements of our world; and to secure its speedy triumph, the concurrence of distillers is obviously indispensable. They must cease to provide the destroying element. This they are urged to do by the following considerations:

1. The business of distilling *confers no benefits on your fellow-men* Ardent spirit is not needed as an article of living. In the first ages of the world, when human life was protracted to hundreds of years, it was unknown. By the first settlers of this country it was not used. It was scarcely used for a whole century. And those temperate generations were remarkably robust, cheerful, and enterprising. To this we may add, that several hundred thousand persons, accustomed to use it, have given it up entirely within a few years past; and their united testimony is, that they have made no sacrifice either of health, or

strength, or any real comfort. Indeed few, if any, except such as have the intemperate appetite, will now seriously contend that distilled liquor is necessary or useful. The little that may perhaps be desirable as medicine, might be made by the apothecary, or the physician.

The talents God has given you *might* be applied to advance the welfare of your fellow-men. It is your duty—your highest *honor*—thus to apply them. And on the bed of death, in near prospect of the judgment, it will surely be a melancholy reflection that, as regards the happiness of mankind, your life has been an utter *blank*.

2. The business of distilling is not only useless, but *is the occasion of many and great evils*. Recent examination has developed a number of appalling facts, which few, if any, pretend to question. It is admitted that the use of ardent spirit has been a tax on the population of our country, of from *fifty to a hundred millions of dollars* annually. It is admitted that three-fourths of all the *crimes* of the land result from the use of intoxicating liquor. It is admitted that at least three-fourths of all the sufferings of *poverty* arise from the same source. It is admitted that upwards of *thirty thousand* of our citizens have annually descended to the *drunkard's grave*. It is admitted, by those who believe the Bible, that *drunkards shall not inherit eternal life*, but must *have their part in the lake that burneth with fire and brimstone*. In a word, it is admitted that health, fortune, social happiness, intellect, conscience, heaven, are all swept away by the tide of intemperance.

And now, what you are specially bound to ponder is, that this burning tide, with all its desolations, flows from those very fountains *you* have opened—the boiling flood can be perpetuated only by those fires which *your* hands kindle, and which it is your daily task to tend.

The position you occupy, then, is one of most fearful responsibility. You are directly and peculiarly accessary to a degree of guilt and misery which none but the infinite mind can comprehend. I hear for you a loud remonstrance from every court of justice, from every prison of collected crime, from every chamber of debasement, and from every graveyard, as well as from the dark world of despair. I hear the cries of unnumbered mothers, and widows, and orphans, all with one voice imploring you to extinguish those fires, to dry up those fountains, and to abandon an occupation pregnant with infamy, and death, and perdition.

3. The business of distilling *destroys, to a great extent, the bounties of Providence.* Many of the substances converted into ardent spirit are indispensable to the comfort of man—some of them the very staff of life. But the work of distillation not only destroys them as articles of food, but actually converts them to poison. An incalculable amount of grain, and tens of thousands of hogsheads of sugar and molasses, besides enormous quantities of other useful articles, are every year thus wickedly perverted in this Christian land. Who does not know the odious fact that, in many places, the *distillery* has regulated the price of bread? Who does not know that this engine of iniquity has at times so consumed the products of industry as to make it difficult for the poorer classes to get a supply? "The poor we have always with us;" and cries of the suffering are often heard from other lands. Such facts, it would seem, might reach the conscience of all who are wantonly destroying Heaven's gifts. Can you, for a little selfish gain, persist in converting the bread of multitudes into pestilential fire? How utterly unlike the example of Him who, while feeding thousands by miracle, could still say, "Gather up the fragments which remain, that nothing be lost."

4. By continuing this destructive business, *you greatly offend the virtuous and respectable part of the community.* The temperance reformation has been commenced and prosecuted by enlightened men. It is not the enterprise of any political party or religious sect. It has the general support of ministers and Christians of different denominations, of statesmen, judges, lawyers, physicians, and hundreds of thousands in the walks of private life. They regard the enterprise as one, on the success of which hang the liberties of our republic and the happiness of future millions.

You cannot be surprised, then, that they look with pain on operations directly adapted to defeat their plans, and perpetuate the dread evil they deplore. You cannot suppose that their eye will light on the *fountains* of this mighty evil but with inexpressible grief, disgust, and indignation. And if you have the common magnanimity of our nature, you will surely cease to outrage the feelings of the virtuous throughout the nation.

5. You pursue a pernicious calling, *in opposition to great light.* The time was when good men extensively engaged in the distilling business, and when few seemed to be aware of its fearfully mischievous tendency. The matter had not been a subject of solemn and extensive discussion. The sin was one of comparative ignorance. But circumstances have changed. Inquiry has thrown upon the community a flood of light. The evil of intemperance has been exhibited in its complicated horrors. Ardent spirit has been found to be not only useless, but fearfully destructive; so that the guilt of manufacturing it is now enormously aggravated.

Good men were once engaged in importing slaves. They suspected not the iniquity of the business; and an apology can be offered for them, on the ground of ignorance. But their trade has now come to be regarded by the civilized world in the same odious light as piracy and murder. The man who engages in it is stamped with everlasting infamy. And the reason is, that, like the distiller, he now sins amid that fulness of light which an age of philanthropy has poured around him.

6. Perseverance in the business of distilling *must necessarily be at the expense of your own reputation and that of your posterity.* You are creating and sending out the materials of discord, crime, poverty, disease, and intellectual and moral degradation. You are contributing to perpetuate one of the sorest scourges of our world. And the scourge can never be removed till those deadly fires you have kindled are all put out. That public sentiment which is worthy of respect calls upon you to extinguish them. And the

note of remonstrance will wax louder and louder till every smoking distillery in the land is demolished. A free and enlightened people cannot quietly look on while an enemy is working his engines and forging the instruments of national bondage and death.

Without a prophet's vision, I foresee the day when the manufacture of intoxicating liquor, for common distribution, will be classed with the arts of counterfeiting and forgery, and the maintenance of houses for midnight revelry and corruption. Like these, the business will become a work only of darkness, and be prosecuted only by the outlaw.

Weigh well, then, the bearing of your destructive employment on personal and family *character*. The employment may secure for you a little gain, and perhaps wealth. But, in a day of increasing light and purity, you can never rid treasures, thus acquired, of a *stigma*, which will render him miserably poor who holds them. Upon the dwelling you occupy, upon the fields you enclose, upon the spot that entombs your ashes, there will be fixed an indescribable gloom and odiousness, to offend the eye and sicken the heart of a virtuous community, till your memory shall perish. Quit, then, this vile business, and spare your name, spare your family, spare your children's children such insupportable shame and reproach.

7. By prosecuting this business *in a day of light and reform, you peculiarly offend God, and jeopard your immortal interests.* In "times of ignorance," God, in a sense, "winked at" error. But let the error be persisted in under a full blaze of light, and it must be the occasion of a dread retribution from his throne.

The circumstances of the distiller are now entirely changed. His sin was once a sin of ignorance, but is such no longer. He *knows* he is taking bread from the hungry, and perverting the bounties of Providence. He *knows* he is undermining the very pillars of our republic. He *knows* that, by distilling, he confers no benefits upon mankind. He *knows* he is directly accessary to the temporal wretchedness and the endless wailing of multitudes. And knowing these things, and keeping on his way, he accumulates guilt which the Holy One cannot overlook. If endless exclusion from heaven be the drunkard's doom, can *he* be held guiltless who deliberately prepared for him, and perhaps placed in his hand, the cup of death and damnation? This is not the decision either of Scripture or of common sense. Wilfully persevering to furnish the sure means of death, you carry to the judgment the murderer's character as clearly as the midnight assassin.

And now, what is the APOLOGY for prosecuting a business so manifestly offensive to God, and ruinous to yourself, as well as others? Do you say, *It is necessary as a means of support?* But whence have you derived authority to procure a living at the sacrifice of conscience, character, and the dearest interests of others? And is the maintenance of a *public nuisance* really necessary to your support? In a country like this, the plea of necessity for crime is glaringly impious. Many and varied departments of honest and honorable industry are before you, all promising a generous reward; and, neglecting them for a wicked and mischievous occupation, you must bear the odium of a most sordid avarice, or implacable malignity.

You virtually, too, impeach the character of God. You proclaim that he has made your comfort, and even subsistence, to depend upon the practice of iniquity. It is an imputation he must repel with abhorrence and wrath. Nor is it sustained by the conscience, reason, or experience of any man.

But possibly you urge, in self-justification, *Others will manufacture spirit, if I do not.* But remember, the guilt of one is no excuse for another. "Every one of us shall give account of *himself* to God." If others pursue a business at the sacrifice of character and of heaven, it becomes you to avoid their crime, that you may escape their doom.

It is not certain, however, that others will prosecute the destructive business, if you abandon it. Men of forethought will not now embark their silver and gold on a pestilential stream, soon to be dried up under that blaze of light and heat which a merciful God has enkindled. They will not deem it either wise or safe to kindle unholy and deadly fires where the pure river of the water of life is so soon to overflow. In the eye of thousands, the distillery on your premises adds nothing to their value. Indeed, should they purchase those premises, the filthy establishment would be demolished as the first effort of improvement. And every month and hour is detracting from its value, and blackening the curse that rests upon it.

Let the thousands now concerned in distilling at once put out their fires, and the act would cause one general burst of joy through the nation; and any effort to rekindle them would excite an equally general burst of indignation and abhorrence. None but a monster of depravity would ever make the attempt.

But again, perhaps you say, *No one is obliged to use the spirit that is made.* But remember, that you make it only to be used. You make it with the desire, with the hope, with the expectation that it will be used. You know it has been used by thousands—by millions—and has strewed the land with desolation, and peopled hell with its victims; and you cannot but acknowledge that you would at once cease to make the liquor, did you not *hope it would continue to be used.* Indeed, you must see that *just in proportion to your success* will be the amount of mischief done to your fellow-men.

It seems hardly needful to say that the foregoing considerations are all strictly applicable to SUCH AS FURNISH THE MATERIALS for the distiller. Were these withheld, his degrading occupation would of course cease. By suffering, then, the fruits of your industry to pass into his hands, you perpetuate his work of death. You share all his guilt, and shame, and curse. And remember, too, that the bushel of grain, the barrel of cider, the hogshead of molasses, for which you thus gain a pittance, may be returned from the fiery process only to hasten the infamy and endless ruin of a beloved son, or brother, or friend.

Nor is the crime of the RETAILER of ardent spirit essentially different. He takes the poison from the distiller, and insidiously deals it out to his fellow-men. It is truly stirring to one's indignation to notice his variety of artifice for rendering it enticing. His occupation is one which the civil authorities have, in some places, with a noble consistency, ceased to tolerate; and one which must soon be put down by the loud voice of public sentiment.

Indeed, the *retailer*, the *distiller*, and he who *furnishes the materials*, must be looked upon as forming a TRIPLE LEAGUE, dangerous alike to private and social happiness, and to the very liberties of the nation. And an awakened people cannot rest till the deadly compact is sundered. Why not, then, anticipate a little the verdict and the vengeance of a rising tone of public sentiment, and at once proclaim the *unholy alliance* dissolved? Why not anticipate the verdict of an infinitely higher tribunal—why not believe God's threatening, and escape the eternal tempest that lowers for *him who putteth the cup to his neighbor's lips?* Why not coöperate promptly in a public reform that is regarded with intense interest in heaven, on earth, and in hell?

O review, as men of reason, and conscience, and immortality, this whole business. And if you have no ambition to *benefit your fellow-men*—if you can consent *to ruin many for both worlds*—if you can persist in *wasting and perverting the bounties of a kind Providence*—if you can outrage the feelings of the most *enlightened and virtuous*—if you can pursue a work of darkness *amid noonday light*—if you can sacrifice a *good name*, and entail *odium on all you leave*—and if you can deliberately *offend God*, and jeopard *your immortal interests* for paltry gain, then go on—go on a little longer; but, "O MY SOUL, COME NOT THOU INTO THEIR SECRET; UNTO THEIR ASSEMBLY, MINE HONOR, BE NOT THOU UNITED."

NOTE.—A premium, offered by a friend of temperance, was awarded to the author of this Tract.

PUBLISHED BY THE AMERICAN TRACT SOCIETY.

PUTNAM AND THE WOLF;

OR,

THE MONSTER DESTROYED.

AN ADDRESS ORIGINALLY DELIVERED AT POMFRET, CONN.,

BY REV. JOHN MARSH.

I REMEMBER, when a boy, reading a story which chilled my blood in my veins; but which taught me never to sit down and try to bear an evil which might, by bold and persevering effort, be remedied. The story was this. A certain district of country was infested by a wild beast. The nuisance was intolerable. The inhabitants rallied, and hunted it day and night, until they drove it into a deep den. There, with dogs, guns, straw, fire, and sulpher, they attacked the common enemy; but all in vain. The hounds came back badly wounded, and refused to return. The smoke of blazing straw had no effect; nor had the fumes of burnt brimstone. The ferocious animal would not quit its retirement. And now the shadows of evening gathered around them. The clock struck nine, and ten. And should they lose their prey? They must, unless some one should be so daring as to descend into this den of monsters and destroy the enemy. One man offered to go; but his neighbors remonstrated against the perilous enterprise. Perilous indeed it was; but live so they could not, and stripping off his coat and waistcoat and having a long rope fastened round his legs, by which he might be pulled back, he entered with a flaming torch in his hand, head foremost. The most terrifying darkness appeared in front of the dim circle afforded by his light. It was still as the house of death. But proceeding onwards with unparalleled courage, he discovered the glaring eyeballs of the ferocious beast, who was sitting at the extremity of the cavern. For a moment he retreated; but again descended with his musket. The beast howled, rolled its eyes, snapped its teeth, and threatened him with instant death, when he levelled, fired, and brought it forth dead, to the view of his trembling and exulting neighbors.

Little did I then think that I should one day see the country rallied on the same spot, to hunt a more terrible monster, whose destruction will require Putnam courage.

The old enemy, gentlemen, which your fathers hunted about these hills and dales, was visible to the eye, and could be reached with powder and ball; but the enemy whom you assault is, like the foe of human bliss which entered the garden of Eden, invisible, and therefore not to be described, and not to be destroyed by force of arms. That enemy did, indeed, to effect his purpose, assume the form of a serpent; and ours has been said, as belonging to the same family, to have occasionally the same aspect. A gentleman in Missouri has recently described a dreadful worm which, he says, infests that country. "It is of a dead lead color, and generally lives near a spring, and bites the unfortunate people who are in the habit of going there to drink.

The symptoms of its bite are terrible. The eyes of the patient become red and fiery; the tongue swells to an immoderate size and obstructs utterance, and delirium of the most horrid character ensues. The name of this reptile is, 'THE WORM OF THE STILL.'" I suspect it is one of the same family which is infesting the peaceful villages of New England, and whose ravages have alarmed the country, and caused you this day to leave your homes and seek its destruction. I would not here inquire minutely into its history. It is said to have originated in Arabia, the country of the false prophet. The aborigines of our forests never knew it. They could proudly tread on the rattlesnake and copperhead, but never fell before the worm of the still. O woful day when it found its way to our coasts; when here it first generated its offspring.

Yet there are men who think we belie it; who say that we are needlessly alarmed; that we are hunting a friend; that we are driving one from our country without whose aid we can never check the ravages of disease, or perform our labor, or have any hilarity. It is not, say they, a poisonous foe. It is a pleasant cordial; a cheerful restorative; the first friend of the infant; the support of the enfeebled mother; a sweet luxury, given by the parent to the child; the universal token of kindness, friendship, and hospitality. It adorns the sideboards and tables of the rich, and enlivens the social circles of the poor; goes with the laborer as his most cheering companion; accompanies the mariner in his long and dreary voyage; enlivens the carpenter, the mason, the blacksmith, the joiner, as they ply their trade; follows the merchant to his counter, the physician to his infected rooms, the lawyer to his office, and the divine to his study, cheering all and comforting all. It is the life of our trainings, and town-meetings, and elections, and bees, and raisings, and harvests, and sleighing-parties. It is the best domestic medicine, good for a cold and a cough, for pain in the stomach, and weakness in the limbs, loss of appetite and rheumatism, and is a great support in old age. It makes a market for our rye and apples; sustains 100,000 families who are distilling and vending, and pours annually millions of dollars into our national treasury. Had the wolf possessed the cunning of the fox, she would have told Putnam as smooth a story as this. But it would have made no difference. The old man's cornfields were fattened by the blood of his sheep, and he would give no quarter. And the blood of our countrymen has been poured out at the shrine of the demon Intemperance, and we must give none. Talk we of alcohol as a friend! As well may a mother praise the crocodile which has devoured her offspring.

Look, my countrymen, at the ravages of intemperance. Fix your eye on its waste of property.

At the lowest calculation, it has annually despoiled us of a hundred millions of dollars—of thirty millions for an article which is nothing worth, and seventy or eighty millions more to compensate for the mischiefs that article has done—money enough to accomplish all that the warmest patriot could wish for his country, and to fill, in a short period, the world with Bibles and a preached Gospel. What farmer would not be roused, should a wild beast come once a year into his borders and destroy the best cow in his farmyard? But 6¼ cents a day for ardent spirit wastes $22 81 cents a year, and in 40 years nearly $1,000, which is a thousand times as much as scores of drunkards are worth at their burial.

See the pauperism it has produced. We have sung of our goodly heritage, and foreign nations have disgorged their exuberant population that they might freely subsist in this land of plenty. But in this granary of the world are everywhere seen houses without windows, fields without tillage, barns without roofs, children without clothing, and penitentiaries and almshouses filled to overflowing; and a traveller might write—BEGGARS MADE HERE. We are groaning under our pauperism, and talking of taxes, and hard times, and no trade; but intemperance has stalked through our land and devoured our substance. It has entered the houses of our unsuspecting inhabitants as a friend, and taken the food from their tables, and the clothing from their beds, and the fuel from their fire, and turned their lands over to others, and drove them from their dwellings to subsist on beggary and crime, or drag out a miserable existence in penitentiaries and almshouses. Two-thirds, or 150,000 of the wretched tenants of these abodes of poverty in the United States, were reduced by intemperance. So themselves confess. It was rum, brandy, and whiskey, that did it. And the Prison Discipline report tells of 50,000 cases of imprisonment for debt annually in the United States, in consequence of the use of ardent spirits. O, its sweeps of property can never be known.

Look at the crime it has occasioned.

It is said that there is a spring in China which makes every man that drinks it a villain. Eastern tales are founded on some plain matter of fact. This spring may be some distillery or dram-shop; for this is the natural effect of alcohol. It breaks down the conscience, quickens the circulation, increases the courage, makes man flout at law and right, and hurries him to the perpetration of every abomination and crime. Excite a man by this fluid, and he is bad enough for any thing. He can lie, and steal, and fight, and swear, and plunge the dagger into the bosom of his nearest friend. No vice is too filthy, no crime too tragical for the drunkard. The records of our courts tell of acts committed under the influence of rum, which curdle the blood in our veins. Husbands butcher their wives; children slaughter their parents. Far the greater part of the atrocities committed in our land, proceed from its maddening power. "I declare in this public manner, and with the most solemn regard to truth," said Judge Rush, some years ago in a charge to a grand jury, "that I do not recollect an instance since my being concerned in the administration of justice, of a single person being put on his trial for manslaughter which did not originate in drunkenness; and but few instances of trial for murder where the crime did not spring from the same unhappy cause." Of 895 complaints presented to the police court in Boston in one year, 400 were under the statute against common drunkards. Of 1,061 cases of criminal prosecution in a court in North Carolina, more than 800 proceeded from intemperance. Five thousand complaints are made yearly in New York to the city police of outrages committed by intoxicated persons; and the late city attorney reports, that of twenty-two cases of murder which it had been his duty to examine, every one of them had been committed in consequence of intemperate drinking. "Nine-tenths of all the prisoners under my care," says Captain Pillsbury, warden of our own state prison, "are decidedly intemperate men, and were brought to their present condition, directly or indirectly, through intoxicating liquor. Many have confessed to me with tears, that they never felt tempted to the commission of crime, thus punishable, but when under the influence of strong drink." And the Prison Discipline report states, "that of 125,000 criminals committed to our prisons in a single year, 93,750 were excited to their commission of crime by spirituous liquors.

Look at its destruction of intellect.

It reduces man to a beast, to a fool, to a devil. The excessive drinker first becomes stupid, then idiotic, then a maniac. Men of the finest geniuses, most acute minds, and profound learning, have dwindled under the touch of this withering demon to the merest insignificance, and been hooted by boys for their silly speeches and silly actions, or chained in a madhouse as unsafe in society. Of eighty-seven admitted into the New York hospital in one year, the insanity of twenty-seven was occasioned by ardent spirit; and the physicians of the Pennsylvania hospital report, that one-third of the insane of that institution were ruined by intemperance. What if one-sixth of our maniacs were deprived of their reason by the bite of the dogs, the friendly inmates of our houses, or by some vegetable common on our table; who would harbor the dangerous animal, or taste the poisonous vegetable? But, one-third of our maniacs are deranged by alcohol. Indeed, every drunkard is in a temporary delirium; and no man who takes even a little into his system, possesses that sound judgment, or is capable of that patient investigation or intellectual effort, which would be his without it. Just in proportion as man comes under its influence, he approximates to idiotism or madness.

Look at its waste of health and life.

The worm of the still, says the Missouri gentleman, never touches the brute creation, but as if the most venomous of all beings, it seizes the noblest prey. It bites man. And where it once leaves its subtle poison, farewell to health—farewell to long life. The door is open, and in rush dyspepsia, jaundice, dropsy, gout, obstructions of the liver, epilepsy—the deadliest plagues let loose on fallen man—all terminating in delirium tremens or mania a potu, a prelude to the eternal buffetings of foul spirits in the world of despair. One out of every forty, or three hundred thousand of our population, have taken up their abode in the lazar-house of drunkenness, and thirty thousand die annually the death of the drunkard. These sweeps of death mock all the ravages of war, famine, pestilence, and shipwreck. The yellow-fever in Philadelphia, in 1793, felt to be one of the greatest curses of heaven, destroyed but four thousand. In our last war the sword devoured but five hundred a year: intemperance destroys two hundred a week. Shipwrecks destroy suddenly, and the country groans when forty or fifty human beings are suddenly engulfed in the ocean; but more than half of all the sudden deaths occur in fits of intoxication. It needed not a fable to award the prize of greatest ingenuity in malice and murder to the demon who invented brandy, over the demon who invented war.

Look at its murder of souls.

Not satisfied with filling jails, and hospitals, and graveyards, it must people hell. Every moral and religious principle is dissipated before it. The heart becomes, under its influence, harder than the nether mill-stone. It has gone into the pulpit and made a Judas of the minister of Christ. It has insinuated itself into the church, and bred putrefaction and death among the holy. It has entered the anxious room in seasons of revival, and quenched conviction in the breast of the distressed sinner, or sent him, exhilarated with a false hope, to profess religion, and be a curse to the church. It has accompanied men, Sabbath after Sabbath, to the house of God, and made them insensible as blocks of marble to all the thunders of Sinai and sweet strains of Zion. It has led to lying, profane swearing, Sabbath-breaking, tale-bearing, contention; and raised up an army, I may almost say, in every village, who wish for no Sabbath, and no Bible, and no Saviour, and who cry out with stammering tongues, "Away with him, crucify him." It has, without doubt, been the most potent of all the emissaries of Satan, to obliterate the fear of the Lord, turn men away from the Sabbath and the sanctuary, steel them against the word, the providence, and grace of God, stupefy the conscience, bring into action every dark and vile passion, and fill up with immortal souls the dark caverns of eternal night. Let a man, day by day, hover around a dram-shop, and sip and sip at his bottle, and the devil is sure of him. No ministers, no Sabbaths, no prayers, no tears from broken-hearted and bleeding relatives, can avail to save him. He holds that man by a chain which nothing but Omnipotence can break.

And look, too, at its waste of human happiness.

Yes, look—look for yourselves. The woes of drunkenness mock all description. Some tell of the happiness of drinking. O, if there is a wretched being on earth, it is the drunkard. His property wasted, his character gone, his body loathsome, his passions wild, his appetite craving the poison that kills him, his hopes of immortality blasted for ever; it is all

> "Me miserable,
> Which way I fly is hell, myself am hell."

And his family. I can never look at it but with feelings of deepest anguish.

> "Domestic happiness, thou only bliss
> Of paradise that hast escaped the fall,"

thou art shipwrecked here. Sorrow, woe, wounds, poverty, babblings, and contention, have entered in and dwell here. Yet we have 300,000 such families in the land; and if each family consists of four individuals, more than a million persons are here made wretched by this curse of curses.

And his death. O, to die in our houses, amid our friends, and with the consolations of religion, strips not death of its character as the king of terrors. But to die as the drunkard dies, an outcast from society, in some hovel or almshouse, on a bed of straw, or in some ditch, or pond, or frozen in a storm; to die of the *brain-fever*, conscience upbraiding, hell opening, and foul spirits passing quick before his vision to seize him before his time—this, this is woe; this is the triumph of sin and Satan. Yet, in the last ten years, 300,000 have died in our land the death of the drunkard; rushing, where?—"Drunkards shall not inherit the kingdom of God"—rushing into hell, where their worm dieth not, and their fire can never be quenched. And if the demon is suffered to continue his ravages, 300,000 more of our existing population will, in the same way, rush into eternal burnings.

And his funeral. Have you ever been at a drunkard's funeral? I do not ask, did you look at his corpse? It was cadaverous before he died. But did you look at his father as he bent over the grave and exclaimed in agony, "O, my son, my son, would to God I had died for thee, my son." Did you look at his widow, pale with grief, and at his ragged, hunger-bitten children at her side, and see them turn away to share the world's cold pity, or, perhaps, rejected and forlorn, follow the same path to death and hell?

Such are the ravages of the demon we hunt. Its footsteps are marked with blood. We glory in our liberties, and every fourth of July our bells ring a merry peal, as if we were the happiest people on earth. But O, our country, our country! She has a worm at her vitals, making fast a wreck of her physical energies, her intellect, and her moral principle; augmenting her pauperism and her crime; nullifying her elections—for a drunkard is not fit for an elector—and preparing her for subjection to the most merciless tyranny that ever scourged any nation under heaven. We talk of our religion, and weep over the delusions of the false prophet and the horrors of Juggernaut; but a more deceitful prophet is in our churches than Mahomet, and a more bloody idol than Juggernaut rolls through our land, crushing beneath its wheels our sons and our daughters. Woe, woe, woe to Zion. Satan is in Eden. And if no check is put to the ravages of the demon, our benevolent institutions must die, our sanctuaries be forsaken, our beautiful fields be wastes, and the church will read the history of her offspring in the third of Romans: *Their throat is an open sepulchre; their mouth is full of cursing and bitterness; their feet are swift to shed blood*—all, blasting our bright hope of the speedy approach of millennial glory.

There is cause, then, for the general alarm that has been excited in our country; reason for this extensive and powerful combination to hunt and destroy the monster. Much, by divine help, has been done. He has been routed and brought to the light of day; the mischief he has done has been exposed; his apologists have been confronted; he is driven into his den, and now how can he be destroyed? That he must be destroyed there can be no question. The man who does not wish for the suppression of intemperance must have the heart of a fiend; especially, if he wishes to grow rich on the miseries of his fellow-men. And he must be destroyed now. It is now or never. Men may say enough has been done, and talk about his being held where he is. He cannot be held there. He has the cunning of a serpent, and he will escape through some fissure in the rock. He is now in our power. The temperance movement, which has on it the impress of the finger of God, has brought him within our grasp; and if we let him escape, the curse of curses will be entailed upon our children. How then can he be destroyed? I answer, and thousands answer, by starvation. No weapon can reach him so long as you feed him. But who has a heart so traitorous to humanity as to feed this monster? Every man who now, in the face of the light that is shed upon this subject, distils, or vends, or uses intoxicating liquor; every distillery, and every dram-shop in the land, nourishes this foe to human peace; every man who takes the alcoholic poison into his system, or imparts it to others, except as he takes and imparts other poisons to check disease, gives life to the beast. I need not stop to prove it. It is manifest to the child. Let every distillery in the land cease, and every dram-shop be closed, and total abstinence become the principle of every individual, and the demon will be dead; yes, take away from him his wine, his brandy, and his whiskey, and he will perish for ever. But here is the very brunt of the battle. We have hunted the monster through the land, and driven him into his den; and now we must stand at the very mouth of the cavern, and contend with our fellow-men and fellow-sufferers—yes, and fellow-Christians too—who are either afraid to attack the monster, or are determined he shall live.

And first, we are met by a body of men who tell us that alcohol is useful. And what if it is? What if every benefit that the moderate and immoderate drinker can think of, flows from it? What will this do to compensate for its giant evils which are desolating our land? Is man so bent on self-gratification that he will have every sweet, though it be mingled with poison? Will he exercise no reason; make no discrimination between unmixed good and good followed by desolating woes? Tea was good. But, said our fathers, if with it we must have all the horrors of British tyranny, away with it from our dwellings. My countrymen, "the voice of your fathers' blood cries to you from the ground, 'My sons, scorn to be slaves!'" Away with the shameful plea that you cannot do without an article which subjects you to an evil ten thousand times worse than all the horrors of British tyranny. You kindle the fires of liberty by pointing to the woes of the prison-ship, and the bones of your countrymen whitening on the shores of New Jersey. O, crouch not to a tyrant who binds a million in his chains, and demands thirty thousand annually for his victims. I blush for the imbecility of the man who must have an article on his farm which eats up his substance and his vitals, and may turn his son into an idiot and a brute. Better have no farm. Better go at once, with his family, into the poor-house, and be supported by public charity.

Next comes canting Hypocrisy, with his Bible in his hand, telling us that "every creature of God is good, and nothing to be refused, if it be received with thanksgiving." What does he mean; that ardent spirit is the gift of God?

Pray, in what stream of his bounty, from what mountain and hill does it flow down to man? O, it is in the rye, and the apple, and the sugar, and the Mussulman has taught us Christians how to distil it. And so the poet tells us Satan taught his legions how to make gunpowder. "There are," said he,

"Deep under ground, materials dark and crude,
Of spirituous and fiery spume.
These, in their dark nativity, the deep
Shall yield us, pregnant with internal flame;
Which, into hollow engines, long and round,
Thick ramm'd, at th' other bore with touch of fire
Dilated and infuriate, shall send forth
From far, with thundering noise, among our foes
Such implements of mischief as shall dash
To pieces and o'erwhelm whatever stands
Adverse.
Th' invention all admired; up they turn'd
Wide the celestial soil; sulphurous and nitrous foam
They found, they mingled; and, with subtle art
Concocted and adjusted, they reduced
To blackest grain."

And now, to carry out the argument, gunpowder, and guns, and swords, are the gift of God, and men must needs use them, and kill one another as fast as possible.

But nothing, it is plead, was made in vain. Spirit is good for something, and to banish it from use, and promise that we will "touch not, taste not, handle not," is contempt of the works of God. I should like to have seen what the Pomfret hero would have done with a man who should have stood before him, and said, Don't you destroy that wolf; God made it, and it may be good for something.

Next, we are checked in our principle of starvation by a set of thoughtless youth and presumptuous men, who say there is no danger from the demon if we keep him low. All his ravages have been occasioned by his being full fed. Let him sip but little, feed him *prudently*, and he will do no harm.

"Good," says the demon, growling in his den; "that is all I want. The doctrine of prudent use is the basis of my kingdom. Temperate drinking has made all the drunkards in the land, and keep it up in all your towns and villages, and I shall be satisfied."

O the delusion! Prudent use! What is the testimony of every chemist and physician in the land? Alcohol is a *poison*.

"Not a bloodvessel," says Dr. Mussey, "however minute, not a thread of nerve in the whole animal machine escapes its influence. It disturbs the functions of life; it increases for a time the action of the living organs, but lessens the power of that action; hence the deep depression and collapse which follow preternatural excitement. By habitual use it renders the living fibre less and less susceptible to the healthy operation of unstimulating food and drink, its exciting influences soon become incorporated with all the living actions of the body, and the diurnal sensations of hunger, thirst, and exhaustion, are strongly associated with the recollection of its exhilarating effects, and thus bring along with them the resistless desire for its repetition." More than fifty per cent. of common spirits are alcohol, this deadly substance, holding rank with henbane, hemlock, prussic acid, foxglove, poison sumach. Nausea, vertigo, vomiting, exhilaration of spirits for a time, and subsequent stupor, and even total insensibility and death, are their accompaniments. Broussais remarks, "A single portion of ardent spirit taken into the stomach produces a temporary phlogosis." Now, I submit it to every considerate man, whether there can be any prudent use of a poison, a single portion of which produces the same disease of which the drunkard dies, and a disease which brings along with it a resistless desire for a repetition of the draught.

Thoughtless, self-sufficient men say, they can control this desire, can govern their appetite, can enjoy the exhilaration of strong drink, and yet be temperate. Let them look at the poor inebriate wallowing in his pollution. He once stood just where they stand; boasted just as they boast; had as fair character, and as kind friends, and as precious a soul and bright hopes of heaven as they have. Let them tell why he does not control his appetite. Perhaps they say, he is a fool. Ah, what made him a fool? Or, his reason is gone. And what took away his reason? Or, he has lost his character. And what took away his character? Or, his sense of shame is departed. And what took away his sense of shame? Ah, here is the dreadful secret, which it may be well for all, boasting of their power of self-control, to know. At the very moment when the man thinks he stands firm, and reason can control appetite, his moral sense departs, his shame is gone, and he turns, through the power of his morning bitters and oft-repeated drams, into the brute and the maniac. With the moral sensibilities laid waste, reason here has only the power of the helmsman before the whirlwind. "Twenty years ago," says Nott, "a respectable householder came in the morning with a glass of bitters in his hand, and offered it to his guest, saying, 'Take it; it will do you good. I have taken it for some years, and I think it does me good; and I never want any more.' Time passed on, and presently the bottle of bitters in the closet was exchanged for the barrel of whiskey in the cellar; and the poor man was often at the tap for just as much as would do him good, and he never wanted any more. Time passed on, and a hogshead was needful; and its contents were exhausted with the same intent, and the same self-deceivings. At length the home of his family was relinquished to his creditors; his polluted body was lodged in a jail, from which he presently issued a drunken vagabond, and wandered a wretched being, until he found a drunkard's grave." It is but the history of thousands. No laws of nature act with more uniformity than the laws of intemperance. No inoculation sends with more certainty disease into the system than drinking strong drink. Hundreds have made an agonizing struggle to escape from perdition. They have seen their sin and danger; they have walked the streets in agony; they have gone to their homes and looked at their wives and children, and into the pit of despair. But their feverish stomach has cried, Give, give! and they have drank often and often, with the solemn promise that it should be the last time; until they have exclaimed, with a once interesting youth, "I know I am a ruined man, but I cannot stop."

Some, indeed, through much care and strength of constitution, may escape; but the plague, if it appear not in their skin and their bone, may break out in their children. "I will drink some," said an aged deacon of a church of Christ; "for it does me good." God was merciful, though he tempted Heaven, and it is said that he died with his character untarnished; but six loathsome sons drank up his substance, with the leprosy in their foreheads. What a meeting must there be between that deacon and his sons on the judgment-day! The doctrine of prudent use must be abandoned. It can have no standard. Every man thinks he drinks prudently, whether he takes one glass a day or five, and is just as much excited and just as liable to drunkenness as all drunkards were when they stood where he now stands. He only that entirely abstains can properly be called a temperate man. And he only is clear from the guilt of spreading intemperance through the land. Moderate drinkers are the life of this bloody system which is wringing with agony the hearts of thousands. Did all at once drink to excess, alcohol would be viewed with dread, as is laudanum and arsenic. Better that all who tasted it were at once made drunkards; then, drunkards would be as scarce as suicides. But men now sip moderately and are reputable; they think themselves safe, but one in every forty sinks to drunkenness; and thus, among twelve millions of people, drinking moderately, the demon has perpetually 300,000 victims. And for these, while all are thus paying homage to the bottle, what is the hope? The lost wretch may wake from his brutality and crime, and resolve that he will reform, and his broken-hearted wife may hope that the storms of life are over, and his babes may smile at his strange kindness and care; but the universal presence of the intoxicating fluid, and the example of the wise and the good around him, will thwart all his resolutions, and he will go back, like the dog to his vomit. All the drunkenness, then, that shall pollute our land, must be traced to moderate drinkers. They feed the monster. They keep in countenance the distillery and the dram-shop, and every drunkard that reels in the streets. Moderate use is to this kingdom of blood what the thousand rivulets and streams are to the mighty river. O how have we been deceived. We long searched for the poison that was destroying our life. The drop said, It is not in me—I am but a drop, and can do no harm. The little stream said, It is not me. Am I not a little one, and can do no harm? And the demon Intemperance, as she prowled around us, said, Let my drops and my rivulets alone; they can do no harm. Go stop, if you can, the mighty river. We believed her. But the river baffled our efforts. Its torrents rolled on, and we contented ourselves with snatching here and there a youth from destruction. But we now see that the poison is in the drops and the rivulets; and that without these, that river of death, which is sweeping the young and the old into the ocean of despair, would cease for ever. And we call upon these self-styled prudent, temperate drinkers, to pause and look at the tremendous responsibility and guilt of entailing drunkenness upon their country for ever.

But we are met with more serious opposers to the plan of starvation. They are, they say, the bone and muscle of the country. They come from the farms, the shipyards, and workshops, and say, If you starve out this monster, *we* shall be starved out, for we cannot do our work and get a living without rum or whiskey; though, according to their own confession, they have found it hard living with. Their rum and their whiskey have cost them double and treble their other taxes—their sons have become vile, their workmen turbulent, their tools have been broken, and many of themselves are already sinking under its enfeebling influence.

With such it is hard to reason. They have tried but one side, and are incapable of judging the case. We can only tell them there is no danger. Not a particle of nourishment does spirit afford them. The hard drinker totters as he walks. The poor inebriate can neither stand nor go. We can point them to hundreds and thousands of their own profession, honest men, who solemnly testify that they are healthier and stronger, can perform more labor, and endure the frosts of winter and heat of summer better without it than with it. We can ask them whether they fully believe that the God of heaven, a God of love, has put them under the dire necessity of using daily an article which, with such awful certainty, makes drunkards; and whether, when he has said, Woe to him that giveth his neighbor drink, he has said, too, you must all drink it; it is necessary for you. But such never can be taught and convinced but by experience; and to such we would say, Try it for yourselves.

Our next opposition, gentlemen, is from a band clothed in white—professors of our holy religion—enlisted soldiers of Christ, engaged to every work of benevolence: they come—O tell it not in Gath!—to intercede for the monster, and oppose our enterprise. Is not this, you ask, a libel? Alas, too often, reports of temperance societies tell of opposition from professors of religion.

What can be the meaning of this? Has not intemperance been the greatest curse to the church? Has it not caused her to bleed at every pore? And have not her members cried to heaven that the destroyer might perish? And now, when God has put into their hands a weapon by which it may at once be exterminated, will they hesitate? Will they hang back? Will they say, we cannot make the sacrifice? O where lies this astonishing witchery? What has put the church to sleep? What has made her angry at the call to come out from the embrace of her deadliest foe? O what has he, who drinks the cup of the Lord, to do with the cup of devils? Does he need it to make him serious or prayerful, or to enable him better to understand the word of God, or bear reproach for Christ, or discharge his Christian duties, or open his heart in charity? Does it not palsy the heart, quench the spirit of prayer, seal up every holy and benevolent feeling, and turn many from Christ, that they walk no more with him? What can a professor mean who refuses to enlist under the temperance banner? Does he really want the monster to live? Does he pray that he may? Will he stand aloof from this conflict? Is he determined to deny himself in nothing? To care not if others perish? To risk shipwreck of character and conscience, and to keep in countenance every drunkard and dram-shop around him? Is it nothing to him that intemperance shall spread like a *malaria*, to every city, and village, and neighborhood, until the land shall send up nothing but the vapors of a moral putrefaction, and none shall here pray, or preach, or seek God; but ignorance, and crime, and suffering, withering comfort and hope, shall go hand in hand, until we can be purified only by a rain of fire and brimstone from heaven? O for shame, for shame! Let the Christian, pleading for a little intoxicating liquor, be alarmed; let him escape as for his life from the kingdom of darkness. "Come out of her, my people, that ye be not partakers of her sins, and that ye receive not of her plagues."

Next to diseased appetite, the love of money is the most potent principle in the breast of depraved man. Thirty-six thousand distillers, and eighty-five thousand venders of ardent spirits in our land, form a tremendous host in opposition to our enterprise. They live everywhere.

> "Pass where we may, through city or through town,
> Village or hamlet, of this merry land,
> * * * * every twentieth pace
> Conducts the unguarded nose to such a whiff
> Of stale debauch, forth issuing from the sties
> That law has licensed, as makes Temperance REEL."

They live wherever the demon has his haunts. Or rather, he lives where they live; for they feed him. And while he fattens on the article they make and vend, they receive in return the silver and gold of his deluded victims. Now, how can this formidable host, who cry out, Our craft is in danger, by this demon we have our wealth—how can they be met? Can they be met at all? Yes, they can—for they are men; generally reputable men; in cases not a few, pious men; and all have consciences, and may be made to feel their accountableness to God. Now let them be told that they keep this monster alive; that to their distilleries and shops may be traced all the poverty, and contention, and tears, and blood, which drunkenness produces; that their occupation is to poison the young and the old; and by dealing out gallons, and quarts, and pints, and gills, they fill up, with drunkards, the highway to hell; that they do all this to get the money of the wretched victims; that the tears of broken-hearted widows and orphan children are entering into the ears of the Lord of Sabaoth, and that neither God nor their consciences will hold them guiltless in this thing, and sure I am that they will be filled with horror at their own doings, and quit their business.

If there are some so hardened and dead to all the best interests of men as to persist, against the light of the age, in the business of making drunkards, let public indignation burn against them till they can no longer stand before its fires. Let a distillery be viewed as a man would view the inquisition, where the racks, the tortures, and the fires, consume the innocent. Let the dram-shop be ranked, as Judge Dagget says it should be, with the haunts of counterfeiters, the depositories of stolen goods, and the retreats of thieves; and over its door let it be written, "The way to hell, leading down to the chambers of death." The time has been when a vender could deal out, day by day, the liquid poison to the tottering drunkard, attend his funeral, help lay him in the grave; then go home, post up his books, turn the widow and her babes into the streets to perish with hunger or be supported by charity, and yet sustain a good reputation. But in future, whenever the community shall stand around the grave of a drunkard, let the eyes of all be fixed on the inhuman vender; let him be called to take one solemn look into the grave of the slain and the pit of the damned; and if he will return to the ruin of his fellow-men, let the voice of his brother's blood cry to him from the ground, and his punishment be greater than he can bear.

Perhaps some reputable vender is offended at the freedom of these remarks. I would ask him if he has never been offended at the smell of that filthy drunkard who has hung around him? I would ask him if his conscience has never stung him as ragged children have come to him in bleak November to have him fill their father's bottle? I would ask him if his soul has never shook within him as he passed, in the darkness of night, the graveyard where three, four, or five of his neighbors lie without even a tombstone, who found their death at his counter? His traffic may be profitable, but let him beware lest while he feeds the monster it turns and devours him and his offspring. At least, let him solemnly inquire, before God, whether he can be a virtuous man and knowingly promote vice; or an honest man, and rob his neighbor by selling an article which promotes sorrow, disease, and death.

I congratulate you, gentlemen, on the stand which you have taken against the monster Intemperance, and on the success with which your efforts have been crowned. You are doing a work for this country for which future generations will call you blessed. Let your watchword be onward, extermination, death; and victory will be yours. Our weapons are simple, but mighty. O what a discovery is this principle of entire abstinence! Let the name of its author be embalmed with that of Luther, and Howard, and Raikes, and Wilberforce. What has it not already done for our suffering country! What a change meets the eye as it wanders from Georgia to Maine—from the Atlantic to our western borders. Here we see farms tilled; there buildings raised; here churches built; there vessels reared, launched, and navigated too; manufactories conducted; fisheries carried on; prisons governed; commercial business transacted; journeys performed; physicians visiting their patients; legislators enacting laws; lawyers pleading for justice; judges deciding the fate of men, and ministers preaching the everlasting Gospel—without intoxicating liquor. Here we see importers unwilling to risk the importation of spirituous liquor into the land; there distillers abandoning their distilleries as curses to themselves and the community; and merchants, not a few, expelling the poison from their stores, and some pouring it upon the ground, choosing that the earth should swallow it rather than man. And all this in the short space of three years. What has done it? Entire abstinence. What then will not be done, when, instead of 50,000 who now avow it, 500,000 shall give their pledge, that they will abandon a kingdom founded in blood. And can they not be found in this land of humane men, and patriots, and Christians? Yes, they can. Onward then, gentlemen. Listen not to those who say you are carrying matters too far. So said the wolf. She loved life, and she loved blood. But did she ever regard the cry of the sheep? The monster Intemperance has been glutted with blood; and never spared, and had no pity. He still howls for blood; and many plead that he may have some. But depend upon it, their pleas are only those of debased appetite and avarice. Rally the community against them. Enlighten the public mind. Collect facts. Let your towns and villages be searched with candles. Go into the dens. Bring the monster and his suffering victims to light, and the public indignation will no longer slumber.

Of one thing I will remind you. The demon will daunt the timid. It is noisy and fiery. Attack it, and it will roll its eyes, and snap its teeth, and threaten vengeance. Attempt to starve it, and it will rave like the famished tiger. Thousands have fed it against their consciences, rather than meet its fury. But fear not. The use of ardent spirit meets no support in the Bible or the conscience, and the traffic meets none. Be firm. Be decided. Be courageous. Connect your cause with heaven. It is the cause of God; the cause for which Immanuel died. O, as men and patriots, banish intemperance, with all its sources, from your country and the land. As ministers and Christians, banish it for ever from the churches of the living God. Let the demon no longer hide in the sanctuary. Let ENTIRE ABSTINENCE be written in capitals over the door of every church. Expel for ever the accursed enemy, that the Spirit of the Lord may descend and bless us with life and peace.

To those not connected with the Temperance Association, I would say, Look at this enterprise. It injures no man, wrongs no man, defrauds no man, has no sectarian or political object in view; it would only relieve our infant nation of a burden and a curse which is fast placing it side by side with buried Sodom. As wise men, judge ye of its importance and merits. As men hastening to judgment, act in relation to it. A solemn responsibility rests upon you. Shall the land now be rid of intemperance? You reply, Yes—and talk of wholesome laws, and high licenses, and prudent use. Three green withes on Samson! *Entire abstinence* is the only weapon which will destroy the monster. "But we can practise that without giving our pledge." True. But until you give it, he will count you his friend and haunt your dwelling. In this cause there is no neutrality. Have you supported this cruel kingdom of darkness and death? Will you do it longer? Shall conscience be riven by the act? Shall the land that bears you be cursed; the young around you be sporting with hell; the awakened sinner be drowning conviction at his bottle; the once fair communicant be disgraced; the once happy congregation be rent; its ministry be driven from the altar, and its sanctuary crumble to ruin? Shall our benevolent institutions fail, and our liberties be sacrificed? Shall God be grieved? Shall wailings from the bottomless pit hereafter reproach and agonize you as the cause of the ruin, perhaps of your children and children's children? Methinks one common pulsation beats in your hearts, and you answer, No—no. Methinks I see you rising in the majesty of freemen and Christians, in behalf of an injured country and church, and destroying at once the demon among you.

ARGUMENT AGAINST THE MANUFACTURE

OF

ARDENT SPIRITS:

ADDRESSED TO

THE DISTILLER AND THE FURNISHER OF THE MATERIALS.

BY REV. EDWARD HITCHCOCK, D. D.

A SENSE of duty impels me to address this portion of my fellow-citizens, in the hope that I may persuade them to abandon the employment by which they furnish ardent spirits to the community. I am not about to charge them as the intentional authors of all the evils our country suffers from intemperance, nor wholly to clear myself from the guilt; for some of these men are my neighbors and personal friends, and I know them to be convinced that the excessive use of ardent spirits is a frightful evil among us, and that they would cheerfully join in some measures for its suppression, though not yet satisfied that those now in train are judicious or necessary. Not long ago, I was in essentially the same state of mind, and encouraged these men in the manufacture of spirits, by the purchase and use of them. Now I would fain believe that the minds of all these individuals are open to conviction, and that the same arguments which satisfied me that I was wrong, will satisfy them.

In the first place, therefore, I would reason with these men *as a chemical philosopher*. The distiller is a practical chemist; and although he may never have studied chemistry in the schools, he cannot but have often thought of the theory of his operations. And the farmer who receives at the distillery, in return for his rye, cider, or molasses, a liquid powerful substance, obtained from them, will very naturally inquire by what strange transformation these articles have been made to yield something apparently so very different from their nature. Probably, some of them may have concluded that the spirits exist naturally in the grain, and apples, and sugar-cane, just as flour, and cider, and molasses do. And hence they have inferred, first, that God intended the spirits for the use of man, as much as the flour, the apples, or the molasses; and that it is just as proper to separate the spirits by distillation, as it is to obtain the flour by grinding and bolting. Secondly, that there can be nothing injurious or poisonous in the spirits, any more than in the apples, the grain, or the molasses; the only injury, in either case, resulting from using too much. Thirdly, that spirits must be nourishing to the body, constituting, as they seem to do, the very essence of the fruit, grain, and molasses, which are confessedly nutritious.

Now, these inferences are all rendered null and void by the fact that ardent spirits, or alcohol, which is their essence, do not exist naturally in apples, grain, or sugar-cane. No one ever perceived the odor or the taste of alcohol in apples, or the cider obtained from them, while it was new and sweet; but after it had fermented for a time, by a due degree of warmth, the sweetness in a measure disappeared, and alcohol was found to be present. And just so in obtaining spirits from rye, or any other substance; a sweet liquor is at first obtained, which, by fermentation, is found to be partly converted into alcohol. This sweetness results from the sugar which the substances naturally contain, or which is formed by the process. This sugar is next destroyed, or decomposed, by the fermentation, and its parts go to make up a new substance, then first brought into existence, called alcohol. If the fermentation be carried on still farther, another new substance is produced, viz., vinegar. Carried still farther, putrid, unhealthy exhalations are the result, such as we find rising from swamps and other places where vegetable matter is decaying. If, then, we may conclude, because alcohol is obtained from grain and other nutritious substances, that therefore God intended it for the use of man, the same reason will show that he intended man should breathe these poisonous exhalations. If alcohol cannot be poisonous or injurious, because derived from harmless and salutary substances, neither can these exhalations be so; nor, indeed, those more putrid and deadly ones arising from the putrefaction of sweet animal food. And if alcohol must be nutritious, because apples, grain, and molasses are so, it follows that these exhalations are nutritious.

Having thus explained the chemistry of this subject, I would, secondly, address these men as a *physician.* I mean merely, that I wish to present before them the views of the most distinguished and impartial physicians concerning ardent spirits. It is important, then, to remark, that physicians have decided that alcohol is a powerful *poison.* And how do they prove this? Simply by comparing its effects with those of other poisons—particularly the poisons derived, as alcohol is, from vegetables—such as henbane, poison hemlock, prussic acid, thorn-apples, deadly nightshade, foxglove, poison sumach, oil of tobacco, and the essence of opium. These poisons, taken in different quantities, according to their strength, produce nausea, dizziness, exhilaration of spirits with subsequent debility, and even total insensibility; in other cases, delirium and death; and alcohol does the same. These poisons weaken the stomach, impair the memory and all the powers of the mind, and sometimes bring on palsy, apoplexy, and other violent disorders; and so does alcohol. Do you say that ardent spirits, as they are commonly drank, do not produce these effects except in a very slight degree? Neither do these substances, when much weakened by mixture with other things. Even rum and brandy, of the first proof, contain only about fifty parts of alcohol in the hundred ; and even the *high wines*, as they are called, are by no means pure alcohol ; yet less than an ounce of proof spirits, given to a rabbit, killed it in less than an hour. Three quarters of an ounce of alcohol, introduced into the stomach of a large and robust dog, killed him in three and a half hours. In larger quantities, as almost every one knows, this same substance has proved immediately fatal to men. Do you say that many drink spirits for years, and are not destroyed ; and do you hence inquire how they can be poisonous ? So I reply, not a few take small quantities of other poisons every day for years, and continue alive. A horse, indeed, may take the eighth part of an ounce of arsenic every day, and yet be thriving. But how many are there, do you suppose, who habitually drink ardent spirits, and yet suffer no bad effects from it ? Have they no stomach complaints, no nervous maladies, no headaches ? Do they live to a great age ? Not one out of a hundred of those who daily drink ardent spirits, escapes uninjured ; though their sickness and premature decay, resulting from this cause, are generally imputed to other causes ; and as many as this would escape if arsenic were used, in moderate quantities, instead of spirits.

Farmers and distillers, whom I address, pause, I beseech you, and meditate upon this fact. It is poison into which you convert your rye and apples ; it is poison which, under the name of whiskey and cider-brandy, you put into your cellars ; it is poison which you draw out from the brandy and whiskey casks for drink, and which you offer your children and friends for drink ; it is poison which you sell to your neighbors ; it is producing the same effects as other poisons upon you and upon them ; that is, it is undermining your constitutions, and shortening your lives and happiness. You would not dare thus to manufacture and distribute among the community calomel or arsenic, if these were in use, leaving it to every man to determine how large doses he should take. Yet it would not be half as dangerous for men of all descriptions to deal out and administer these substances to themselves and others, for there would be none of that bewitching temptation to excess, in the case of calomel and arsenic, which attends ardent spirits. But if by carelessly distributing calomel or arsenic in society, you had destroyed only one life, your conscience would be exceedingly burdened with the guilt. And who is to bear the guilt of destroying the thirty or forty thousand who are cut off annually in this country by intemperance? Suppose the distilleries were all to stop, how many would then die from hard drinking?

But if alcohol is poisonous in a degree, yet it is often necessary, you say. Physicians say not, except in a very few cases as a medicine; and even in these cases it is doubtful whether they have not other remedies as good, or better. Spirits are necessary, you say, to enable a man to endure great extremes of heat, cold, fatigue, and in exposure to wet, and attendance upon the sick. If this be correct, farmers will sometimes need them. But many of the most hard-working and thorough farmers in the land have, within a few years past, tried the experiment of laboring without spirits; and their unanimous testimony is, that they are stronger, healthier, and better able to bear all extremes and severe fatigue without them. Have you ever tried the same experiment? Be persuaded to make the trial, at least for one year, before you reject so much substantial testimony.

If spirits are necessary for any class, we should suppose it would be the West Indian slave. But "on three contiguous estates," says Dr. Abbot, "of more than four hundred slaves, has been made, with fine success, the experiment of a strict exclusion of ardent spirits at all seasons of the year. The success has very far exceeded the proprietor's most sanguine hopes. Peace, and quietness, and contentment, reign among the negroes; creoles are reared in much greater numbers than formerly; the estates are in the neatest and highest state of cultivation; and order and discipline are maintained with very little correction, and the mildest means."

Sailors are another class who must sometimes need spirits, if they are needed in case of great exposure to cold and wet. But several crews have attempted to winter in high northern latitudes, and those furnished with spirits have nearly all perished, while those not furnished with them have nearly all survived. When exposed to cold and wet, and partially immersed in the sea for hours, those who have not used spirits have commonly outlived those who drank them.

Soldiers are exposed to even more and severer extremes and vicissitudes than sailors. But Dr. Jackson, a most distinguished physician in the British army, asserts that spirits are decidedly injurious to soldiers on duty, rendering them less able to endure labor and hardship. And a general officer in the same army thus testifies: "But, above all, let every one who values his health, avoid drinking spirits when heated; that is adding fuel to the fire, and is apt to produce the most dangerous inflammatory complaints." "Not a more dangerous error exists, than the notion that the habitual use of spirituous liquors prevents the effects of cold. On the contrary, the truth is, that those who drink most frequently of them are soonest affected by severe weather. The daily use of these liquors tends greatly to emaciate and waste the strength of the body," etc.

The Roman soldiers marched with a weight of armor upon them which a modern soldier can hardly stand under; and they conquered the world. Yet they drank nothing stronger than vinegar and water.

"I have worn out two armies in two wars," says the Dr. Jackson mentioned above, "by the aids of temperance and hard work, and probably could wear out another before my period of old age arrives. I eat no animal food, drink no wine or malt liquor, or spirits of any kind; I wear no flannel, and neither regard wind nor rain, heat nor cold, when business is in the way."

Those men in Europe who are trained for boxing-matches would require spirits if they were necessary for giving bodily strength and health, since the object of this training is to produce the most perfect health, and the greatest possible strength. But ardent spirits are not used by them at all; and even wine is scarcely allowed.

In protracted watching by the bed of sickness, food and intervals of rest are the only real securities against disease and weakness. Spirits peculiarly expose a man to receive the disease, if it be contagious, and if not, they wear out the strength sooner than it would otherwise fail.

The most exposed and trying situations in life, then, need not the aid of ardent spirits; nay, they are in such cases decidedly injurious. They are not, therefore, necessary, but injurious for men in all other situations. The distiller must, therefore, give up the necessity of using them in the community as a reason for continuing their manufacture.

But spirits, it may be said, do certainly inspire a man with much additional strength. Yes; and physicians tell us how. It is by exciting the nervous system, and thus calling into more vigorous action the strength that God has given the constitution to enable it to resist heat, cold, and disease. If this strength do not previously exist in the system, spirits can never bestow it; for they do not afford the least nourishment, as food does. They merely call into action the stock of strength which food has already implanted in the body. Hence the debility and weakness which always succeed their use when the excitement has passed by. Hence, too, it follows, that spirits can never give any additional permanent strength to the body.

But this is not all; for physicians infer from this statement, that the use of spirits, even in moderate quantities, tends prematurely to exhaust and wear out the system. It urges on the powers of life faster than health requires, and thus wears them out sooner, by a useless waste of strength and spirits. True, a moderate drinker may not notice any striking bad effects upon his health, from this cause, for many years; nay, the excitement it produces may remove, for the time being, many uncomfortable feelings which he experiences, and which are the early warnings that nature gives him that she is oppressed, for the secret poison is at work within; and if such a man is attacked by a fever, or other acute disease, physicians know that he is by no means as likely to recover as the water-drinker, because the spirits have partially exhausted the secret strength of his constitution, all of which is now wanted to resist the disease. Let every man who indulges in the use of spirits ponder well the declaration of a committee of one of the most *enlightened medical societies* in our land: "Beyond comparison greater is the risk of life, undergone in nearly all diseases, of whatever description, when they occur in those unfortunate men who have been previously disordered by these poisons." Such men, too, it may be added, are much more liable to the attacks of disease than those who totally abstain from alcohol. In both these ways, therefore, the use of spirits, even in the greatest moderation, tends to shorten life.

Distillers of ardent spirits, I entreat you, think seriously of these things, as you tend the fires under your boilers. Farmers, as you drive your load of cider or rye to the distillery, meditate upon them, I beseech you. You have here the opinions and advice of the most able and impartial physicians in this country and in Europe. True, you may find here and there one, of little or no reputation and learning, who, either because he thinks it for his interest, or is attached to ardent spirits himself, will oppose such views of the subject. But no physician of distinction and good moral character would dare, at this day, to come out publicly in opposition to the principles above advanced, sanctioned as they are by the united testimony of science and experience. O, shut not your ears against this powerful voice.

In the third place, I would expostulate with these men *as a friend to my country.* Can it be that they are acquainted with the extent of the mischiefs which our country already suffers from intemperance? Do they know that fifty-six millions of gallons of ardent spirits are annually consumed in the United States, or more than four and an half gallons to each inhabitant; and that about forty-four millions of this quantity are prepared in the distilleries of our own country; that ten millions of gallons are distilled from molasses, and more than nine million bushels of rye are used for this purpose? Do they know that these forty-four millions of gallons, as retailed, must cost the community not less than $22,000,000; that they render from two hundred to three hundred thousand of our citizens intemperate; that in consequence of this intemperance the country sustains an annual loss, in the productive labor of these drunkards, of not far from $30,000,000; and a loss of more than twenty-five thousand lives, from her middle-aged citizens, who are thus cut off prematurely? That two-thirds of the pauperism in the country, costing from $6,000,000 to $8,000,000, and two-thirds of the crime among us, perpetrated by an army of eighty or ninety thousand wretches, result from the same cause; and that from forty to fifty thousand of the cases of imprisonment for debt, annually, are imputed to the same cause? That the pecuniary losses proceeding from the carelessness and rashness of intemperate sailors, servants, and agents, are immense; and that the degradation of mind, the bodily and mental sufferings of drunkards and their families, and the corruption of morals and manners, are altogether beyond the reach of calculation to estimate, and of words to express?*

Can it be that these men have ever soberly looked forward to see what must be the ultimate effects, upon our free and beloved country, of this hydra-headed evil, unless it be arrested? Can they be aware that, judging by the past proportion of deaths from intemperance in the most regular and moral parts of the land, one third of the six million adults now living will die from the same cause? Do they know how the intemperate entail hereditary diseases and a thirst for ardent spirits upon their descendants, and how rapidly, therefore, the bodily vigor of our citizens is giving way before their deadly influence? And can they doubt that vigor of mind will decay in the same proportion? Corruption of manners and morals too, how rapidly it will spread under the operation of this poison! Nor can religious principle stand long before the overwhelming inundation; and just in the degree in which alcoholic liquors are used, will the Sabbath, and the institutions of religion, and the Bible be neglected and trodden under foot. And when the morality, and religion, and the conscience of the majority of our nation are gone, what but a miracle can save our liberties from ruin? Corrupt the majority, and what security is there in popular elections? Corrupt the majority, and you have collected together the explosive materials that need only the touch of some demagogue's torch to scatter the fair temple of our independence upon the winds of heaven.

But admitting that this picture is not overdrawn, yet the distiller and the furnisher of materials may perhaps say, that all this does not particularly concern them. They are

* In order to obtain the result in this paragraph, the well-established estimates that have often been made, concerning the cost and evils of ardent spirits in our country, have been reduced about one fourth or fifth part, to make allowance for the amount imported from abroad.

not intemperate, they force no man to drink, or even to buy their spirits: nay, they generally refuse to sell to the intemperate. The intemperate are the persons to whom these expostulations should be addressed. As for the distiller and the farmer, who manufacture the poison, they are following a lawful calling, and have a right to the honest proceeds of their business.

The principle, then, which I understand you to advocate, is this: that provided your employment be not contrary to the laws of the state, you are under no obligation to inquire particularly as to its influence upon the public happiness after the products of your labor get out of your own hands. If this be a correct principle for your guidance, it is certainly a correct one for others. Let us apply it to the intemperate man.

I expostulate with him on the destructive influence of his habits upon his country. "But have I not a right," says he, "to use my own property in such a way as I choose, provided I do not violate the laws of the land? If I may not employ a portion of my money in purchasing spirits, neither have you a right to lay out yours for a carriage, or for painting your house, or for any thing else which some of your neighbors may regard as unnecessary. I buy no more spirits than my health and comfort require; and I have as good a right to judge of the quantity, as you have in respect to the needless articles of dress and furniture which you procure."

I urge the man who keeps a licensed gambling-house to abandon a pursuit that is ruining his country. "But I am not violating the laws," he replies, "nor compelling any man to gamble and drink to excess in my house. The whole responsibility, therefore, rests upon those who do it. Expostulate with them. I have a right to my earnings."

You see where this principle leads. Is it one that a true patriot ought to adopt? No: he alone is a true patriot who is ready to abandon every pursuit that is injuring his country, however profitable it may be to himself, and however tolerated by the civil law. Nor I would not attempt to extenuate the guilt of the intemperate man, nor of the merchant who sells him spirits; but I do say, that if those who distil, and those who furnish the materials, were to abandon the business altogether, it would almost put an end to intemperance in the land. For only a small proportion of the spirits used is imported; and its price must always continue so high that but few could afford to be drunkards were the domestic manufacture to cease. You have it in your power, then, to put a stop to this most dreadful national evil, and thus to save our liberties and all that is dear to us from ruin. Your fathers poured out their blood like water to purchase our independence, and to build up a bulwark around our rights. But the ten thousand distilleries which you ply are so many fiery batteries, pouring forth their forty-four million discharges every year, to level that bulwark in the dust. All Europe combined against us in war could not do us half as much injury as your distilleries are doing every year. Oh, abandon them—tear them down—melt your boilers in the furnace—give your grain and molasses to the poor, or to the fowls of heaven—make fuel of your fruit-trees, rather than destroy your country.

Some may say, that if they cease to manufacture spirits, others will take up the business and carry it on as extensively as they do. And since, therefore, the country will gain nothing by their discontinuance of distillation, they may as well have the profit of it as others. But what course of wickedness will not such reasoning justify? A highwayman robs you, or an assassin invades your dwelling at midnight and slaughters your wife and children. Now, would you think them justified, should they plead that they knew of others about to commit the same outrages, and therefore they thought their commission of these deeds was not wrong, since they needed the avails of the robbery and murder as much as any body? A man could pursue the slave-trade year after year on this principle, with no upbraidings of conscience, if he only suspected that the business would be carried on were he to stop. And a traitor might sell his country for gold, could he only ascertain that some one else was about to do it, and yet be exonerated from blame, if this principle be proper to act upon. Oh, how can any decent man plead a moment for a principle that leads to such monstrous results!

Some will say, however, that they sell the spirits which they manufacture only to those whom they know to be temperate, and therefore they are not accessory to the intemperance in the land; for they are not accountable for the sins of those who sell spirits to improper persons.

You supply them only to the temperate! The greater the blame and the guilt; for you are thus training up a new set of drunkards to take the place of those whom death will soon remove out of the way. Were you to sell only to the intemperate, you would do comparatively little injury to the community. For you would only hasten those out of the way who are a nuisance, and prevent the education of others to fill their places. But let not any man think that no blame attaches to himself because the poison goes into other hands before it is administered. *A man is to blame for any evil to his fellow-men which he could prevent.* Now, by stopping all the distilleries in the land, you could prevent men from becoming drunkards. The very head and front of the offending, therefore, lies with you. It is as idle for you to attempt to cast all the guilt upon others, in this way, as it was for Pilate, when he endeavored to fix the blood of Christ upon the people by washing his hands before them and declaring himself innocent, and then going back to his judgment-seat and passing sentence of death upon him. Good man! He did not touch a hair of the Saviour's head. It was the cruel soldiers who executed his orders, that, according to this plea, were alone guilty!

Some distillers will probably say that they cannot support themselves and families if they abandon this business; and some farmers will say, if we cannot sell our cider and rye to the distillers, the products of our orchards must all be lost, and rye is the only article which we can raise upon our farms with any profit. And if I were not to purchase these articles, says the distiller, their price must be so low that no farmer could afford to raise them. Thus to reduce a large class of the yeomanry of our country—its very sinews—to poverty, would be a greater evil than even the intemperance that is so common.

Is it indeed true, that in this free and happy country an industrious, temperate, and economical man, cannot find any employment by which he can support himself and family in a comfortable manner without manufacturing poison and selling it to his countrymen? In other words, cannot he live without destroying them? Is land so scarce, or so eaten up with tithes and taxes, that he cannot thence derive subsistence unless he converts its products into money at the expense of others' comfort, reputation, and life? Is every honest calling so crowded, or so unproductive, that every avenue is closed? Have the men who make this plea tried, even for a single year, to live without the manufacture of spirits? It may be, indeed, that for a time they will find other pursuits less productive than this. And is not this, after all, the true reason why they shrink from the sacrifice? But if superior profits be a sufficient reason for continuing distillation, it is a reason that will justify the robber, the thief, and every other depredator upon the rights of others.

But how does it appear that the stoppage of all the distilleries in the land will reduce the price of cider and rye? Their operation has produced a great demand for these articles, and that demand has thrown into the market an immense supply: the consequence is, that the prices are reduced as low as the articles can be afforded, at a very moderate profit, and the great complaint now among farmers is, that they are so low. Let the distilleries cease to exist, and the special demand for these articles will cease; and consequently the market will not be glutted with them, because no extra efforts will be made to raise them: the result will probably be, that in a very short time their price will be very nearly or quite as high as it now is.

But even if we suppose the worst, that the distiller and some farmers should be reduced to absolute beggary by the cessation of this manufacture; no reasonable, or patriotic, or Christian man can for a moment regard this as a reason why he should continue in any business that is productive of immense mischief to his country. Is it not better that he and his family should come to want, than that hundreds of thousands should be ruined, soul and body, for time and eternity? If he has a right to derive his subsistence from the ruin of others, then others, as the thief, the swindler, and the robber, have a right to obtain their subsistence from his ruin.

In the fourth place, I appeal to these men *as a neighbor and a parent, and in behalf of the drunkard's wife and children.* When Providence cast our lot in the same neighborhood, I considered, and doubtless you thought the same, that a regard to our mutual welfare bound us to do every thing in our power to make the community in which we lived intelligent, virtuous, and happy; and to avoid every thing that would mar its peace, degrade its character, or stain its purity. My complaint is, that by the manufacture of ardent spirits you have violated these obligations. The facilities for obtaining spirits, and the temptations to their use and abuse, have been thus so multiplied, and brought so near, that very many who were once kind neighbors and valuable members of society are ruined, or in different stages of the path to ruin. One has got as far as an occasional visit to the grog-shop and the bar-room: another is rarely seen there; but the wretched condition of his house, barn, and farm, his impatience of confinement at home, and his many foolish bargains, tell me, in language not to be mistaken, that the worm which is preying upon the root of his prosperity is the worm of the still. The frequent visits of the sheriff to the house of another neighbor, whose family is healthy and industrious; his bitter complaints of the hardness of the times; his constant efforts to borrow money to prevent executions from being levied; the mortgaging of his farm to the bank; his pimpled face, and bloated body, and dry hacking cough, are painful testimonies of his familiarity with the products of the distillery. It is distressing to look around upon our once happy neighborhood—did you ever do it?—and to see what havoc your manufactory of spirits has made upon the peace, property, reputation, intelligence, morality, and good order of the community. No wasting sickness, no foreign or domestic war, no premature frost; no drought, blasting, or mildew; nor any other visitation of God; no, not all of them combined have been the tenth part as fatal to our prosperity and happiness, as this one self-inflicted curse. And this curse we should never have felt, had not some of you put into operation your distilleries, and others fed them with the products of your farms: I mean, such would have been the happy effect, had the manufacture of spirits ceased in our land before these evils had followed: and I am now supposing that some one in every town and neighborhood throughout the land, where there is a distillery, is addressing the same language to those who conduct it as I am addressing to you. We make a united and earnest appeal to you, in view of the ruin that rises around us, that you would stop the work of destruction and strengthen the things that remain, which are ready to die. You stand at the fountain-head of that fiery stream which is spreading volcanic desolation over the land. Oh, shut up the sluices before every verdant spot is buried beneath the inundation.

But to come again into our own neighborhood: I have a family of beloved children growing up in the vicinity of your distillery; and when I recollect that every fortieth individual among us is a drunkard, and that about every third person above the age of twenty dies prematurely through intemperance, I cannot but feel a deep anxiety lest my boys should be found at length among the number. True, one of the earliest lessons I teach them is total abstinence, and I try to excite in their minds a disgust towards every species of alcoholic mixture. But they go to one of my neighbors and hear him telling of the whiskey and cider-brandy that have been produced upon his farm, and they see him mixing and circulating the bowl among his laborers, his visitors, and even his own children; and it is offered also to mine, accompanied with some jeer against cold water societies. They see the huge accumulations of cider and rye at the distillery, and mark the glee of the men who conduct its operations, and of those who come to fill their barrel or keg with spirits. They go also to the store in the vicinity, and see one after another filling their jugs with the same article. Now, these neighbors who thus distil, and vend, and drink whiskey and brandy, my children are taught to respect; and how is it possible that they should not feel that their father is too rigid in his requirements, and hence be tempted to taste; and tasting, to love; and loving, to be destroyed by the poison? Oh, is there no guilt in thus spreading a snare for my children? Should they fall, will none of their blood be upon your heads? Shall not the entreaties of a parent be felt by those who are themselves parents, and whose days may yet be rendered intolerable by the cruelty of drunken children?

I would invite the manufacturer of spirits, and the farmer who supplies the materials, to go around with me among the people in the vicinity of the distillery, that they may have some nearer views of the miseries produced by their employment. Let us stop for a moment at this tavern.

MYSELF. You seem, landlord, to be quite full of business to-day. What is the occasion?

LANDLORD. Neighbors X and Y have their case tried here, to-day, before Esquire Z, and you know that these matters cannot go on well with dry throats.

MYSELF. What is the point in dispute between your neighbors?

LANDLORD. Something about swapping a horse, I believe; but it is my opinion that both of them hardly knew what they were about, when they made the exchange. It was last town-meeting day, and I recollect that both of them called quite frequently at my bar that day. They are none of your cold water folks, I assure you.

MYSELF. Are these court days generally profitable to you, landlord?

LANDLORD. Better, even, than a town meeting; for those who come on such occasions have no qualms of conscience about drinking, if they have occasion, I assure you. But on town-meeting days, some of the pale-faced temperance men are always about, to frighten away honest people.

MYSELF. Do not these court occasions often lay the foundation for other courts?

LANDLORD. Oh, very frequently: but so much the better, you know, for my business; and so I must not complain.

Let us next call at Mr. A's, who has so fine a farm and orchard, and every means, one would think, of independence and happiness. But hark; there is a family dialogue going on between farmer A, his wife, and son.

SON. What; boozy so early, mother? and father too, and quarrelling, as usual, I perceive. O, I wish our orchard were all burnt down, and the distillery too, rather than live in such a bedlam.

MOTHER. But do you not like a little yourself, son, when eleven o'clock comes?

FATHER. Aye, and at four, and some bitters in the morning. We are old, you must remember, son, and require more to warm us and support nature than you do.

SON. If you would drink only moderately, as I do, I would not complain. For I am not one of your cold water scarecrows, I assure you. But to have you drink half the time, is what vexes me.

What a fine picture is here, my neighbors, for the men to look at who expect to reform the world by *moderate drinking*, without adopting the principle of *total abstinence.*

But look at the sheriff yonder, pointing about neighbor B's house, from which he seems to be excluded.

SHERIFF. You are too late, gentlemen; all the property is attached for twice its value. Rum, bad bargains, and negligence, have done the business with poor B. But I pity his wife and children most, for they have struggled hard to prevent it.

DISTILLER. Is every thing gone? The fellow owed me two hundred dollars.

MYSELF. For whiskey, I suppose.

DISTILLER. He was formerly a partner in my still, you recollect.

Yonder comes from the store the mechanic, neighbor D. Well, neighbor D, how do the times go with you now?

D. Was there ever such a scarcity of money? When the rich are failing all around, how can a poor mechanic stand it?

MYSELF. What have you, friend D, bound up so carefully in your handkerchief?

D. Aye, you belong to the cold water society, I believe. But I do know that a *little* now and then does me good.

MYSELF. I should suppose that, shut up as you are in your shop most of the time, you could not be much exposed to heat or cold, or great fatigue, and therefore would hardly need spirits.

D. Well, but I have a weak and cold stomach, and often feel so faint and sick that I must either take an emetic or a glass of spirits. But the latter cures all my bad feelings.

Myself. Ah, friend D, I fear the times will prove too hard for you. But why do you try to conceal your jug when you go to the store for whiskey?

D. Why—why—it is more convenient to carry it tied up in this way.

Let us stop next at this skeleton of a house, which you know used to look so tidy before its owner became intemperate. Oh, was misery ever more perfectly personified than in his wife and children, whom you see through the doors and window-frames! And there lies the wretch himself, dead-drunk.

Myself. Pray, madam, do these children attend school?

Wife. Ah, sir, I am ashamed to say it, they have not decent clothes. But it was not always as you see it to-day. When we were first married our prospects were good; and by industry and economy our little farm supported us, and we made some headway. But (turning towards the farmer) yet I would not hurt any one's feelings.

Farmer. Tell your story, madam.

Wife. Well, sir, you recollect that five years ago your orchard produced abundantly, and you proposed to my husband to assist you in making the cider, and getting it to the distillery, and to take his pay in brandy. He did so, and soon a barrel of the poison, which he could not sell, was deposited in our cellar. Oh, what a winter followed! I have known no peace or comfort since, nor shall I, till I find them in the grave. Were it not for these poor naked children, I could wish to rest there soon. But O, what will become of them? Oh, sir, can you think it strange if all these things should come into my mind every time you and I sit down together at the same communion-table?

We must not return home without calling at the next miserable hovel, where the widow of a drunkard, with half a dozen ragged, squalid children, is dragging out a miserable existence. Hark, she is reading the Bible. Did you hear that stifled groan, as she read in that holy book, *Be not deceived: neither fornicators, nor idolaters, nor drunkards, shall inherit the kingdom of God.*

Myself. I believe I have not seen you, madam, since the death of your husband. I hope you find support.

Widow. Oh, sir, resignation is easy if we feel a confidence, or even a feeble hope, that our friends who are taken away will escape the agonies of a second death. But how can we hope against the express declarations of the word of God?

Distiller. And yet, madam, your husband had many excellent qualities.

Widow. And he would still have lived to bless me and the world by their exhibition, had it not been for your distillery.

Distiller. I have no idea of sitting in judgment upon our departed friends, and sending them to hell because they had a few failings.

Widow. Ah, sir, if my husband has gone there, it was your distillery that sent him. Before that was built no man was more kind, temperate, and happy. But you persuaded him to labor there, and paid him in whiskey; and it ruined him, and ruined us all. Look at me—look at these children, without food, without raiment, without fire, without friends, except their Friend in heaven. I do not ask you to bestow upon us any articles for the supply of our temporal necessities; but look at us, and be entreated to tear down your distillery, so that you may not multiply upon you the execrations of the widow and the orphan, wrung from them by the extremity of their sufferings.

Gentlemen, let me exhort you to take such a tour of observation as this once a month. Oh, I entreat every one in the land, who has any concern in the manufacture of ardent spirits, to do the same; and ere long, I am persuaded, you would either abandon every claim to humanity, or abandon for ever your pernicious employment.

In the fifth place, I advise and forewarn these men *as their personal friend.* If you distil ardent spirits, or furnish the materials, you must use them yourselves and allow of their use in your families; otherwise your inconsistency, not to say dishonesty, would subject you to universal contempt. Now, to have your children familiar with the sling, the toddy, and the flip, as they grow up! Is here no danger that the temptation will prove too strong for them? *Can a man take fire in his bosom, and his clothes not be burned? Can one go upon hot coals, and his feet not be burned?* And what compensation for the intemperance of a wife, or a child, would be the highest profits of an orchard, a field of rye, or a distillery? Oh, to be a drunkard is to destroy the soul as well as the body: and *what shall a man give in exchange for his soul?* And are you yourselves in no danger of intemperance, plied as you are by so many allurements? Look around you and see how many strong men, how many of the wise, the moral, the amiable, and the apparently pious, have fallen before the fascinations of this prince of serpents. And are you safe who stand even within the reach of his forky tongue, and lay the bait for his victims, and lure them into his jaws by tasting of it yourselves? Oh, the history of distillers and temperate drinkers, in their last days, furnishes an awful warning for you.

But there is another danger before you, of which, as a faithful friend, I wish to forewarn you. I see a dark storm gathering over your heads. You cannot be ignorant of the mighty movement that is making in our land on the subject of temperance. You must have felt the heavy concussion, and heard the rolling thunder. The religious, the moral, the patriotic, the learned, and the wise, as intemperance has been developing its huge and hateful features more and more, have been aroused to effort; they have closed together in a firm phalanx; and as they move on with the standard of *total abstinence* waving before them, the great, and the good, and the valiant of every name, are swelling their ranks. The cry is waxing louder and louder, "Where are the strong holds of the monster; point out to us the fountains that supply his insatiable thirst, and who it is that feeds them; and who it is that opens the enormous flood-gates? and thither we will march, and against such men will we point our heaviest artillery." And to this cry there is an answer more and more distinctly breaking out: "To the distilleries—to the distilleries." My friends, wait not till this storm of public indignation bursts upon you, nor fancy that you can face it. Oh, no; it will be a steady, fiery blast, that will bear you down; and you will find that none but the dregs of the community will be left with you to sustain you. You will be left with the drunkards, to be distinguished from them only as their abettors and supporters; and from you will every virtuous and patriotic man turn away in disgust, as enemies to himself, his children, and his country. Think not that all this is imagination: look up, and you will see the cloud blackening, and the lightning beginning to play, and hear the thunder roaring. But it is not yet too late to escape from the fury of the storm.

Finally, I would entreat these men *as a Christian.* Some of them profess a personal and experimental knowledge of vital Christianity, and are members of the visible church. What, can it be that a real Christian should, at this day, be concerned in the manufacture of ardent spirits for general use? When I think of the light that now illuminates every man's path on this subject so clearly, and think how the horrors of intemperance must flash in his face at every step, I confess I feel disposed indignantly to reply, No; this man cannot be a Christian. But then I recollect David, the adulterer; Peter, the denier of his master, profanely cursing and swearing; and John Newton, a genuine convert to Christianity, yet for a long time violating every dictate of conscience and of right; and I check my hasty judgment, and leave the secret character of the manufacturer of ardent spirits to a higher and more impartial tribunal. But if such a man be really a Christian, that is, if he do really love God supremely and his neighbor as himself, in what a state of awful alienation and stupidity must he be living! Remaining in such a state, that is, while persevering in so unchristian an employment, can he have any evidence himself, or afford any evidence to others, of possessing a Christian character?

I would not apply these remarks in their unqualified severity to every professor of religion who supplies the distillery with materials, or who vends or uses wine or ardent spirits; for we shall find some of this description who really suppose that, instead of being condemned for such conduct in the Bible, they are rather supported by some parts of it: they not only find Christ converting water into wine at a marriage, and Paul directing Timothy to use a little wine for his health, but that, in one case, the Jews had liberty to convert a certain tithe into money, and bring it to Jerusalem and bestow it for what their *soul lusted after, for oxen, or for sheep, or for wine, or strong drink,* and they were to *eat there before the Lord their God, and rejoice, they and their household.* Deut. 14 : 26. But before any one settles down into a conclusion that this passage warrants the use of wine and ardent spirits, in our age and country, let him consider that there may have been, as there doubtless were, peculiar reasons, under the Levitical dispensation, for permitting the Jews to partake of what their soul desired *before the Lord,* which would not apply to mankind generally; as was the case in respect to several other things. But not to urge this point, I would say, further, that the fact that *Judea was a wine country,* that is, a country where the grape for the manufacture of wine was easily and abundantly raised, puts a different aspect upon this permission. In our country, the apple takes the place of the grape, and our cider is nearer equivalent to the wine of Judea; because there the apple does not flourish, and here the grape cannot be extensively cultivated. *To use wine in wine countries, therefore, is essentially the same thing as to use cider in cider countries;* and it does not appear that the one, in such cases, is much more productive of intemperance than the other. The fact is, the wines used in countries where they are manufactured, contain but little more then half as much alcohol as most of the wine sold in this country, where, as a very respectable authority states, "for every gallon of pure wine which is sold, there is perhaps a pipe, or fifty times the quantity of that, which is adulterated, and in various manners sophisticated—the whole, without exception, the source of a thousand disorders, and in many instances an active poison, imperfectly disguised."

But after all, I am not obliged, in this place, to prove that God has forbidden the use of wine, though led into this digression from the desire to correct a general misapprehension of the Scriptures on this subject; for the inquiry now relates to ardent spirits. And what shall we say concerning the permission, above pointed out, for the Jews to use *strong drink?* I say, it was merely a permission to use wine; for the strong drink several times mentioned in the Bible was, in fact, *nothing more than a particular kind of wine,* made of dates and various sorts of seeds and roots, and called strong drink, merely to distinguish it from the wine made from grapes. Nor is there any evidence that it was in fact any stronger, in its intoxicating qualities, than common wine. The truth is, *ardent spirits were not known until many centuries after Christ:* not until the art of distillation was discovered, which was not certainly earlier than the dark ages. *Not a word, therefore, is said in the Bible concerning distilled spirits.* All its powerful descriptions of drunkenness, and awful denunciations against it, were founded upon the abuse men made of wine. How much louder its notes of remonstrance and terror would have risen, had distillation thus early taught men how to concentrate the poison, may be imagined by the reader.

After these statements, I trust none of those whom I address will any longer resort to the Bible for proofs of a divine permission to manufacture or use ardent spirits. But do the principles of the Bible *condemn* such use and manufacture?

What do you think of the golden rule of *doing unto others as we would they should do unto us?* Should you suppose your neighbors were conducting towards you according to this rule, were they unnecessarily to pursue such a business, or to set such an example as would inevitably lead any of your children or friends into confirmed drunkenness? If not, then how can you, consistently with this rule, distil, use, or furnish materials for the manufacture of ardent spirits, when you thereby, directly or indirectly, render intemperate from two hundred thousand to three hundred thousand of your fellow-citizens, and every year also raise up new recruits enough to supply the dreadful ravages which death makes in this army? This you are certainly doing; for were your distilleries to stop, and you to stop drinking, few would become drunkards, from want of the means.

How would you like to have your neighbors one after another break down your fences, and turn their cattle into your corn-fields, cut down your fruit and ornamental trees, set your house or barn on fire, and threaten you with poverty and slavery? If you would not have your neighbor do thus to you, provided he had the power, then how can you, by preparing the food for intemperance, subject the property, the peace, the morality, the religion, and the liberties of your country to those dangers and fearful depredations which you are now inflicting upon her?

How would you like to have your neighbors, directly or indirectly, but unnecessarily, cause the premature death of every fortieth of your children and friends, and of one in three of those above the age of twenty? I know you would not that they should do thus to you, and yet your manufacture of spirits causes the premature death of five hundred of your fellow-citizens every week; in other words, about that number die every week through the intemperance produced by your distilleries.

Again, I ask the men whom I am addressing, how they reconcile their manufacture and sale of spirits with another command of the Bible? *Woe unto him that giveth his neighbor drink, that puttest thy bottle to him, and makest him drunken also, that thou mayest look on their nakedness.* True, this applies most emphatically to the retailer of spirits: but what could the retailer do if there were no distillery; and what could the distiller do if the farmer withheld the materials? All these men are engaged, directly or indirectly, in giving their neighbors drink; and though it may pass through many hands before it reaches all their mouths, yet where must the burden of the guilt rest, if not upon those who stand at the head of the series, and first convert the articles which God has given to nourish and sustain life into active poison for its destruction; and then, for the sake of a paltry pecuniary profit, send it round amongst their neighbors, accompanied with all the plagues that issued from the fabled Pandora's box?

Finally, let me ask these men how the business of preparing ardent spirits for the community appears to them when they think most seriously of another world? In the hours of sober reflection, on the Sabbath, during seasons of devotion, when sickness overtakes you, and death seems near, or you stand by the dying-bed of some one of your family or neighbors; at such seasons can you look back upon this pursuit with pleasure? If conscience then tells you that this business ought to be given up, Oh remember, that conscience is an honest and faithful friend at such times, and that, as this pursuit then appears to you, so will it appear when you come actually to die. Test this business, I beseech you, by bringing it in imagination to the scrutiny of your dying hour. Whether it be lawful or unlawful.

certain it is that it sends five hundred drunkards into eternity every week; and you have the express testimony of the Bible, that no drunkard shall inherit the kingdom of God. As the Bible is true, then, are not the manufacturers of ardent spirits in our land the means of sending five hundred souls to hell every week? Tell me, my friends, how will this awful truth appear to you on the bed of death? And how does it appear when you look forward to the final judgment, and realize that you must meet there fifty or an hundred, or five hundred times five hundred drunkards, made such through your instrumentality, for one, or two, or ten years, and must there justify yourselves for this instrumentality, or go away with them into perdition, covered with their blood and followed by their execrations?

Oh, my friends, these are realities; and they are near. Do you begin to doubt whether you are in the path of duty? Listen, I beseech you, to the first whispers of the faithful monitor in your bosom.

By the reasonings of philosophy, by the testimony of physicians, by the expostulations of your bleeding country, by the tears, the rags, and the wretchedness of three hundred thousand drunkards, with their wives and children; by the warnings of personal friendship, and by the sanctions of the divine law, the solemnities of death and the judgment, and the groans of ten thousand drunkards, rising from the pit, I entreat you, abandon at once and for ever this most unrighteous employment, and save yourselves from the eternal agonies of conscience, the execrations of millions, and the wrath of Omnipotence.

ADDRESS

TO

THE YOUNG MEN OF THE UNITED STATES,

ON

TEMPERANCE.

BY RT. REV. C. P. M'ILVAINE, D. D.

In addressing the Young Men of the United States in regard to the great enterprise of promoting the universal prevalence of Temperance, we are not aware that any time need be occupied in apology. Our motives cannot be mistaken. The magnitude of the cause, and the importance of that coöperation in its behalf which this address is designed to promote, will vindicate the propriety of its respectful call upon the attention of those by whom it shall ever be received.

It is presumed that every reader is already aware of the extensive and energetic movements at present advancing in our country in behalf of Temperance. That an unprecedented interest in this work has been recently excited, and is still rapidly strengthening in thousands of districts; that talent, wisdom, experience, learning, and influence are now enlisted in its service, with a measure of zeal and harmony far surpassing what was ever witnessed before in such a cause; that great things have already been accomplished; that much greater are near at hand; and that the whole victory will be eventually won, if the temperate portion of society are not wanting to their solemn duty, must have been seen already by those living along the main channels of public thought and feeling. Elevated, as we now are, upon a high tide of general interest and zeal—a tide which may either go on increasing its flood till it has washed clean the very mountain tops, and drowned intemperance in its last den; or else subside, and leave the land infected with a plague, the more malignant and incurable from the dead remains of a partial inundation—it has become a question of universal application, which those who are now at the outset of their influence in society should especially consider: "What can *we* do, and what *ought* we to do in this cause?" For the settlement of this question we invite you to a brief view of the whole ground on which temperance measures are now proceeding.

It cannot be denied that our country is most horribly scourged by intemperance. In the strong language of Scripture, *it groaneth and travaileth in pain, to be delivered from the bondage of this corruption.* Our country is free; *with a great price obtained we this freedom.* We feel as if all the force of Europe could not get it from our embrace. Our shores would shake into the depth of the sea the invader who should presume to seek it. One solitary citizen led away into captivity, scourged, chained by a foreign enemy, would rouse the oldest nerve in the land to indignant complaint, and league the whole nation in loud demand for redress. And yet it cannot be denied that our country is enslaved. Yes, we are groaning under a most desolating bondage. The land is trodden down under its polluting foot. Our families are continually dishonored, ravaged, and bereaved; thousands annually slain, and hundreds of thousands carried away into a loathsome slavery, to be ground to powder under its burdens, or broken upon the wheel of its tortures.

What are the statistics of this traffic? Ask the records of madhouses, and they will answer, that one-third of all their wretched inmates were sent there by Intemperance. Ask the keepers of our prisons, and they will testify that, with scarcely an exception, their horrible population is from the schools of Intemperance. Ask the history of the 200,000 paupers now burdening the hands of public charity, and you will find that two-thirds of them have been the victims, directly or indirectly, of Intemperance. Inquire at the gates of death, and you will learn that no less than 30,000 souls are annually passed for the judgment-bar of God, driven there by Intemperance. How many slaves are at present among us? We ask not of slaves to man, but to Intemperance, in comparison with whose bondage the yoke of the tyrant is freedom. They are estimated at 480,000! And what does the nation pay for the honor and happiness of this whole system of ruin? *Five times as much, every year, as for the annual support of its whole system of government.* These are truths, so often published, so widely sanctioned, so generally received, and so little doubted, that we need not detail the particulars by which they are made out. What, then, is the whole amount of guilt and of woe which they exhibit? Ask Him "unto whom all hearts are open, all desires known, and from whom no secrets are hid." Ask *Eternity!*

The biographer of Napoleon, speaking of the loss sustained by England on the field of Waterloo, says, "Fifteen thousand men killed and wounded, threw half Britain into mourning. It required all the glory and all the solid advantages of that day to reconcile the mind to the high price at which it was purchased." But what mourning would fill *all* Britain, if every year should behold another

Waterloo? But what does every year repeat in our peaceful land? Ours is a carnage not exhibited only once in a single field, but going on continually, in every town and hamlet. Every eye sees its woes, every ear catches its groans. The wounded are too numerous to count. Who is not wounded by the intemperance of this nation? But of the dead we count, year by year, more than double the number that filled half Britain with mourning. Ah, could we behold the many thousands whom our destroyer annually delivers over unto death, collected together upon one field of slaughter, for one funeral, and one deep and wide burial-place; could we behold a full assemblage of all the parents, widows, children, friends, whose hearts have been torn by their death, surrounding that awful grave, and loading the winds with tales of woe, the whole land would cry out at the spectacle. It would require something more than "*all the glory*," and "*all the solid advantages*" of Intemperance, "*to reconcile the mind to the high price at which they were purchased.*"

But enough is known of the intemperance of this country to render it undeniable by the most ignorant inhabitant, that a horrible scourge is indeed upon us.

Another assertion is equally unquestionable. *The time has come when a great effort must be made to exterminate this unequalled destroyer.* It was high time this was done when the first drunkard entered eternity to receive the award of Him who has declared that no drunkard shall enter the kingdom of God. The demand for this effort has been growing in the peremptory tone of its call, as "the overflowing scourge" has passed with constantly extending sweep through the land. But a strange apathy has prevailed among us. As if the whole nation had been drinking the cup of delusion, we saw the enemy coming in like a flood, and we lifted up scarcely a straw against him.

As if the magicians of Egypt had prevailed over us by their enchantments, we beheld our waters of refreshment turned into blood, and a destroying sword passing through till "there was a great cry" in the land, for there was scarcely "a house where there was not one dead;" and still our hearts were hardened, and we would not let go the great sin for which these plagues were brought upon us. It seems as if some foul demon had taken his seat upon the breast of the nation, and was holding us down with the dead weight of a horrid nightmare, while he laughed at our calamity and mocked at our fear—when our fear came as desolation, and our destruction as a whirlwind.

Shall this state continue? Is not the desolation advancing? Have not facilities of intemperance, temptations to intemperance, examples to sanction intemperance, been fast increasing ever since this plague began? Without some effectual effort, is it not certain they will continue to increase, till intemperate men and their abettors will form the public opinion and consequently the public conscience and the public law of this land—till intemperance shall become, like leviathan of old, "king over all the children of pride," whose breath kindleth coals, and a "flame goeth out of his mouth?" Then what will effort of man avail? "Canst thou draw out leviathan with a hook? His heart is as firm as a stone; yea, as hard as a piece of the nether millstone. He drinketh up a river, and hasteth not. When he raiseth up himself, the mighty are afraid."

It is too late to put off any longer the effort for deliverance. It is granted by the common sense, and urged by the common interest; every feeling of humanity and every consideration of religion enforces the belief that the time has come when a great onset is imperiously demanded to drive out intemperance from the land.

This, to be great, *must be universal.* The whole country is enslaved; and the whole country must rise up at once, like an armed man, and determine to be free. Of what lasting avail would it be for one section of territory, here and there, to clear itself, while the surrounding regions should remain under the curse? The temperance reformation has no quarantine to fence out the infected. Geographical boundaries are no barriers against contagion. Rivers and mountains are easily crossed by corrupting example. Ardent spirits, like all other fluids, perpetually seek their level. In vain does the farmer eradicate from his fields the last vestige of the noisome thistle, while the neighboring grounds are given up to its dominion, and every wind scatters the seed where it listeth. The effort against intemperance, to be effective, *must be universal.*

Here, then, are three important points which we may safely assume as entirely unquestionable: that *our country is horribly scourged by intemperance;* that *the time has come when a great effort is demanded for the expulsion of this evil;* and that *no effort can be effectual without being universal.* Hence is deduced, undeniably, the conclusion that it is the duty, and the solemn duty of the people, in every part of this country, to rise up at once, and act vigorously and unitedly in the furtherance of whatever measures are best calculated to promote reformation.

Here the question occurs, *What can be done? How can this woe be arrested?* The answer is plain. Nothing can be done, but in one of the three following ways. You must either suffer people to drink *immoderately;* or you must endeavor to promote *moderation* in drinking; or you must try to persuade them to drink *none at all.* One of these plans must be adopted. Which shall we choose? The first is condemned already.

What say we to the second, *the moderate use* of intoxicating drinks? It has unquestionably the sanction of high and ancient ancestry. It is precisely the plan on which intemperance has been wrestled with ever since it was first discovered that "wine is a mocker," and that "strong drink is raging." But hence comes its condemnation. Its long use is its death-witness. Were it new, we might hope something from its adoption. But it is old enough to have been tried to the uttermost. The wisdom, the energy, the benevolence of centuries have made the best of it. The attempt to keep down intemperance by endeavoring to persuade people to indulge only moderately in strong drink, has been the world's favorite for ages; while every age has wondered that the vice increased so rapidly.

At last we have been awakened to a fair estimate of the success of the plan. And what is it? So far from its having shown the least tendency to exterminate the evil, it is the mother of all its abominations. All who have attained the stature of full-grown intemperance, were once children in this nursery, sucking at the breasts of this parent. All the "men of strength to mingle strong drink," who are now full graduates in the vice, and "masters in the arts" of drunkenness, began their education and served their apprenticeship under the discipline of moderate drinking. All that have learned to lie down in the streets, and carry terror into their families, and whom intemperance has conducted to the penitentiary and the madhouse, may look back to this as the beginning of their course—the author of their destiny. No man ever set out to use strong drink with the expectation of becoming eventually a drunkard. No man ever became a drunkard without having at first assured himself that he could keep a safe rein upon every disposition that might endanger his strict sobriety. "*I am in no danger while I only take a little,*" is the first principle in the doctrine of intemperance. It is high time it were discarded. It has deluged the land with vice, and sunk the population into debasement. The same results will ensue again, just in proportion as the moderate use of ardent spirits continues to be encouraged. Let the multitude continue to drink a little, and still our hundreds of thousands will annually drink to death.

It is settled, therefore, that to encourage moderate drinking is not the plan on which the temperance reformation can be successfully prosecuted. The faithful experiment of generation after generation, decides that it must be abandoned. A cloud of witnesses, illustrating its consequences in all the tender mercies of a drunkard's portion, demand that it should be abandoned. Its full time is come. Long enough have we refused to open our eyes to the evident deceitfulness of its pretensions. At last the country is awaking, and begins to realize the emptiness of this dream. Let it go as a dream, and only be remembered that we may wonder how it deceived, and lament how it injured us.

But, if this be discarded, what plan of reformation remains? If nothing is to be expected from endeavoring to promote a *moderate* use of ardent spirits, and still less from an *immoderate* use, what can be done? There is but one possible answer. *Persuade people to use none at all. Total abstinence* is the only plan on which reformation can be hoped for. We are shut up to this. We have tried the consequences of encouraging people to venture but moderately into the atmosphere of infection; and we are now convinced that it was the very plan to feed its strength and extend its ravages. We are forced to the conclusion, that, to arrest the pestilence, we must starve it. All the healthy must abstain from its neighborhood. All those who are now temperate must give up the use of the means of intemperance. The deliverance of this land from its present degradation, and from the increasing woes attendant on this vice, depends altogether upon the extent to which the principle of total abstinence shall be adopted by our citizens.

But suppose this principle universally adopted, would it clear the country of intemperance? Evidently it is the only, but is it the effectual remedy? Most certainly, if all temperate persons would disuse ardent spirits, they could not cease to be temperate. Many a drunkard, under the powerful check of their omnipresent reproof, would be sobered. His companions would totter, one after another, to their graves. A few years would see them buried, and the land relinquished to the temperate. Then what would be the security against a new inroad of the exterminated vice? Why, public opinion would stand guard at every avenue by which it could come in.

Consider the operation of this influence. Why is it now so easy to entice a young man into the haunts of drunkenness? Because public opinion favors the use of the very means of his ruin. He may drink habitually, and fasten upon himself the appetite of drink, till he becomes enchained and feels himself a slave; but if he has never fallen into manifest intoxication, he has forfeited no character in public opinion. All this is a direct result of the fact, that those considered as temperate people set the example, and patronize the snare of moderate drinking. But suppose them to take the ground proposed, and bear down with the whole force of their example and influence on the side of entire abstinence, would they not create an immense force of public opinion against the least use of ardent spirits? How then could a temperate man ever become a drunkard? He has not yet contracted the desire for ardent spirits; and how will he contract it? Will he risk his character; fly in the face of public feeling and opinion; despise all the warnings in the history of intemperance, to get at the use, and put himself under the torture of that for which, as yet, he has no disposition? Only post a wakeful public sentiment at the little opening of moderate drinking, and the whole highway to the drunkard's ruin will be closed up. All its present travellers will soon pass away, while none will be entering to keep up the character of the road.

Most assuredly, then, the reformation of the land is in the power of public opinion. It is equally certain, that public opinion will accomplish nothing but by setting its influence directly in opposition to *any* indulgence in strong drink. And it is just as plain, that in order to accomplish this, the temperate part of the population must create a power of example by setting out upon the firm and open ground of total abstinence. In proportion, then, as the temperate throughout the country shall come up to this ground, will the redemption of our enslaved republic be accomplished.

Thus have we arrived at the last refuge of this cause. ABSTAIN ENTIRELY, is the grand principle of life, to be written upon the sacred standard of all temperance movements, and under which the contending host may be as sure of victory as if, like Constantine, they saw inscribed with a sunbeam upon the cloud, *In hoc signo vinces.** But such being the eminent importance of total abstinence, it deserves to be presented in detail. We begin, therefore, with the position, that

Entire abstinence from ardent spirits is essential to personal security. Such is the insidious operation of strong drink upon all the barriers we may set up against excess; so secretly does it steal upon the taste, excite the appetite, disorganize the nervous system, and undermine the deepest

* Under this standard you shall conquer.

resolutions of him who imagines himself in perfect security; so numerous and awful have been its victories over every barrier, and every species of mental and bodily constitution, that we may lay it down as an assertion, which none who know the annals of intemperance will dispute, that no individual who permits himself to use ardent spirits moderately, has any valid security that he will not become a victim to its power.

We know the remarks which instantly mount to the lips of many at the sight of such an assertion: "Surely the little we take can never hurt us. Look around and see how many have done the same, and continued the habit to the end of life, without having ever been betrayed into drunkenness." We do look around, and are constrained to remark, how many have seemed to live temperately to the end, who, if the reality were known, would be quoted as warnings against the insidiousness of the poison, instead of examples of the security with which it may be used in moderation. They were never delirious; but were they never fevered? Fever is often fatal, without delirium. Ah, did every disease with which human beings are fevered, and swollen, and slain, receive a candid name; were every gravestone inscribed with a true memorial, as well of the life, as the death of him at whose head it stands; could every consumption, and dropsy, and liver-complaint, disclose its secret history; did every shaking nerve, and palsied stomach, and aching temple, and burning brain, and ruptured blood-vessel, relate how it began, and grew, and triumphed, we should hear, indeed, of many who died in consumption, or dropsy, and other diseases, without any impulse towards the grave from the use of strong drink; but of how many, never regarded as intemperate, should we learn that the real, though slow and silent cause of their death was *drink.* They lingered long, and their malady was called a disease of the lungs; or they fell suddenly, and it was a case of apoplexy; or they were greatly swollen, and it was considered dropsy; they lost their powers of digestion, and were said to be troubled with dyspepsia; every vital function refused its natural action, and the poor victim was treated or a liver-complaint. But why? what produced the disease? Alcohol! They were poisoned. They died of the intemperate use of ardent spirits, however moderately they may have had the credit of indulging in them.

But again, we look at the world, and while we cannot acknowledge that they have habitually indulged in even a moderate use of ardent spirits without receiving some injury—for alcohol must hurt a healthy man in some way or other—we do acknowledge that many have thus indulged with no very perceptible injury. They have continued sober. But so it must be acknowledged, that many have breathed the air and mingled with the victims of a pestilence, without being infected; or stood amidst the carnage of battle, without receiving a wound. But were they in no danger? Because they came off unhurt, shall *we* be willing to rush into the streets of an infected city, or join the conflict of charging battalions?

But again, we look at the world, and see how many have been slain, while many have lived; how many who, if exalted station, eminent talents, great attainments, excellent feelings, and heavy responsibilities, are any security, might, with more than usual reason, have flattered themselves with the assurance of safety: men of all professions, of strong nerves, and numerous resolutions and precautions, at last reduced to a level with the brutes; and this spectacle forces the conviction that entire abstinence is the only security against final ruin. Had you a tree in your gardens, the fruit of which should be discovered to have inflicted disease as often as the prudent use of ardent spirits has resulted in the sorrows of intemperance, that tree would be rooted up. Its fruit would be entitled *poison*. The neighborhood would be afraid of it. Children would be taught to beware of so much as venturing to try how it tastes.

Again: *The total disuse of ardent spirits, on the part of parents, is the only plan of safety in bringing up their children.* How many are the parents whose lives are cursed with children who, were it not that "no drunkard hath any inheritance in the kingdom of God," they would be relieved to hear were dead! But how were those children ruined? "*Ah, by those corrupting companions; by that vile dram-shop,*" the parents would answer. But what first inclined their way to that house of seduction? By what avenue did evil associates first effect a lodgment in those children's hearts? How many parents must turn and look at home for an answer! They have not been intemperate; but while the tastes and habits of their children were forming, they used to drink moderately of ardent spirits. The decanter containing it had an honorable place on the sideboard and on the table. It was treated respectfully, as a fountain of strength to the feeble, of refreshment to the weary; and as perfectly safe when used in moderation. To offer it to a friend was a debt of hospitality. Thus the whole weight of parental example was employed in impressing those children with a favorable idea of the pleasure, the benefit, and the security, not to speak of the necessity, of the use of ardent spirits. Thus the parents presented the decanter of strong drink to their children, with a recommendation as forcible as if every day they had encircled it with a chaplet of roses, and pronounced an oration in its praise.

And what consequences were to be expected? Children who revere their parents will honor what their parents delight to honor. It was not to be supposed that those children would do else than imitate the high example before them. Most naturally would they try the taste, and emulate to acquire a fondness for strong drink. They would think it sheer folly to be afraid of what their parents used. In a little while the flavor would become grateful. They would learn to think of it, ask for it, contrive ways of obtaining it, and be very accessible to the snares of those who used it to excess. Thus easily would they slide into the pit. And thus the history of the decline, and fall, and death of multitudes must commence, not at the dram-shop, but at the tables of parents; not with describing the influence of seductive companions, but with a lamentation over the examples of inconsiderate parents, who furnished those companions with their strongest argument, and wreathed their cup of death with a garland of honor.

Such consequences must be looked for wherever parental example is expected to be held in reverence among children. A father may venture to the brink of a precipice, and stand without giddiness upon the margin of the torrent that rushes by and plunges into a deep abyss; but will he trust his child to occupy the same position? But if the child see him there, is there no danger that when the parent's eye is away, he too will venture, and go and play upon the frightful verge, and be amused with the bubbles as they dance along the side of the cataract, and at last become giddy, and be drawn in with the rush of the tide?

Entire abstinence from the drink of drunkards is the parents' only plan in training up their children.

Again: *The total disuse of ardent spirits is essential to the beneficial influence of the example of the temperate upon society at large.*

However novel the assertion to some, it can be easily shown that the example of all who use ardent spirits, except as they use prescribed medicine, *is in the scale of intemperance.* As far as its influence extends, it helps directly to fill up the ranks of the intemperate, and annually to launch a multitude of impenitent souls into a hopeless eternity. Can this be true? Suppose all the rising generation, in imitation of their elders, should commence the moderate use of strong drink. They are thus attracted into the current of the stream which is setting silently, smoothly, powerfully, towards the roaring whirlpool. But now they are urged by those whose example they have thus far followed, to go no farther. "Beware," they cry, "the tide is strong; do like us; drop the anchor, ply the oar." Ah, but now their influence fails. It was strong enough to persuade the thoughtless into danger; but now it is perfectly impotent to keep them from ruin. They have none of the strength or prudence by which others have been enabled to keep their place. They have no anchor to drop, nor skill at the oar. They yield, and go down, and perish. But where must we look for the prime cause of this destruction? To those whose example enticed them into the way—*the example of prudent drinkers.*

Such, unquestionably, was the influence by which a great portion of those now intemperate were first drawn into the snares of death. It is not, as many suppose, the odious example of those already under the dominion of intemperate habits, by which others are seduced; the operation of such disgusting precedents is rather on the side of entire abstinence from the means of their debasement. But it is to the honor given the degrading cup, by those who can drink without what is considered excess, that we must ascribe, in a great degree, the first seduction of all who receive the ultimate wages of intemperance.

Again: Entire abstinence from strong drink should be the rule of all; because, *to one in health, it never does good, but, on the contrary, it always, of its very nature, does harm.* We know the general idea, that hard labor, and cold weather, and a hot sun demand its use; that a little to stimulate the appetite, and a little to help digestion, and a little to compose us to sleep, and a little to refresh us when fatigued, and a little to enliven us when depressed, is very useful, if not necessary. And we know how soon so many little matters make a great amount. We have often been called to "behold how great a matter a little fire kindleth." A more unfounded idea never was adopted, than that a man in health can need such medicine. Is there any nourishment in drinking alcohol? About as much as in eating fire.

But why should not the opinions of physicians suffice on this point? If we take their advice as to what will cure us when sick, why not also as to what will injure us when well? The first medical men throughout the land do not more perfectly agree, that to breathe a foul atmosphere is pernicious, than that the use of strong drink, in any quantity, is hurtful. *Abstain entirely,* is their loud and reiterated advice. Many of them will even maintain that it can easily and profitably be dispensed with in medicine.

But how speaks experience on this head? Who works the longest under the sun of August, or stands the firmest against the winter, or abides the safest amidst abounding disease, or arrives last at the infirmities of old age? The experiment of total abstinence has been fairly tried in thousands of cases, by those who once imagined they must drink a little every day; and invariably have they borne a grateful testimony to its happy effects upon the health of their bodies and the peace of their minds. Farms are tilled, harvests gathered, ships built, companies of militia parade, associations of firemen labor, fishermen stand their exposure, the student trims his lamp, the hungry eat their bread, and the weary take their rest, with no debt of thanks to the aid of the distillery.

We say no more upon the plan of entire abstinence. But we will mention four reasons which should embolden any friend of temperance in urging it upon others.

1. It is extremely *simple.* All can comprehend, all can execute it. It requires no labor; costs no study; consumes no time.

2. It contains no *coercion.* Its whole force is that of reason. The influence of laws and of magistrates it does not embrace. No man can complain of a trespass upon his liberty, when we would persuade him to escape the drunkard's slavery by not tasting the drunkard's cup.

3. *In this cure there is no pain.* It is recommended to whom? *the temperate*—to those who, having formed no strong attachment to ardent spirit, can feel no great self-denial in renouncing its use.

4. In this remedy *there is no expense.* To those who complain of other works of usefulness because of their cost, this is without blame. To drink no spirits, will cost no money. But what will it save? It will save the majority of the poorer class of the population, in most of our towns, one half their annual rent. It will empty all our alms-houses and hospitals of two thirds their inhabitants, and support the remainder. Yes, such is the tax which the consumption of ardent spirits annually levies upon this nation, that the simple disuse of strong drink, throughout the land, would save in one year the value of at least five times the whole national revenue.

It is too late to say that a general adoption of the great principle of total abstinence is too much to be hoped for. A few years ago, who would not have been considered almost deranged had he predicted what has already been accomplished in this cause? Great things, wonderful things, have already been effected. The enemies of this reformation, whose pecuniary interests set them in opposition, are unable to deny this fact. It is felt from the distillery to the dram-shop. It is seen from Maine to the utmost South and West. Every traveller perceives it. Every vender knows it. The whole country wonders at the progress of this cause. It is rapidly and powerfully advancing. *One thing*, and only one, can prevent its entire success. The frenzy of drunkenness cannot arrest its goings. The hundreds of thousands in the armies of intemperance cannot resist its march. But the *temperate* can. If backward to come up to the vital principle of this work, *they will* prevent its accomplishment. But the banner of triumph will wave in peace over all the land, hailed by thousands of grateful captives from the gripe of death, in spite of all the warring of the "mighty to drink wine," if those who abhor intemperance, and think they would be willing to make a great sacrifice to save their children or friends from its blasting curse, will only come up to the little effort of entire abstinence. This is the surest and shortest way to drain off the river of fire now flowing through the land. It is the moderate use of the temperate that keeps open the smoking fountains from which that tide is poured.

To YOUNG MEN who have not yet been brought under the dominion of intemperate habits, we address the urgent exhortation of this cause. Consider the immense responsibility that devolves upon you. It is not too much to say that the question, whether this nation is to be delivered from the yoke of death—whether the present march of reformation shall go on till the last hiding-place of this vice shall be subdued, or else be arrested and turned back, with the sorrow of beholding the vaunting triumph, and the emboldened increase of all the ministers of woe which attend in the train of intemperance, rests ultimately with you. You compose the muscle and sinew of this nation. You are to set the example by which the next generation is to be influenced. By your influence its character will be formed. By your stand its position will, in a great measure, be determined. You are soon to supplant those who have passed the state of life which you now are occupying. Soon the generation that is to grow up under the influence of your example and instruction, will have reached your place. Thus are you the heart of the nation. Corruption and debasement here must be felt to the extremities of the national body. Temperance here will eventually expel, by its strong pulsations, the last remnant of the burning blood of drunkenness from the system, and carry soberness and health to every member of our political constitution.

Are these things so? Suppose them exaggerations. Grant that the importance of your vigorous and unanimous coöperation in this work of reformation is unreasonably magnified; still, how much can you do. Were our coasts invaded by a powerful enemy, come to ravage our cities, chain our liberties, poison our fountains, burn our harvests, and carry off our youth into perpetual slavery, what could young men do? To whom would the trump of battle be sounded so effectually? Who else would feel upon themselves the chief responsibility for their country's rescue? What excuse could they find for supineness and sloth? Such indeed is the enemy by which the country is already desolated. And now it is to the warm hearts, and the strong hands, and the active energies, and the powerful example of young men, that the dearest interests of the nation look for deliverance.

Young men, shall we not enlist heartily and unitedly in promoting the extermination of intemperance? What question have we to decide? Is it a question whether the country is cursed with this plague to a most horrible and alarming extent? No. Is it a question whether the present power and the progressive character of intemperance among us demand an *immediate* rising up of all the moral force of the nation to subdue it? No. Is it a question whether the most important part of the strength and success of such an effort depends upon the part in it which the young men in the United States shall take? No. Then what does the spirit of patriotism say to us? If we love our country; if we would rise in arms to shake off the hosts of an invader from our shores; if every heart among us would swell with indignation at the attempt of an internal power to break in pieces our free constitution, and substitute a government of chains and bayonets; what does the love of country bid us do, when by universal acknowledgment an enemy is now among us whose breath is pestilence and whose progress desolation—an enemy that has already done and is daily doing a more dreadful work against the happiness of the people than all the wars and plagues we have ever suffered?

What does the voice of common humanity say to us? Can we feel for human woe, and not be moved at the spectacle of wretchedness and despair which the intemperance of this country presents? Let us imagine the condition of the hundreds of thousands who are now burning with the hidden flame, and hastening to utter destruction by this most pitiless of all vices; let us embrace in one view the countless woes inflicted by the cruel tempers, the deep disgrace, the hopeless poverty, and the corrupting examples of all these victims, upon wives, children, parents, friends, and the morals of society; let us stand at the graves of the thirty thousand that annually perish by intemperance, and there be still, and listen to what the *voice of humanity* speaks.

What does the exhortation of religion say to us? What undermines more insidiously every moral principle of the heart; what palsies so entirely every moral faculty of the soul; what so soon and so awfully makes man *dead while he liveth;* what spreads through the whole frame-work of society such rottenness, or so effectually opens the door to all those powers of darkness by which the pillars of public order are crumbled and the restraints of religion are mocked; what so universally excludes from the death-bed of a sinner the consolations of the Gospel, or writes upon his grave such a sentence of despair, as *intemperance?* Behold the immense crowd of its victims! Where are they not seen? Read in the book of God that declaration, "nor thieves, nor *drunkards,* shall inherit the kingdom of God;" then listen to what the exhortation of Christian benevolence speaks to us. Is it asked, *What can young men do?* We can do this one thing at least. *We can continue temperate.* What if every one of us, now free from the appetite of strong drink, should hold on to our liberty; how would the ranks of intemperance, which death is continually wasting, be filled up? But how shall we continue temperate? Not by using the means of destruction. Not by a moderate indulgence in the cup of seduction. Not by beginning where all those began who have since ended in ruin. But by *entire abstinence from strong drink.* Let us renounce entirely what cannot profit us, what forms no important item in our comforts, what may bring us, as it has brought such multitudes as strong as we, to the mire and dirt of drunkenness.

But we can do something more. We can contribute the influence of our example to help bring into disrepute the use of ardent spirits for any purposes but those of medicine. If any of us are confident that we could go on in the moderate, without ever coming to the immoderate use of strong drink, we know that the deliverance of the country from its present curse is utterly hopeless while ardent spirit is in the hands of the people. It must be banished. Public opinion must set it aside. Young men must contribute to form that opinion. It cannot be formed without the total abstinence of the temperate. Let us not dare to stand in its way.

But we can do something more. We have an influence which, in a variety of ways, we may use in the community to diminish the temptations which, wherever we look, are presented to the unwary to entice them to intemperance. We can employ the influence of example, of opinion, and of persuasion, to drive out of fashion and into disrepute, the common but ensnaring practice of evincing hospitality by the display of strong drink, and of testifying friendship and good-will over the glass. We can contribute much powerful coöperation in the effort to make the use of ardent spirits for the ordinary purposes of drink so unbecoming the character of temperate people, that he who wishes to have his reputation for temperance unsuspected, will either renounce the dangerous cup, or wait till no eye but that of God can see him taste it. We can do much, in union with those of more age and more established influence, to create a public feeling against the licensing of those innumerable houses of corruption where seduction into the miseries of drunkenness is the trade of their keepers, and the means of destruction are vended so low, and offered so attractively, that the poorest may purchase his death, and the strongest may be persuaded to do so. These horrible abodes of iniquity not only facilitate the daily inebriation of the veteran drunkard, but they encourage, and kindle, and nourish, and confirm the incipient appetite of the novice, and put forth the first influence in that system of persuasion by which the sober are ultimately subdued and levelled to the degradation of wretches, from whose loathsomeness they once turned away in disgust. Why are these instruments of cruelty permitted? Not because the authorities will not refuse to license them. Public opinion is the conscience of those authorities. Let the opinions and feelings of that portion of the community where the strength and patronage of society reside, be once enlisted in opposition to such houses, and the evil will be remedied; the morals of society will not be insulted, nor the happiness of families endangered at every step by the agents and means and attractions of intemperance. Young men have much to do, and are capable of doing a great work in creating such a public opinion.

In order to exert ourselves with the best effect in the promotion of the several objects in this great cause to which young men should apply themselves, let us associate ourselves into *Temperance Societies.* We know the importance of associated exertions. We have often seen how a few instruments, severally weak, have become mighty when united. Every work, whether for evil or benevolent purposes, has felt the life, and spur, and power of coöperation. The whole progress of the temperance reformation, thus far, is owing to the influence of *societies;* to the coming together of the temperate, and the union of their resolutions, examples, and exertions, under the articles of temperance societies. Thus examples have been brought out, set upon a hill, and made secure. Thus the weak have been strengthened, the wavering confirmed, the irresolute emboldened. Thus public attention has been awakened, public feeling interested, and public sentiment turned and brought to bear. Thus works have been performed, information distributed, agencies employed, and a thousand instruments set in motion which no industry of individual unassociated action could have reached. Let temperance societies be multiplied. Every new association is a new battery against the stronghold of the enemy, and gives a new impulse to the hearts of those who have already joined the conflict. Let us arise, and be diligent, and be united; and may the God of mercy bless our work.

THE DRUNKARD IN HIS FAMILY.

His example is seen daily in the house, and in the parent. It is seen by children so soon as they can see any thing, and long before their minds are capable of distinguishing its nature, or its tendency. The parent visibly regards spirituous liquors as a peculiarly interesting enjoyment of sense, at a time when they know no enjoyments but those of sense: of course they cannot but think it eminently valuable. The means of intoxication are also provided to their hand; and their own home, so far as a dangerous and malignant influence is concerned, is changed into a dram-shop. The mother, in the meantime, not unfrequently contracts the same evil habit from the father; and thus both parents unite in the unnatural and monstrous employment of corrupting their children.

What a prospect is here presented to our view! A husband and wife, to whom God has given children to be trained up by them for heaven, united together in taking them by the hand, and leading them coolly to perdition. What heart, not made of stone, can look at such a family without feeling exquisite distress, and the most terrible forebodings? Contemplate, for a moment, the innocent, helpless beings, perfectly unconscious of their danger, and incapable of learning it, thus led as victims to the altar of a modern *Moloch*, less sanguinary, indeed, but not less cruel than the heathen god before whom the Israelitish parents burnt their own offspring, and say, whether you most pity the children, or detest the parents.

Dr. Dwight.

No. 247.

WHO SLEW ALL THESE?

AN AUTHENTIC NARRATIVE.

About twenty years ago, Mr. and Mrs. ——, decent and respectable people, removed with a family of children from the country to a neighboring town, where they purchased a small house and lot, and lived very comfortably. Their family, however, increasing to five boys, they removed to the shore—the town being situated on a river—and in addition to their former means of obtaining a living, erected a sign, and provided "entertainment" for such as chose to call on them. They were temperate people, accounted honest, and sent their children to the most respectable school in the place. In a short time it was perceived that they too frequently partook of the "entertainment," as it is called, which they provided for their customers. The habit of daily measuring the poison to others, induced them to taste for themselves; their house was not as respectable as formerly; restraints were removed; and although they were not drunkards, they gave evidence that they used too freely the deadly drug which they fearlessly handled. If the temperance reformation had been at that time commenced, they might have been warned of their danger, and saved from ruin; but nothing arrested their progress in the path of the destroyer.

Their children, who used to be clad with garments which denoted a mother's industry, soon began to bear marks of neglect, and were by degrees withdrawn from the school—their parents, because of *hard times*, not being able to support them there. They consequently lounged about, became acquainted with the customers at the bar, and learned their evil habits, especially that of drinking.

The parents had commenced the sale of intoxicating drinks to become rich; but at the end of a few years it had reduced them to poverty. They had lost their respectability, their honesty, and their property, which was mortgaged for rum; their children had become vagabonds, and their house a receptacle of vice. Of all their five sons, not one escaped the infection; they and their miserable parents wallowed in the mire together.

In consequence of the dreadful excess to which she had abandoned herself, the imagination of Mrs. —— became disordered, and conjured up horrible visions. In her fits of the *delirium tremens*, she fancied herself bound with a belt of brass, to which was attached a chain held by the great enemy of souls, who had indeed enchained her with the most dire and effectual of all his spells. She would cross the room with the rapidity of lightning, screaming that he was winding up the chain, and she *must go*—she *could not* stop. She was afraid to pass her own threshold, and fancied she heard unearthly voices, and saw spirits black and hideous all around her. "There they sit," she would say, "J——, M——," mentioning the names of all her children; "there they sit, grinning at me, and telling me I sent them to hell: they are on the beams and in the corners, and wherever I go."

The writer of this has often witnessed her desperate struggles; has seen her, when a gleam of reason came over her mind, weep in bitterness over her ruin and misery; has heard her confessions of deeds of villany committed under her roof; and has heard also her solemn vows to refrain from that which wrought all this misery and sin; but after all this, has seen her "seek it yet again."

All the arguments which religion can offer were set before her, and she often appeared to feel their force, and resolved to repent; but the deadly wave seemed to have retired to gather new force, and again swept over her and prostrated her lower than "the beasts that perish." There can be no more effectual barrier against the voice of conscience, the powerful influence of natural affection, and the strivings of the blessed Spirit of God, than the use of intoxicating drinks.

Her husband had made himself literally a beast: his appearance was scarcely human; bloated, discolored, tottering, uttering curses, and sometimes threatening her life. Her constitution after a while gave away, and she sunk in death, snoring out the few last days of her existence in a state of stupor, covered with rags and filth. Her husband had so benumbed every feeling of humanity by his excess, that he seemed very little affected by her death; and to one who reminded him of their former respectability, and spoke of the wretched state to which they were reduced, urging him powerfully, over the dead body of the self-murdered wife *now* to desist, he replied stupidly, that there is an *eleventh hour*.

Four or five years have elapsed, and he is still in the same state of beastly degradation—his property entirely gone, and he occasionally earning a few cents, with which to purchase the poison which is consuming his vitals, and rendering him stupid and dead to every motive that can be urged for reformation.

Two of the sons of this unhappy man have gone down to death in an awful manner. Another, in an affray occasioned by intoxication, received such an injury in the head that his intellect has suffered, and he is subject to fits of partial derangement. The other two are very intemperate; one of them apparently lost to all sense of shame.

The circumstances attending the death of one of these young men were extraordinary. He had become subject to fits in consequence of his intemperate life; and his wife following the same course, they were obliged to give up keeping a public-house, and he maintained himself by fishing. He frequently stopped colored people and others who were advertised as runaways, and obtained a reward for returning them to their masters. He was brutally cruel in his treatment of those who thus fell into his hands, and on one occasion, having apprehended a young colored man on suspicion of his being a runaway, he confined him; and taking him in a boat to his master—who had sent him from home on business—as he was returning, he fell from the boat, probably in a fit, and sunk like lead into the mighty waters. On the following day search was made for his body, which was found swollen and disfigured, and laid in the grave.

His brother, the youngest of the five, had not reached his twentieth year, but had given himself up to the influence of the vice which has proved the destruction of his family, until he also was subject to fits. Not many months ago he was seized with one, being then intoxicated; he was recovered by the by-standers, and crawled to a small sloop lying partly on the shore for repairs: he laid himself down there, and was found, ten minutes afterwards, *dead*, with his head partly under water. It was supposed that another fit had seized him, and that in his struggle he had fallen and suffocated.

This is a melancholy history, but a true one. Many circumstances rendering it more striking are suppressed, as some of the parties are living. The old man, but a short time ago, was warned again, and the question put to him, "What are the benefits of this practice?" "It *fattens graveyards!*" he replied. with a distorted countenance and a horrid laugh.

Yes, such are the dire results of intemperance; and of intemperance not born with one, but brought on by a temperate use of ardent spirit. These facts are well known. They are published with the hope of their proving a restraint to some one who, trusting in the strength of principle, may occasionally taste this destructive poison.

"Look not upon the wine when it is red, when it giveth his color in the cup, when it moveth itself aright: at the last it biteth like a serpent, and stingeth like an adder." Go to God for strength to resist temptation; practise entire abstinence from all that can intoxicate; repent of sin, and trust in the mercy of Christ; and you shall be safe for the present life, and that which is to come.

PUBLISHED BY THE AMERICAN TRACT SOCIETY.

THE

EFFECTS OF INTEMPERANCE

ON THE

MORAL, INTELLECTUAL, AND PHYSICAL POWERS.

BY THOMAS SEWALL, M. D.,

PROFESSOR OF ANATOMY AND PHYSIOLOGY IN THE COLUMBIAN COLLEGE, WASHINGTON CITY.

I ADDRESS you, fellow-citizens, to enlist your sympathies and efforts in behalf of an institution which, in accordance with the spirit of the times, has been established through our land by the almost united voice of the nation, and this for the suppression of one of the most alarming evils that ever infested human society; a vice, too, so odious in its nature, so injurious in its consequences, and attended with so many circumstances of suffering, mortification, and disgrace, that it seems difficult to understand how it should ever have become a prevalent evil among mankind; and more especially how it should have come down to us from the early periods of society, gaining strength, and power, and influence, in its descent. That such is the fact, requires no proof. Its devastating effects are but too obvious. In these latter times, more especially, it has swept over our land with the rapidity and power of a tempest, bearing down every thing in its course. Not content with rioting in the haunts of ignorance and vice, it has passed through our consecrated groves, has entered our most sacred enclosures: and O, how many men of genius and of letters have fallen before it; how many lofty intellects have been shattered and laid in ruins by its power; how many a warm and philanthropic heart has been chilled by its icy touch! It has left no retreat unvisited; it has alike invaded our public and private assemblies, our political and social circles, our courts of justice and halls of legislation. It has stalked within the very walls of our capitol, and there left the stain of its polluting touch on our national glory. It has leaped over the pale of the church, and even reached up its sacrilegious arm to the pulpit and dragged down some of its richest ornaments. It has revelled equally on the spoils of the palace and the cottage, and has seized its victims, with an unsparing grasp, from every class of society; the private citizen and public functionary, the high and the low, the rich and the poor, the enlightened and the ignorant: and where is there a family among us so happy as not to have wept over some of its members, who have fallen by the hand of this ruthless destroyer?

As a nation, intemperance has corrupted our morals, impaired our intellect, and enfeebled our physical strength. Indeed, in whatever light we view it, whether as an individual, a social, or national evil, as affecting our personal independence and happiness, our national wealth and industry; as reducing our power of naval and military defence, as enfeebling the intellectual energies of the nation, and undermining the health of our fellow-citizens; as sinking the patriotism and valor of the nation, as increasing paupers, poverty, and taxation, as sapping the foundation of our moral and religious institutions, or as introducing disorder, distress, and ruin into families and society; it calls to us, in a voice of thunder, to awake from our slumbers, to seize every weapon, and wield every power which God and nature have placed within our reach, to protect ourselves and our fellow-citizens from its ravages.

But the occasion will not permit me to dwell on the general effects of intemperance, nor to trace the history of its causes. I shall, therefore, confine myself more particularly to a consideration of its influence on the individual; its effects on the moral, intellectual, and physical constitution of man—not the primary effect of ardent spirit as displayed in a fit of intoxication; it is the more insidious, permanent, and fatal effects of intemperance, as exemplified in the case of the habitual dram-drinker, to which I wish to call your attention.

I. The effects of ardent spirit on THE MORAL POWERS. It is perhaps difficult to determine in what way intemperance first manifests its influence on the moral powers, so variously does it affect different individuals. Were I to speak from my own observation, I should say that it first appears in an alienation of those kind and tender sympathies which bind a man to his family and friends; those lively sensibilities which enable him to participate in the joys and sorrows of those around him. "The social affections lose their fulness and tenderness, the conscience its power, the heart its sensibility, till all that was once lovely, and rendered him the joy and the idol of his friends, retires," and leaves him to the dominion of the appetites and passions of the brute. "Religious enjoyment, if he ever possessed any, declines as the emotions excited by ardent spirit arise." He loses, by degrees, his regard to truth and to the fulfilment of his engagements—he forgets the Sabbath and the house of worship, and lounges upon his bed, or lingers at the tavern. He lays aside his Bible—his family devotion is not heard, and his closet no longer listens to the silent whispers of prayer. He at length becomes irritable, peevish, and profane; and is finally lost to every thing that respects decorum in appearance, or virtue in principle; and it is lamentable to mark the steps of that process by which the virtuous and elevated man sinks to ruin.

II. Its effects on THE INTELLECTUAL POWERS. Here the influence of intemperance is marked and decisive. The inebriate first loses his vivacity and natural acuteness of perception. His judgment becomes clouded and impaired in its strength, the memory also enfeebled and sometimes quite obliterated. The mind is wandering and vacant, and incapable of intense or steady application to any one subject. This state is usually accompanied by an unmeaning stare or fixedness of countenance quite peculiar to the drunkard. The imagination and the will, if not enfeebled, acquire a morbid sensibility, from which they are thrown into a state of violent excitement from the slightest causes: hence, the inebriate sheds floods of tears over the pictures of his own fancy. I have often seen him, and especially on his recovery from a fit of intoxication, weep and laugh alternately over the same scene. The will, too, acquires an omnipotent ascendency over him, and is the only monitor to which he yields obedience. The appeals of conscience, the claims of domestic happiness, of wives and children, of patriotism and of virtue, are not heard.

The different powers of the mind having thus lost their natural relation to each other, the healthy balance being destroyed, the intellect is no longer fit for intense application, or successful effort; and although the inebriate may, and sometimes does, astonish, by the wildness of his fancy and the poignancy of his wit, yet in nine cases out of ten he fails, and there is never any confidence to be reposed in him. There have been a few who, from peculiarity of constitution, or some other cause, have continued to perform intellectual labor for many years, while slaves to ardent spirits; but in no instance has the vigor of the intellect or its ability to labor been increased by indulgence; and where there is one who has been able to struggle on under the habits of intemperance, there are thousands who have perished in the experiment, and some among the most powerful minds that the world ever produced. On the other hand, we shall find, by looking over the biography of the great men of every age, that those who have possessed the clearest and most powerful minds, neither drank spirits nor indulged in the pleasures of the table. Sir Isaac Newton, John Locke, Dr. Franklin, John Wesley, Sir William Jones, John Fletcher, and President Edwards, furnish a striking illustration of this truth. One of the secrets by which these men produced such astonishing results, were enabled to perform so much intellectual labor, and of so high a grade, and to arrive at old age in the enjoyment of health, was a rigid course of abstinence. But I hasten to consider more particularly,

III. Its effects on THE PHYSICAL POWERS. In view of this part of the subject, the attention of the critical observer is arrested by a series of circumstances, alike disgusting and melancholy.

1. The *odor of the breath* of the drunkard furnishes the earliest indication by which the habitual use of ardent spirit becomes known. This is occasioned by the exhalation of the alcoholic principle from the bronchial vessels and air-cells of the lungs—not of pure spirit, as taken into the stomach, but of spirit which has been absorbed, has mingled with the blood, and has been subjected to the action of the different organs of the body; and not containing any principle which contributes to the nourishment or renovation of the system, is cast out with the other excretions, as poisonous and hurtful. This peculiar odor does not arise from the accidental or occasional use of spirit; it marks only the habitual dram-drinker—the one who indulges daily in his potation; and although its density varies in some degree with the kind of spirit consumed, the habits and constitution of the individual, yet it bears generally a close relation to the degree of intemperance.

These observations are confirmed by some experiments made on living animals by the celebrated French physiologist, Magendie. He ascertained that diluted alcohol, a solution of camphor, and some other odorous substances, when subjected to the absorbing power of the veins, are taken up by them, and after mingling with the blood, pass off by the pulmonary exhalants. Even phosphorus injected into the crural vein of a dog, he found to pass off in a few moments from the nostrils of the animal in a dense white vapor, which he ascertained to be phosphoric acid. Cases have occurred, in which the breath of the drunkard has become so highly charged with alcohol as to render it actually inflammable by the touch of a taper. One individual in particular is mentioned, who often amused his comrades by passing his breath through a small tube, and setting it on fire as it issued from it. It appears, also, that this has been the source of that combustion of the body of the drunkard which has been denominated spontaneous, many well-authenticated cases of which are on record.

2. The perspirable matter which passes off from the skin becomes charged with the odor of alcohol in the drunkard, and is so far changed, in some cases, as to furnish evidence of the kind of spirit drank. "I have met with two instances," says Dr. McNish, "the one in a claret, and the other in a port drinker; in which the moisture that exhaled from their bodies had a ruddy complexion, similar to the wine on which they had committed their debauch."

3. The *whole system* soon bears marks of debility and decay. The voluntary muscles lose their power, and cease to act under the control of the will; and hence, all the movements become awkward, exhibiting the appearance of stiffness in the joints. The positions of the body, also, are tottering and infirm, and the step loses its elasticity and vigor. The muscles, and especially those of the face and lips, are often affected with a convulsive twitching, which

produces the involuntary winking of the eye, and quivering of the lip, so characteristic of the intemperate. Indeed, all the motions seem unnatural and forced, as if restrained by some power within. The extremities are at length seized with a tremor, which is more strongly marked after recovery from a fit of intoxication. The lips lose their significant expression, and become sensual; the complexion assumes a sickly, leaden hue, or is changed to an unhealthy, fiery redness, and is covered with red streaks and blotches. The eye becomes watery, tender, and inflamed, and loses its intelligence and its fire. These symptoms, together with a certain œdematous appearance about the eye, bloating of the whole body, with a dry, feverish skin, seldom fail to mark the habitual dram-drinker; and they go on increasing and increasing, till the intelligence and dignity of the man is lost in the tameness and sensuality of the brute.

But these effects, which are external and obvious, are only the "signals which nature holds out, and waves in token of internal distress;" for all the time the inebriate has been pouring down his daily draught and making merry over the cup, morbid changes have been going on within; and though these are unseen, and, it may be, unsuspected, they are fatal, irretrievable. A few of the most important of these changes I shall now describe.

4. The *stomach* and its functions. This is the great organ of digestion. It is the chief instrument by which food is prepared to nourish, sustain, and renovate the different tissues of the body, to carry on the various functions, and to supply the waste which continually takes place in the system. It is not strange, therefore, that the habitual application to the organ of any agent, calculated to derange its functions, or change its organization, should be followed by symptoms so various and extensive, and by consequences so fatal. The use of ardent spirit produces both these effects; it deranges the functions of the stomach,

and if persisted in, seldom fails to change its organic structure.

The inebriate first loses his appetite, and becomes thirsty and feverish; he vomits in the morning, and is affected with spasmodic pains in the region of the stomach. He is often seized with permanent dyspepsia, and either wastes away by degrees, or dies suddenly of a fit of cramp in the stomach.

On examining the stomach after death, it is generally found irritated, and approaching a state of inflammation, with its vessels enlarged, and filled with black blood; and particularly those of the mucous coat, which gives to the internal surface of the stomach the appearance of purple or reddish streaks, resembling the livid patches seen on the face of the drunkard.

The coats of the stomach become greatly thickened and corrugated, and so firmly united as to form one inseparable mass. In this state, the walls of the organ are sometimes increased in thickness to the extent of ten or twelve lines, and are sometimes found also in a scirrhous or cancerous condition.

The following case occurred in my practice several years since. A middle-aged gentleman, of wealth and standing, had long been accustomed to mingle in the convivial circle, and though by no means a drunkard, had indulged at times in the use of his old cogniac, with an unsparing hand. He was at length seized with pain in the region of the stomach, and a vomiting of his food an hour or two after eating. In about eighteen months he died in a state of extreme emaciation.

On opening the body after death, the walls of the whole of the right extremity of the stomach were found in a scirrhous and cancerous condition, and thickened to the extent of about two inches. The cavity of the organ was so far obliterated as scarcely to admit the passage of a probe from the left to the right extremity, and the opening which remained was so unequal and irregular as to render it evident that but little of the nourishment he had received could have passed the lower orifice of the stomach for many months.

I have never dissected the stomach of a drunkard, in which the organ did not manifest some remarkable deviation from its healthy condition. But the derangement of the stomach is not limited to the function of nutrition merely. This organ is closely united to every other organ, and to each individual tissue of the body, by its sympathetic relations. When the stomach, therefore, becomes diseased, other parts suffer with it. The functions of the brain, the heart, the lungs, and the liver, become disordered; the secretions are altered, and all the operations of the animal economy are more or less affected.

5. The *liver* and its functions. Alcohol, in every form and proportion, has long been known to exert a strong and speedy influence on this organ, when used internally. Aware of this fact, the poultry-dealers of England are in the habit of mixing a quantity of spirit with the food of their fowls, in order to increase the size of the liver; so that they may be enabled to supply to the epicure a greater abundance of that part of the animal, which he regards as the most delicious.

The influence of spirit on the liver is exerted in two ways: first, the impression made upon the mucous coat of the stomach is extended to the liver by sympathy; the second mode of action is through the medium of the circulation, and by the immediate action of the alcoholic principle on the liver itself, as it passes through the organ, mingling with the blood. In whichsoever of these ways it operates, its first effect is to increase the action of the liver, and sometimes to such a degree as to produce inflammation. Its secretion becomes changed from a bright yellow to a green or black, and from a thin fluid to a substance resembling tar in its consistence. There soon follows also an enlargement of the liver, and a change in its organic structure. I have met with several cases in which the liver has become enlarged from intemperance, so as to occupy a greater part of the cavity of the abdomen, and weighing from eight to twelve pounds, when it should have weighed not more than four or five.

The liver sometimes, however, even when it manifests great morbid change in its organic structure, is rather diminished than increased in its volume. This was the case in the person of the celebrated stage-actor, George Frederick Cook, who died a few years since in the city of New York. This extraordinary man was long distinguished for the profligacy of his life, as well as for the native vigor of his mind and body. At the time of his death, the body was opened by Dr. Hosack, who found that the liver did not exceed its usual dimensions, but was astonishingly hard, of a lighter color than natural, and that its texture was so dense as to make considerable resistance to the knife. The blood-vessels, which, in a healthy condition, are extremely numerous and large, were in this case nearly obliterated, evincing that the regular circulation through the liver had long since ceased; and tubercles were found throughout the whole substance of the organ.

I have met with several cases in the course of my dissections, in which the liver was found smaller than natural, shrivelled, indurated, its blood-vessels diminished in size and number, with the whole of its internal structure more or less changed. In consequence of these morbid changes in the liver, other organs become affected, as the spleen, the pancreas, etc., either by sympathy or in consequence of their dependence on the healthy functions of the liver for the due performance of their own.

6. Of *the brain* and its functions. Inflammation and engorgement of this organ are frequent consequences of intemperance, and may take place during a debauch—or may

arise some time after, during the stage of debility, from a loss of the healthy balance of action between the different parts of the system. This inflammation is sometimes acute, is marked by furious delirium, and terminates fatally in the course of a few days, and sometimes a few hours. At other times it assumes a chronic form, continues much longer, and then frequently results in an effusion of serum, or an extravasation of blood, and the patient dies in a state of insensibility, with all the symptoms of compressed brain. Sometimes the system becomes so saturated with ardent spirit, that there is good reason to believe the effusions, which take place in the cavities of the brain, and elsewhere, are composed, in part at least, of the alcoholic principle. The following case occurred, not long since, in England, and is attested by unquestionable authority.

A man was taken up dead in the streets of London, soon after having drank a quart of gin, on a wager. He was carried to the Westminster Hospital, and there dissected. "In the ventricles of the brain was found a considerable quantity of limpid fluid, distinctly impregnated with gin, both to the sense of smell and taste, and even to the test of inflammability. The liquid appeared to the senses of the examining students, as strong as one-third gin, and two-thirds water."

Dr. Armstrong, who has enjoyed very ample opportunity of investigating this subject, speaks of the chronic inflammation of the brain and its membranes, as frequently proceeding from the free use of strong liquors.

It is a fact familiar to every anatomist, that alcohol, even when greatly diluted, has, by its action on the brain after death, the effect of hardening it, as well as most of the tissues of the body which contain albumen; and it is common to immerse the brain in ardent spirit for a few days, in order to render it the firmer for dissection.

On examining the brain after death of such as have long

been accustomed to the free use of ardent spirit, it is said the organ is generally found harder than in temperate persons. It has no longer that delicate and elastic texture. Its arteries become diminished in size, and lose their transparency, while the veins and sinuses are greatly distended and irregularly enlarged.

This statement is confirmed by my own dissections, and they seem also to be in full accordance with all the intellectual and physical phenomena displayed in the drunkard, while living.

7. The *heart* and its functions. It has generally been supposed, that the heart is less frequently affected by intemperance, than most of the other great vital organs; but, from the history of the cases which have come under my own observation, I am convinced that it seldom escapes disease under the habitual use of ardent spirit. And why should it, since it is thrown almost perpetually into a state of unnatural exertion, the very effect produced by the violent agitation of the passions, the influence of which upon this organ is found so injurious?

The following case came under my notice, a few winters since. A large athletic man, long accustomed to the use of ardent spirit, on drinking a glass of raw whiskey, dropped instantly dead. On carefully dissecting the body, no adequate cause of the sudden cessation of life could be found in any part, except the heart. This organ was free from blood, was hard and firmly contracted, as if affected by spasms. I am convinced that many of those cases of sudden death which take place with intemperate persons, are the result of a spasmodic action of the heart, from sympathy with the stomach, or some other part of the system. The use of ardent spirit, no doubt, promotes also the ossification of the valves of the heart, as well as the development of other organic affections.

8. *The lungs* and their functions. Respiration in the

inebriate is generally oppressed and laborious, and especially after eating or violent exercise; and he is teased with a cough, attended with copious expectoration, and especially after his recovery from a fit of intoxication; and these symptoms go on increasing, and unless arrested in their progress, terminate in consumption.

This affection of the lungs is produced in two ways: first, by the immediate action of the alcoholic principle upon the highly sensible membrane which lines the trachea, bronchial vessels, and air-cells of the lungs, as poured out by the exhalants; and second, by the sympathy which is called into action between the lungs and other organs already in a state of disease, and more especially that of the stomach and liver.

I have met with many cases in the course of my practice, of cough and difficult breathing, which could be relieved only by regulating the functions of the stomach, and which soon yielded, on the patient ceasing to irritate this organ with ardent spirit. I have found the liver still more frequently the source of this affection; and on restoring the organ to its healthy condition, by laying aside the use of ardent spirit, all the pulmonary symptoms have subsided.

On examining the lungs of the drunkard after death, they are frequently found adhering to the walls of the chest; hepatized, or affected with tubercles.

But time would fail me, were I to attempt an account of half the pathology of drunkenness. *Dyspepsia, Jaundice, Emaciation, Corpulence, Dropsy, Ulcers, Rheumatism, Gout, Tremors, Palpitation, Hysteria, Epilepsy, Palsy, Lethargy, Apoplexy, Melancholy, Madness, Delirium-tremens, and premature old age,* compose but a small part of the catalogue of diseases produced by ardent spirit. Indeed, there is scarcely a morbid affection to which the human body is liable, that has not, in one way or another, been produced by it; there is not a disease but it has aggravated, nor a predisposition to disease, which it has not called into action; and although its effects are in some degree modified by age and temperament, by habit and occupation, by climate and season of the year, and even by the intoxicating agent itself; yet, the general and ultimate consequences are the same.

But I pass on to notice one state of the system, produced by ardent spirit, too important and interesting to leave unexamined. It is that *predisposition to disease and death* which so strongly characterizes the drunkard in every situation of life.

It is unquestionably true, that many of the surrounding objects in nature are constantly tending to man's destruction. The excess of heat and cold, humidity and dryness, noxious exhalations from the earth, the floating atoms in the atmosphere, the poisonous vapors from decomposed animal and vegetable matter, with many other invisible agents, are exerting their deadly influence; and were it not that every part of his system is endowed with a self-preserving power, a principle of excitability, or, in other words, a vital principle, the operations of the economy would cease, and a dissolution of his organic structure take place. But this principle being implanted in the system, reäction takes place, and thereby a vigorous contest is maintained with the warring elements without, as well as with the principle of decay within.

It is thus that man is enabled to endure, from year to year, the toils and fatigues of life, the variations of heat and cold, and the vicissitudes of the seasons—that he is enabled to traverse every region of the globe, and to live with almost equal ease under the equator and in the frozen regions of the north. It is by this power that all his functions are performed, from the commencement to the close of life.

The principle of excitability exists in the highest degree in the infant, and diminishes at every succeeding period of life; and if man is not cut down by disease or violence, he struggles on, and finally dies a natural death—a death occasioned by the exhaustion of the principle of excitability. In order to prevent the too rapid exhaustion of this principle, nature has especially provided for its restoration by establishing a period of sleep. After being awake for sixteen or eighteen hours, a sensation of fatigue ensues, and all the functions are performed with diminished precision and energy. Locomotion becomes feeble and tottering, the voice harsh, the intellect obtuse and powerless, and all the senses blunted. In this state the individual anxiously retires from the light, and from the noise and bustle of business, seeks that position which requires the least effort to sustain it, and abandons himself to rest. The will ceases to act, and he loses in succession all the senses; the muscles unbend themselves, and permit the limbs to fall into the most easy and natural position; digestion, respiration, circulation, secretion, and the other functions, go on with diminished power and activity; and consequently the wasted excitability is gradually restored. After a repose of six or eight hours, this principle becomes accumulated to its full measure, and the individual awakes and finds his system invigorated and refreshed. His muscular power is augmented, his senses are acute and discriminating, his intellect active and eager for labor, and all his functions move on with renewed energy. But if the stomach be oppressed by food, or the system excited by stimulating drinks, the sleep, though it may be profound, is never tranquil and refreshing.

The system being raised to a state of feverish excitement, and its healthy balance disturbed, its exhausted excitability is not restored. The individual awakes, but finds himself fatigued rather than invigorated. His muscles are relaxed, his senses obtuse, his intellect impaired, and his whole system disordered; and it is not till he is again under the influence of food and stimulus that he is fit for the occupations of life. And thus he loses the benefits of this wise provision of repose, designed for his own preservation.

Nothing, probably, tends more powerfully to produce premature old age, than disturbed and unrefreshing sleep.

It is also true, that artificial stimulus, in whatever way applied, tends constantly to exhaust the principle of excitability of the system, and this in proportion to its intensity, and the freedom with which it is applied.

But there is still another principle on which the use of ardent spirit predisposes the drunkard to disease and death. It acts on the blood, impairs its vitality, deprives it of its red color, and thereby renders it unfit to stimulate the heart and other organs through which it circulates; unfit, also, to supply the materials for the different secretions, and to renovate the different tissues of the body, as well as to sustain the energy of the brain—offices which it can perform only while it retains the vermilion color, and other arterial properties. The blood of the drunkard is several shades darker in its color than that of temperate persons, and also coagulates less readily and firmly, and is loaded with serum; appearances which indicate that it has exchanged its arterial properties for those of the venous blood. This is the cause of the livid complexion of the inebriate, which so strongly marks him in the advanced stage of intemperance. Hence, too, all the functions of his body are sluggish, irregular, and the whole system loses its tone and its energy. If ardent spirit, when taken into the system, exhausts the vital principle of the solids, it destroys the vital principle of the blood also; and if taken in large quantities, produces sudden death; in which case the blood, as in death produced by lightning, by opium, or by violent and long-continued exertion, does not coagulate.

The principles laid down are plain, and of easy application to the case before us.

The inebriate having, by the habitual use of ardent spirit, exhausted to a greater or lesser extent the principle of excitability in the solids—the power of reäction—and the blood having become incapable of performing its offices also, he is alike predisposed to every disease, and rendered liable to the inroads of every invading foe. So far, therefore, from protecting the system against disease, intemperance ever constitutes one of its strongest predisposing causes.

Superadded to this, whenever disease does lay its grasp upon the drunkard, the powers of life being already enfeebled by the stimulus of ardent spirit, he unexpectedly sinks in the contest, and but too frequently to the mortification of his physician, and the surprise and grief of his friends. Indeed, inebriation so enfeebles the powers of life, so modifies the character of disease, and so changes the operation of medical agents, that unless the young physician has studied thoroughly the constitution of the drunkard, he has but partially learned his profession, and is not fit for a practitioner of the present age.

These are the true reasons why the drunkard dies so easily, and from such slight causes.

A sudden cold, a pleurisy, a fever, a fractured limb, or a slight wound of the skin, is often more than his shattered powers can endure. Even a little excess of exertion, an exposure to heat or cold, a hearty repast, or a glass of cold water, not unfrequently extinguishes the small remains of the vital principle.

In the season that has just closed upon us, we have had a melancholy exhibition of the effects of intemperance in the tragical death of some dozens of our fellow-citizens; and had the extreme heat which prevailed for several days continued for as many weeks, we should hardly have had a confirmed drunkard left among us.

Many of those deaths which came under my notice seemed almost spontaneous, and some of them took place in less than one hour from the first symptoms of indisposition. Some died apparently from a slight excess of fatigue, some from a few hours' exposure to the sun, and some from a small draught of cold water; causes quite inadequate to the production of such effects in temperate persons.

Thus, fellow-citizens, I have endeavored to delineate the effects of ardent spirit upon man, and more especially to portray its influence on his moral, intellectual, and physical powers. And now let me mention a few things which MUST BE DONE in order that the evil may be eradicated.

1. Let us keep in view the objects of the Temperance Society, and the obligation imposed on us, *to use all proper measures to discourage the use of ardent spirit in the social circle, at public meetings, on the farm, in the mechanic shop, and in all other places.* It is not a mere matter of formality that we have put our names to this society's constitution; we have pledged ourselves to be bold, active, and persevering in the cause; to proclaim the dangers of intemperance to our fellow-citizens, and to do what we can to arrest its progress.

In view of these objects and of this pledge, then, let us, if indeed we have not already done it, banish ardent spirit from our houses at once, and for ever; and then we can act with decision and energy, and speak in a tone of authority, and our voice will be heard, if precept be sanctioned by example.

2. Let us use our utmost endeavors to lessen the number, and, if possible, utterly exterminate from among us those establishments which are the chief agents in propagating the evils of intemperance. I refer to those shops which are licensed for *retailing ardent spirit.* Here is the source of the evil. These are the agents that are sowing among us the seeds of vice, and poverty, and wretchedness.

How preposterous, that an enlightened community, professing the highest regard for morality and religion, making laws for the suppression and punishment of vice, and the promotion of virtue and good order, instituting societies to encourage industry, enlighten the ignorant, reclaim the vicious, bring back the wanderer, protect the orphan, feed the hungry, clothe the naked, bind up the broken-hearted, and restore domestic peace, should, at the same time, create and foster those very means that carry idleness, and ignorance, and vice, and nakedness, and starvation, and discord into all ranks of society; that make widows and orphans, that sow the seeds of disease and death among us; that strike, indeed, at the foundation of all that is good and great.

You create paupers, and lodge them in your alms-house—orphans, and give them a residence in your asylum—convicts, and send them to the penitentiary. You seduce men to crime, and then arraign them at the bar of justice—immure them in prison. With one hand you thrust the dagger to the heart—with the other attempt to assuage the pain it causes.

We all remember to have heard, from the lips of our parents, the narration of the fact, that in the early history of our country, the tomahawk and scalping-knife were put into the hands of our savage neighbors, by our enemies at war, and that a bounty was awarded for the depredations they committed on the lives of our defenceless fellow-citizens. Our feelings were shocked at the recital, and a prejudice was created, as well to these poor wandering savages, as to the nation that prompted them to the work, which neither time nor education has eradicated. Yet, as merciless and savage as this practice may appear to us, it was Christian, it was humane, compared with ours: theirs sought only the life-blood, and that of their enemies; ours seeks the blood of souls, and that of our own citizens, and friends, and neighbors. Their avarice was satiated with a few inches of the scalp, and the death inflicted was often a sudden and easy one; ours produces a death that lingers: and not content with the lives of our fellow-citizens, it rifles their pockets. It revels in rapine and robbery; it sacks whole towns and villages; it lays waste fields and vineyards; it riots on domestic peace, and virtue, and happiness; it sets at variance the husband and the wife; it causes the parent to forsake the child, and the child to curse the parent; it tears asunder the strongest bonds of society; it severs the tenderest ties of nature.

And who is the author of all this; and where lies the responsibility? I appeal to my fellow-citizens.

Are not we the authors? Does not the responsibility rest upon us? Is it not so?

The power emanates from us; we delegate it to the constituted authorities, and we say to them, "Go on; cast firebrands, arrows, and death; and let the blood of those that perish be on us and on our children." We put the tomahawk and scalping-knife into the hands of our neighbors, and award to them a bounty. We do more; we share the plunder. Let us arouse, my fellow-citizens, from our insensibility, and redeem our character for consistency, humanity, and benevolence.

3. Let us not confine our views or limit our operations to the narrow boundaries of our own city or district. Intemperance is a common enemy. It exists everywhere, and everywhere is pursuing its victims to destruction: while, therefore, we are actively engaged upon the subject in our own city, let us endeavor to do something elsewhere; and much may be done by spreading through our country correct information on the subject of intemperance. To this end, every newspaper and every press should be put in requisition. Circulate through the various avenues suitable tracts, essays, and other documents, setting forth the causes of intemperance, its evils, and its remedy, together

with an account of the cheering progress now making to eradicate it.

Do this, and you will find thousands starting up in different parts of the country, to lend their influence, and give their money in support of your cause; individuals who have hitherto been unconscious of the extent and magnitude of the evil of intemperance. You will find some who have been slumbering upon the very precipice of ruin, rallying round your standard. Indeed, we have all been insensible, till the voice of alarm was sounded, and the facts were set in array before us.

4. Appeal to *the medical profession* of the country, and ask them to correct the false idea which so extensively, I may say, almost universally prevails, viz., that ardent spirit is sometimes necessary in the treatment of disease. This opinion has slain its thousands and its tens of thousands, and multitudes of dram-drinkers daily shelter themselves under its delusive mask. One takes a little to raise his desponding spirits, or to drown his sorrow; another, to sharpen his appetite, or relieve his dyspepsia: one, to ease his gouty pains; another, to supple his stiffened limbs, or calm his quivering muscles. One drinks to overcome the heat; another, to ward off the cold; and all this as a medicine. Appeal, then, to the medical profession, and they will tell you—every independent, honest, sober, intelligent member of it will tell you—that there is no case in which ardent spirit is indispensable, and for which there is not an adequate substitute. And it is time the profession should have an opportunity to exonerate itself from the charge under which it has long rested, *of making drunkards.* But I entreat my professional brethren not to be content with giving a mere assent to this truth. You hold a station in society which gives you a commanding influence on this subject; and if you will but raise your voice and speak out boldly, you may exert an agency in this matter which

will bring down the blessings of unborn millions upon your memory.

5. Much may be done by guarding the *rising generation* from the contagion of intemperance. It is especially with the children and youth of our land, that we may expect our efforts to be permanently useful. Let us, then, guard with peculiar vigilance the youthful mind, and with all suitable measures, impress it with such sentiments of disgust and horror of the vice of intemperance, as to cause it to shrink from its very approach. Carry the subject into our infant and Sunday schools, and call on the managers and teachers of those institutions to aid you, by the circulation of suitable tracts, and by such other instructions as may be deemed proper. Let the rising generation be protected but for a few years, and the present race of drunkards will have disappeared from among us, and there will be no new recruits to take their place.

6. Let intelligent and efficient agents be sent out into every portion of our country, to spread abroad information upon the subject of intemperance, to rouse up the people to a sense of their danger, and to form temperance societies; and let there be such a system of correspondence and coöperation established among these associations as will convey information to each, and impart energy and efficiency to the whole. "No great melioration of the human condition was ever achieved without the concurrent effort of numbers; and no extended and well-directed association of moral influence was ever made in vain."

7. Let all who regard the virtue, the honor, and the patriotism of their country, withhold their suffrages from those candidates for office who offer ardent spirit as a bribe to secure their elevation to power. It is derogatory to the liberties of our country, that office can be obtained by such corruption—be held by such a tenure.

8. Let the ministers of the Gospel, wherever called to

labor, exert their influence, by precept and example, in promoting the cause of temperance. Many of them have already stepped forth, and with a noble boldness have proclaimed the alarm, and have led on the work of reformation; but many timid spirits still linger, and others seem not deeply impressed with the importance of the subject, and with the responsibility of their station. Ye venerated men, you are not only called to stand forth as our moral beacons, and be unto us burning and shining lights, but you are placed as watchmen upon our walls, to announce to us the approach of danger. It is mainly through your example and your labors that religion and virtue are so extensively disseminated through our country—that this land is not now a moral waste. You have ever exerted an important influence in society, and have held a high place in the confidence and affections of the people. You are widely spread over the country, and the scene of your personal labors will furnish you with frequent opportunities to diffuse information upon the subject of temperance, and to advance its progress. Let me then ask you, one and all, to grant us your active and hearty coöperation.

9. Appeal to the *female sex* of our country, and ask them to come to your assistance; and if they will consent to steel their hearts against the inebriate, to shut out from their society the man who visits the tippling-shop, their influence will be omnipotent. And by what power, ye mothers, and wives, and daughters, shall I invoke your aid? Shall I carry you to the house of the drunkard, and point you to his weeping and broken-hearted wife, his suffering and degraded children, robed in rags, and poverty, and vice? Shall I go with you to the almshouse, the orphan asylum, and to the retreat for the insane, that your sensibility may be roused? Shall I ask you to accompany me to the penitentiary and the prison, that you may there behold the end of intemperance? Nay, shall I draw back the curtain and

disclose to you the scene of the drunkard's death-bed? No—I will not demand of you a task so painful: rather let me remind you that you are to become the mothers of our future heroes and statesmen, philosophers and divines, lawyers and physicians; and shall they be enfeebled in body, debauched in morals, disordered in intellect, or healthy, pure, and full of mental energy? It is for you to decide this question. You have the future destiny of our beloved country in your hands. Let me entreat you, then, for your children's sake, and for your country's sake, not to ally yourselves to the drunkard, nor to put the cup to the mouth of your offspring, and thereby implant in them a craving for ardent spirit, which, once produced, is seldom eradicated.

10. Call upon all public and private associations, religious, literary, and scientific, to banish ardent spirit from their circle; call upon the agricultural, manufacturing, and commercial establishments, to withhold it from those engaged in their employment; call upon the legislatures of the different states to coöperate by the enactment of such laws as will discourage the vending of ardent spirit, and render licenses to sell it unattainable; call upon the proper officers to banish from the army and navy that article which, of all others, is most calculated to enfeeble the physical energies, corrupt the morals, destroy the patriotism, and damp the courage of our soldiers and sailors; call upon our national legislature to impose such duties on the distillation and importation of ardent spirit as will ultimately exclude it from the list of articles of commerce, and eradicate it from our land.

Finally, call upon every sober man, woman, and child, to raise their voices, their hearts, and their hands in this sacred cause, and never hold their peace, never cease their prayers, never stay their exertions, till intemperance shall be banished from our land and from the world.

BIBLE ARGUMENT

FOR

TEMPERANCE.

BY REV. AUSTIN DICKINSON.

THE Bible requires us to "present our bodies a living sacrifice, holy and acceptable unto God;" to "purify ourselves, even as he is pure;" to "give no occasion of stumbling to any brother;" to "give no offence to the church of God;" to "love our neighbor as ourselves;" to "do good to all as we have opportunity;" to "abstain from all appearance of evil;" to "use the world as not abusing it;" and, "whether we eat or drink, or whatsoever we do, to do all to the glory of God."

A Being of infinite benevolence could not prescribe rules of action less holy, and they are "the same that shall judge us in the last day." Any indulgence, therefore, not consistent with these rules, is rebellion against the great Lawgiver, and must disqualify us for "standing in the judgment."

As honest men, then, let us try by these rules the common practice of drinking or selling intoxicating liquor.

The use of such liquor, instead of enabling us to "present our bodies a living sacrifice, holy and acceptable," *actually degrades, and prematurely destroys both body and mind.* Dr. Rush, after enumerating various loathsome diseases, adds, that these are "the usual, natural, and legitimate consequences of its use." Another eminent physician says, "The observation of twenty years has convinced me, that were ten young men, on their twenty-first birthday, to begin to drink one glass of ardent spirit, and were they to drink this supposed moderate quantity daily, the lives of eight out of the ten would be abridged by ten or fifteen years." When taken freely, its corrupting influences are strikingly manifest. And even when taken moderately, very few now pretend to doubt that it shortens life. But nothing can be clearer, than that he who thus wilfully cuts short his probation five, ten, or twenty years, is as truly a suicide, as if he slew himself violently. Or if he knowingly encourage his neighbor to do this, he is equally guilty. He is, by the law of God, "a murderer."

But besides prematurely destroying the body, alcoholic drink injures the immortal mind. To illustrate the blinding and perverting influence of even a small quantity of such liquor, let a strictly temperate man spend an evening with a dozen others indulging themselves "moderately:" they will be sure to say things which to him will appear foolish, if not wicked; and which will appear so to *themselves* on reflection; though at the time they may not be conscious of any impropriety. And if this "moderate indulgence" be habitual, there must, of course, be an increased mental perversion; till conscience is "seared as with a hot iron," and the mind is lost to the power of being affected by truth, as well as to the capacity for usefulness. And is this destruction of the talents God has given, consistent with the injunction to "glorify God in body and spirit?"

Again, the habit of drinking *is incompatible with that eminent holiness to which you are commanded to aspire.* The great Founder of Christianity enjoins, "Be ye perfect, even as your Father in heaven is perfect." This will be the true Christian's desire. And a soul aspiring to the image and full enjoyment of God, will have no relish for any counteracting influence.

Is it said, that for eminently holy men to "mingle strong drink" may be inconsistent; but not so for those less spiritual? This is making the want of spirituality an excuse for sensuality; thus adding sin to sin, and only provoking the Most High. His mandate is universal: "Be ye holy, for I am holy."

To this end you are charged to "abstain from fleshly lusts, which war against the soul;" to "mortify your members, which are earthly;" to "exercise yourselves rather unto godliness;" to "be kindly affectioned towards all men." But who does not know that "strong drink," not only "eats out the brain," but "taketh away the heart," diminishes "natural affection," and deadens the moral sensibilities, while it cherishes those very passions which the Holy Spirit condemns? And how can one aspiring to the divine image, drink that which thus tends to destroy all that is pure, spiritual, and lovely, while it kindles the very elements of hell?

The use of such liquor *is utterly inconsistent with any thing like high spiritual enjoyment, clear spiritual views, or true devotion.* A sense of shame must inevitably torment the professor who in such a day cannot resist those "fleshly lusts which war against the soul;" his brethren will turn from him in pity or disgust; and, what is infinitely more affecting, the Holy Spirit will not abide with him. Thus, without an approving conscience, without cordial Christian intercourse, without the smiles of the Comforter, how can he enjoy religion?

Abstinence from highly stimulating liquor or food has ever been regarded indispensable to that serenity of soul and clearness of views so infinitely desirable in matters of religion. Hence, the ministers of religion especially, were commanded not to touch any thing like strong drink when about to enter the sanctuary. Lev. 10 : 9. And *this,* it is added, *shall be a statute for ever throughout your generations; that ye may put difference between holy and unholy;* clearly showing God's judgment of the effect of temperance on spiritual discernment.

On the principle of abstinence we may account, in part, for that holy ecstasy, that amazing clearness of spiritual vision, sometimes enjoyed on the deathbed. "Administer nothing," said the eloquent dying Summerfield, "that will create a stupor, not even so much as a little porter and water—*that I may have an unclouded view.*" For the same reason, Dr. Rush, who so well knew the effect of strong drink, peremptorily ordered it not to be given him in his last hours. And it is recorded, that the dying SAVIOUR, "who knew all things," when offered "wine mingled with myrrh," "*received it not.*" The truly wise will not barter visions of glory for mere animal excitement and mental stupefaction.

Equally illustrative of our principle is the confession of an aged deacon, accustomed to drink moderately: "I always, in prayer, felt a coldness and heaviness at heart—*never suspecting it was the whiskey!* but since that is given up, I have *heavenly communion!*" O, what an increase of pure light and joy might there be, would all understand this, and be *temperate in all things.*"

The use of such liquor *is inconsistent with the sacred order and discipline of the church.* A venerable minister, of great experience, gives it as the result of his observation, that *nine-tenths* of all the cases calling for church discipline have in former years been occasioned by this liquor. This is a tremendous fact. But a little examination will convince any one that the estimate is not too high. And can it be right to continue an indulgence that brings tenfold, or even fourfold more trouble and disgrace on the church than all other causes united? Do not these foul "spots in your feasts of charity" clearly say, "Touch not the unclean thing?" Can we countenance that which is certain to bring deep reproach on the church of Christ? "It must needs be that offences come, but woe to that man by whom the offence cometh."

The use of alcoholic liquor by the religious community *is inconsistent with the hope of reforming and saving the intemperate;* and thus shows a *want of love to souls.* The Christian knows, that *drunkards cannot inherit eternal life.* He knows also, that hundreds of thousands now sustain or are contracting this odious character; and that if the evil be not arrested, millions more will come on in the same track, and go down to the burning gulf. But the man who drinks just so much as to make himself "feel well," cannot reprove the drunkard who only does the same thing. The drunkard may say to him, "My appetite is stronger than yours; more, therefore, is necessary, in order to make me '*feel well;*' and if you cannot deny yourself, how can I control a more raging appetite?" This rebuke would be unanswerable.

All agree that total abstinence is the only hope of the drunkard. But is it not preposterous to expect him to abstain, if he sees the minister, the elder, the deacon, and other respectable men indulging their cups? With mind enfeebled and character lost, can he summon resolution to be singular, and live more temperately than his acknowledged superiors?—thus telling to all that *he has been a drunkard!* This cannot be expected of poor sunken human nature. No; let moderate drinking be generally allowed, and in less than thirty years, according to the past ratio of their deaths, armies of drunkards greater than all the American churches, will go from this land of light and freedom to "everlasting chains of darkness." If, then, the drunkard is worth saving, if he has a soul capable of shining with seraphim, and if you have "any bowels of mercies," then give him the benefit of your example. Professing to "do good to *all* as you have opportunity," be consistent in this matter. By a little self-denial you may save multitudes from ruin. But if you cannot yield *a little,* to save fellow-sinners from eternal pain, have you the spirit of Him who, for his enemies, exchanged a throne for a cross?

Could all the wailings of the thousand thousands slain by this poison come up in one loud thunder of remonstrance on your ear, you might then think it wrong to sanction its use. But "let God be true," and those wailings are as real as if heard in ceaseless thunders.

Again, the use of intoxicating drink *is inconsistent with true Christian patriotism.* All former efforts to arrest the national sin of intemperance have failed. A glorious effort is now making to remove it with pure water. Thousands are rejoicing in the remedy. Not a sober man in the nation really doubts its efficacy and importance. Who, then, that regards our national character, can hesitate to adopt it? Especially, who that is a Christian, can cling to that which has darkened the pathway of heaven, threatened our liberties, desolated families and neighborhoods, and stigmatized us as a "nation of drunkards?"

Is it said, that the influence of a small temperance society, or church, is unimportant? Not so; its light may save the surrounding region; its example may influence a thousand churches. And let the thousand thousand professing Christians in this land, with such others as they can enlist, resolve on TOTAL ABSTINENCE—let this great example be held up to view—and it would be such a testimony as the world has not yet seen. Let such a multitude show, that these drinks are unnecessary, and reformation easy, and the demonstration would be complete. Few of the moral would continue the poison; thousands of the immoral abandon it at once; and the nation be reformed.

The use of this liquor is *inconsistent with the proper influence of Christian example.* The Saviour says, "Let your light so shine before men, that they may see your good works, and glorify your Father who is in heaven." But will men esteem Christians the more for *drinking,* and thus be led to glorify God on their behalf? Or will the Saviour praise them for this, "when he shall come to be glorified in his saints, and to be admired in all them that believe?" Rather, will not their drinking lead some to excess, and thus sully the Creator's work? Nay, is it not certain, that if the religious community indulge, the example will lead *millions* to drunkenness and perdition? And, on the other hand, is it not morally certain, that if they abstain, their combined influence will save millions from infamy and ruin? How, then, in view of that day when all the bearings of your conduct shall be judged, can you hesitate on which side to give your influence? It is not a little matter; for who can conceive the results of even *one* impulse, among beings connected with others by ten thousand strings!

The use of this liquor *is inconsistent with that harmony and brotherly love which Christ requires in his professed-*

followers. He requires them to "love one another with a pure heart, fervently;" to "be all of one mind;" to be "of one heart and one soul." But who does not see the utter impossibility of this, if some continue an indulgence which others regard with abhorrence? Since public attention has been turned to the subject, thousands have come to the full conviction, that to use intoxicating liquor is a sinful as well as foolish practice. The most distinguished lights of the church, and such as peculiarly adorn human nature, embrace this sentiment. And how can you associate with these, and yet continue a habit viewed by them with disgust? Ah, the man, however decent, who "will have his glass, *not caring* whom he offends," *must have it;* but he must also "*have his reward.*" "Whoso shall *offend one of these little ones which believe in me,* it were better for him that a millstone were hanged about his neck."

The use of intoxicating drink, in this day of light, *is incompatible with the hope of receiving any general effusion of the Holy Spirit.* Christians are allowed to hope for the Spirit to be poured out only in answer to prayer—true, spiritual, believing prayer. "If they regard iniquity in their heart, the Lord will not hear them." If they wilfully cherish sin, they cannot have faith. Indeed, how odious the spectacle of a company looking towards heaven, but in the posture of devotion breathing forth the foul, fiery element—literally "offering strange fire before the Lord!"

We are not, then, to expect divine influence to come down "like showers that water the earth," till we put away that which we know tends only to wither and consume all the "fruits of the Spirit."

The *waste of property* in the use of alcoholic drink *is inconsistent with faithful stewardship for Christ.* Religious "contributions" are among the appointed means for saving the world. But allow each of the tens of thousands of professing Christians in this land only three cents worth of such liquor daily, and the annual cost is some MILLIONS OF DOLLARS; which would be sufficient to support THOUSANDS OF MISSIONARIES. Let "stewards" of the Lord's bounty, then, who would consume their portion of this "*little*" on appetite, ponder and blush for such inconsistency; and let them hasten to clear off the heavy charge, "*Ye have robbed me, even this whole nation.*"

Again, to indulge in intoxicating liquor *is inconsistent with attempts to recommend the Gospel to the heathen.* Nothing has done more, in former years, to prejudice our Indian neighbors, and hinder among them the influence of the Gospel, than those liquors we have encouraged them to use. Several tribes have set the noble example of excluding them by the strong arm of law; and it is only by convincing such that really consistent Christians do not encourage these evils, that our missionaries have been able to gain their confidence.

The same feeling prevails in some distant heathen nations. They cannot but distrust those who use and sell a polluting drink, which *they,* to a great extent, regard with abhorrence.

Suppose our missionaries should meet the heathen with the Bible in one hand, and the intoxicating cup in the other; what impression would they make? Nature herself would revolt at the alliance. And nothing but custom and fashion have reconciled any to similar inconsistencies at home.

But not only must our missionaries be unspotted, they must be able to testify, that *no real Christians* encourage this or any unclean thing. With *such* testimony they might secure the conviction, that our religion is indeed elevating, and that our God is *the true God.* For saith Jehovah, "Then shall the *heathen* know that I am the Lord, when I shall be sanctified in you before their eyes."

Indulgence in this drink, especially by the church, *is inconsistent with any reasonable hope that the flood of intemperance would not return upon the land, even should it for a season be dried up.* The same causes which have produced it would produce it again, unless there be some *permanent* counteracting influence. Temperance associations are unspeakably important as means of reformation. But they are not permanent bodies; their organization may cease when intemperance is once done away; and unless the principle of TOTAL ABSTINENCE be generally acknowledged and regarded as a Christian duty, by some great association that *is to be perpetual,* it may in time be forgotten or despised; and then drunkenness will again abound. Such an association is found only in "the church of the living God." This will continue while the world stands. Let the principle of ENTIRE ABSTINENCE, then, be recognized by all members of the church, and such others as they can influence; and you have a great multitude to sustain the temperance cause, "till time shall be no longer." And can the real Christian, or patriot, think it hard thus to enlist for the safety of all future generations? If parents love their offspring, if Christians love the millions coming upon the stage, will they not gladly secure them all from the destroyer? Has he a shadow of consistency who will rather do that, which, if done by the church generally, would lead millions to hopeless ruin?

The use of intoxicating drink, as an article of luxury or living, *is inconsistent with the plain spirit and precepts of God's word.* The proper use to be made of it, is so distinctly pointed out in Scripture, that men need not mistake. It is to be used as a *medicine* in *extreme cases.* "Give strong drink unto him that is *ready to perish.*" Its common use is condemned as foolish and pernicious. "Strong drink is raging; and whosoever is deceived thereby, is *not wise.*" "They are out of the way through strong drink; they err in vision; they stumble in judgment." Such passages show clearly the mind of God with respect to the nature and use of this article.

Moreover, it is said, "Woe unto him that giveth his neighbor drink." But does not every man who sells or uses this liquor, as a beverage, encourage his neighbor to drink, and thus contemn God's authority? Does he not aggravate his guilt by sinning against great light? And would he not aggravate it still further, should he charge the blame on the sacred word? O, what a blot on the Bible, should one sentence be added, *encouraging the common use of intoxicating liquor!* "If any man thus add,

God shall add unto him the plagues that are written in this book."

To encourage the manufacture of such liquors *is to abuse the bounties of Providence.* When God had formed man, he kindly said, "Behold, I have given you every herb bearing seed, which is upon the face of all the earth, and every tree, in the which is the fruit of a tree yielding seed; *to you it shall be for meat.*" God, then, it seems, intended men should use the fruits of the earth for *food.* But "they have sought out many inventions." And one of these is, to convert these "gifts of God" into a poison, most insidious in its nature, and destructive both to soul and body. The distiller, the vender, and the consumer, encourage one another in this perversion of God's gifts. And is this "receiving his gifts with thanksgiving?" Better, infinitely better, to cast them at once into the fire, and say unto the Almighty, "We have no need of these." But the ingratitude does not stop here. When men, in abuse of the divine bounty, have made this poison, to give it currency, they call it one of the "*creatures of God.*" With as much propriety might they call gambling establishments and murderous weapons his "creatures." But how awful the *impiety* of thus ascribing the worst of man's inventions to the benevolent God!

For a man to *persevere in making, selling, or using intoxicating liquor, as an article of luxury or living,* WHILE FULLY KNOWING ITS EFFECTS, *and possessing* THE LIGHT PROVIDENCE HAS POURED ON THIS SUBJECT, *is utterly inconsistent with any satisfactory evidence of piety.* "By their fruits ye shall know them." And what are *his* fruits. Why, as we have seen, he wilfully cuts short his own life, or the life of his neighbor; he wilfully impairs memory, judgment, imagination, all the immortal faculties, merely for sensual indulgence or paltry gain; he stupefies conscience, and cherishes all the evil passions; he prefers sordid appetite to pure spiritual enjoyment; he is the occasion of stumbling to those for whom Christ died, and of dark reproach on the church; he neglects the only means Providence has pointed out for saving millions from drunkenness and perdition; he wilfully encourages their downward course; he refuses the aid he might give to a great national reform; he lends his whole weight against this reformation; he is the occasion of offence, grief, and discord among brethren; he grieves the Holy Spirit; he robs the Lord's treasury; he makes Christianity infamous in the eyes of the heathen; he disregards the plain spirit of the Bible; and, in fine, he perverts even the common bounties of Providence. Such are his fruits. And the man, surely, who can do all this in meridian light, while God is looking on, and widows and orphans are remonstrating, *does not give satisfactory evidence of piety.* He shows neither respect for God nor love to man.

Let conscience now solemnly review this whole argument by the infinitely holy law. Is it indeed right and scriptural to impair body and mind, to defile the flesh, cloud the soul, stupefy conscience, and cherish the worst passions? Is it right to bring occasions of stumbling into the church? Is it right to encourage drunkards; right to treat with contempt a great national reform? Is it right to offend such as Christ calls "brethren;" right to grieve the Holy Spirit, and hinder his blessed influence? Is it right to "consume on lust" what would fill the Lord's treasury; and right to make religion odious to the heathen? Is it right to leave the land exposed to new floods of intemperance; to disregard the manifest lessons of God's word and providence; and to convert food to poison? Is it indeed scriptural and right to sanction habits fraught only with wounds, death, and perdition? Can *real Christians*, by example, propagate such heresy?

Let it not be suggested that our argument bears chiefly against the *excessive* use of these liquors; for common observation and candor will testify that the *moderate* use of the poison is the real occasion of all its woes and abominations. Who was ever induced to taste, by the disgusting sight of a drunkard? Or who ever became a drunkard, except by moderate indulgence in the beginning? Indeed, this habit of moderate drinking is, perhaps, tenfold *worse* in its general influence on society than occasional instances of drunkenness; for these excite abhorrence and alarm, while moderate indulgence sanctions the general use, and betrays millions to destruction. O never, since the first temptation, did Satan gain such a victory, as when he induced Christians to sanction everywhere the use of intoxicating liquor. And never, since the triumph of Calvary, has he experienced such a defeat as they are now summoned to accomplish. Let them unitedly pledge themselves against strong drink, and by *diffusing light on this subject*, do as much to expose as they have done to encourage this grand device of Satan, and mighty rivers of death will soon be dried up.

In this work of LIGHT AND LOVE, then, be *generous*, "be sober, be self-denying, be vigilant, be of one mind;" for the great adversary, "as a roaring lion, walketh about." And possibly through apathy, or discord, or treason among professed friends of temperance, "Satan may yet get an advantage," and turn our fair morning into a heavier night of darkness, and tempest, and war. But woe to that man who, in this day of light, shall wilfully encourage the *exciting cause* of such evils. And heaviest woe to him who shall avail himself of a standing in the church for this purpose. I hear for such a loud remonstrance from countless millions yet unborn, and a louder still from the throne of eternal Justice.

But "though we thus speak," we hope better things, especially from the decided followers of the Lamb, of every name; "things which make for peace, things wherewith one may edify another, and things which accompany salvation" to a dying world.

FOUR REASONS

AGAINST THE

USE OF ALCOHOLIC LIQUORS.

BY JOHN GRIDLEY, M. D.

In presenting this subject, it shall be my aim to state and illustrate such facts and principles as shall induce every man, woman, and child, capable of contemplating truth and appreciating motive, to exert the whole weight of their influence in favor of the "Temperance Reform." There are *Four Reasons* which claim special attention.

The first reason we would urge, why the use of alcoholic liquors should be altogether dispensed with, is their *immense cost* to the consumers. It is estimated from data as unerring as custom-house books, and the declarations of the manufacturers of domestic distilled spirit, that previous to 1826, 60,000,000 gallons of ardent spirit were annually consumed in these United States; the average cost of which is moderately stated at fifty cents per gallon, and in the aggregate *thirty millions* of dollars.

Thirty millions of dollars annually! A sum which, if spread out in one dollar bank-notes, end to end, would reach *across the Atlantic.* Or, if in silver dollars piled one upon the other, would form a column nearly *thirty miles* high; and which it would occupy a man twelve hours in each day, for almost two years, to enumerate, allowing him to count one every second. Or to suppose a useful application of this fund, it would support annually from *two to three hundred thousand young men* in preparing for the Gospel ministry. In three years it is a sum more than equal to the supply of a *Bible to every family on the habitable globe.*

One-half the amount would defray all the ordinary expenses incident to the carrying on of our nation's governmental operations every year. Thus I might multiply object upon object, which this vast sum is adequate to accomplish, and carry the mind from comparison to comparison in estimating its immense amount; still the cost, thus considered as involving the *pecuniary* resources of the country, is a mere *item* of the aggregate, when the loss of time, waste of providential bounty, neglect of business, etc., incident to the consumption of this one article, are thrown into the account.

A SECOND REASON why its use should be condemned is, the *entire inadequacy of any property it possesses to impart the least benefit,* either nutrient, or in any other way substantially to the consumer, to say nothing just now of its never-failing injurious effects. *Alcohol* consists chemically in a state of purity of carbon, oxygen, and hydrogen; in the proportions of carbon about 52 parts, oxygen 34, and hydrogen 14 to the 100. The addition of water forms the various proof spirits. It can be generated in no way but by *fermentation:* no skill of art has yet been able to combine the above elements in such proportions, or relations, as to produce alcohol, except by heat and moisture inciting fermentation in vegetable substances. But it should be understood, that vegetables may undergo a certain degree of fermentation without producing alcohol; or, if suffered to produce it, another stage of fermentation will radically destroy it, and produce an acid. Thus, any of the vegetable substances, as corn or rye, subjected to a certain degree of heat and moisture, will soon suffer a decomposition, and a development of sugar, to a greater or less degree, will take place. If removed now from circumstances favorable to its farther fermentation, as is the case with dough for bread, etc., no appreciable quantity of alcohol is created. A *further* degree of fermentation, however, is generative of alcohol, and if arrested here, the alcohol maintains its decided character; while still another stage presents the acetous state, and the alcoholic property is lost in vinegar. As in our opinion, success to the temperance cause depends much upon a right understanding of *what alcohol is*, and the manner of its production, a more simple illustration may not be inappropriate here.

A farmer takes a quantity of apples to the mill in order to convert them into cider. He grinds, then lays them up into a cheese, when pressure is applied, and the juice runs into a vat placed to receive it. Here, at this stage of the business, there is no alcohol in the juice. It is now put into casks, and the sweet or sugar stage of fermentation, which is already begun, soon passes into the vinous or *alcoholic* stage, as it is called, and *alcohol* is formed. The prudent farmer, at this point, when the juice is done *working*, or fermenting, immediately bungs his casks, and does such other things as his skill and experience may suggest, to prevent his cider becoming sour, which it will do if the third stage of fermentation is permitted to succeed. Here, then, he has *perfect alcohol*, though in small proportions; as perfect as it is in brandy, gin, rum, and whiskey. The same results ensue from subjecting corn, rye, barley, etc., to such processes as is customary to prepare them for distillation, namely, to such a degree of fermentation as that alcohol is formed. And when the alcohol is formed by fermentation, then it is drawn off, by distilling, from its union with the other materials in the fermented mass. Alcohol, then, is strictly *the product of fermentation*. It is not, and cannot be produced in any other way. To distil, therefore, is only to lead it off from its union with the vegetable mass, and show it naked with all its virulence.

Having considered the manner in which alcohol is formed, let us examine some of its *properties*. It contains nothing that can afford any nourishment to the body, and consequently it can impart no strength. When taken in certain quantities, diluted with water, as it must be for common use, its effect is, to arouse the energies of the system, and for a while the individual *feels* stronger; but this excitement is always followed by depression and loss of animal and mental vigor. Thus it is a mere provocative to momentary personal effort, without affording any resources to direct or execute. Hence the fallacy of that doctrine held by some, that to accomplish deeds of daring, feats of muscular strength, etc., with success, demands the drinking of spirituous liquors. Were I about to storm an enemy's battery, with no alternative before me but victory or death, I might, principle aside, infuriate my men with the maddening influence of ardent spirit, and let them loose upon the charge, as I would a wounded elephant, or an enraged tiger. But in attaining an object to which the combined energies of mind and body were requisite, I should never think of the appropriateness of spirituous liquor to aid the effort.

But an objector says, "I certainly *feel stronger* upon drinking a glass of spirit and water, and can do more work than I can without it. I can swing a scythe with more nerve, or pitch a load of hay in less time; and feel a general invigoration of my body during the heat of a summer's day, after having drank a quantity of grog. How is this?" We reply, doubtless you *feel* for the moment all that you describe; but your *feeling strength* thus suddenly excited, is far from being proof that you are *really* any stronger. The opposite is the fact; which we infer from the inadequacy of any substance, be it ever so nutritious, to impart strength so suddenly, as it would *seem* ardent spirit did when drank; for there has not been sufficient time for digestion, through which process only can any substantial nourishment be derived to the body. The *apparent* strength which an individual feels upon drinking ardent spirit, is the same in kind, though not in degree, with that which a man feels who has lain sick with a fever fifteen or twenty days, during which time he has taken little food, and been subjected to the weakening influence of medicines; but who on a sudden manifests great strength, striving to rise from his bed, etc., and in his delirious efforts must be restrained perhaps by force. Now no man in his senses will call this any *real* increase of strength in the sick man, who has been starving thus long; but only a rallying of the powers of life under the stimulus of disease, which is always followed by extreme languor and debility, if not by death. So it is with the individual under the influence of ardent spirit: he *feels* the powers of his body excited from the stimulus of the spirit; yet, as we think must be clear to the apprehension of any one, without any addition of *actual* strength.

Again, alcohol is not only innutritious, but is *poisonous*. Taken into the stomach in an undiluted and *concentrated* state, in quantities of two or three teaspoonfulls, it destroys life, as clearly shown in Accum's experiments. Combined with different proportions of water, sugar, etc., it is modified in its effects. Most of the vegetable and mineral poisons may be so diluted and modified as to be capable of application to the bodies of men internally, without producing immediate fatal consequences; which, nevertheless, cannot be used any length of time, even thus disarmed, without producing pernicious effects. So it is with alcohol: like other poisons, it cannot be used any length of time, even diluted and modified, without proving pernicious to health, and if persevered in, in considerable quantities, inevitably destructive to life. This last sentiment, however, we will consider more particularly under the

THIRD REASON for the disuse of alcohol: It *destroys both body and soul.* It is estimated that *thirty or forty thousand* died annually in the United States from the intemperate use of ardent spirit before the Temperance reformation began. Thirty or forty thousand! a sacrifice seldom matched by war or pestilence. The blood which flowed from the veins of our martyred countrymen, in the cause of freedom, never reached this annual sacrifice. And the pestilential *cholera*, ruthless as it is, which has marked its desolating track through many of our towns and cities, numbers not an amount of victims like this plague, much as its virulence has been enhanced by ardent spirit. The destructive influence of immoderate drinking upon the bodily powers of men, is painfully apparent, sometimes long before the fatal catastrophe. The face, the speech, the eyes, the walk, the sleep, the breath, all proclaim the drying up of the springs of life. And although abused nature will often struggle, and struggle, and struggle, to maintain the balance of her powers, and restore her wasted energies, she is compelled to yield at length to suicidal violence.

The effect of the habitual use of ardent spirit upon the health, is much greater than is generally supposed. An individual who is in the habit of drinking spirits daily, although he may not fall under the character of a drunkard, is undermining his constitution gradually, but certainly; as a noble building, standing by the side of a small, unnoticed rivulet, whose current steals along under its foundation, and carries away from its support sand after sand, has its security certainly though imperceptibly impaired, and finally falls into utter ruin. A large proportion of the inmates of our madhouses are the victims of ardent spirit. Our hospitals and poor-houses speak volumes of the ruin that awaits the bodily powers of those who indulge in even moderate tippling. It exposes the system to much greater ravages when disease attacks it. The powers of nature are weakened, and less able to resist disease; and medicines will never act so promptly and kindly upon those who are accustomed to strong drink as upon those who are not.

But where is the *soul*, the disembodied spirit of a deceased drunkard? "No drunkard shall inherit the kingdom of God," is the plain declaration of sacred writ; and were there no such scriptural denunciation of the wretched inebriate, the very nature of his case would render his prospect dark and dismal. In the intervals of his cups, when his animal powers are not goaded by artificial excitement, his distressed spirit partakes of the horrible collapse of its polluted tenement, and can contemplate no motive, however weighty, nor entertain any other thought, be it ever so interesting, than how to relieve its present wretchedness. When, then, can the unhappy man find peace with God -

amid this tumult of his unbalanced faculties, this perturbation of his unholy passions? How utterly unfitted to perform those duties which are requisite to secure a blessed immortality?

Our FOURTH REASON for the disuse of alcoholic liquors is, that *any thing short of entire abstinence exposes to all the dread consequences just named.* Here is the grand hope of our cause. TOTAL ABSTINENCE defies all danger and mocks at consequences. With it, we are safe; without it, in peril.

No man was ever *born* a drunkard; nor are we born with a natural taste or thirst for alcoholic drinks, any more than we are born with an appetite for aloes, assafœtida, or any other drug or medicine. And the child when first taught to take it, is induced to do so only by sweetening it, and thus rendering it palatable, as is the case with other medicines. Neither is it, at any time, the taste or flavor of alcohol, exclusively, that presents such charms for the use of it; but in the effect upon the *stomach and nerves* lie all the magic and witchery of this destructive agent. In proof of this, watch the trembling victim of strong drink while he pours down his morning or mid-day dram, and see him retch and strangle like a sickened child at a nauseous medicine. Ask him, too, and he will confess it is not the taste for which he drinks. Intemperate drinking is ever the result of what has been misnamed *temperate drinking.* "Taking a little" when we are too cold, or too hot, or wet, or fatigued, or low-spirited, or have a pain in the stomach, or to keep off fevers, or from politeness to a friend, or not to appear singular in company, etc., etc., or as is sometimes churlishly said, "when we have a mind to."

And here I shall step aside a little from the main argument, and attempt to *explain* the *effects* which *temperate drinking* has upon the animal system; and how it leads to ruinous drunkenness, BY A LAW OF OUR NATURES, certain and invariable. The nervous system, as I have said, is that department of our bodies which suffers most from stimulants and narcotics. Although the circulation of the blood is increased, and all the animal spirits roused by alcoholic drink; still, the nerves are the organs that must finally bear the brunt and evil of this undue excitement. Thus we see in the man who has been overexcited by these stimulants, a trembling hand, an infirm step, and impaired mental vigor. The *excitability* of our system—and by this term we mean that property of our natures which distinguishes all living from dead matter—is acted upon by stimuli, either external or internal; and it is by various stimuli, applied properly, and in due proportion, that the various functions of life are kept up. Thus a proper portion of food, and drink, and heat, and exercise, serves to maintain that balance of action among all the organs, which secures health to the individual. But if an agent is applied to the system, exerting stimulant powers exceeding those that are necessary for carrying on the vital functions steadily, an excitement ensues which is always followed by a corresponding collapse. This principle is clearly illustrated by the stimulus of alcohol. If a person unaccustomed to its use receives into his stomach a given quantity of distilled spirits, it will soon produce symptoms of universal excitement. The pulse increases in frequency; the action of all the animal functions is quickened; and even the soul, partaking of the impulse of its fleshly tabernacle, is unduly aroused. But this is of short duration, and a sinking, or collapse, proportioned to the excitement, soon takes place, with a derangement, more or less, of all the organs of the body. The stimulus repeated, the same effect ensues. We must, however, notice that the same quantity of any unnatural stimulus, such as opium, spirit, etc., frequently repeated, fails to produce its specific effect. Hence, in order to secure the same effect, it is necessary to increase its quantity. Thus, to a person indulging in the frequent or stated practice of drinking, before he is aware, the repetition becomes pleasant. As the accustomed hour returns for his dram, he regularly remembers it; again and again he drinks; the desire increases; he makes himself believe it is necessary from the very fact that he desires it;

the principle, or law, of which we have been speaking, developes itself; an increased quantity becomes necessary to insure a feeling of gratification; more, and still more becomes necessary, and oftener repeated, until without it he is miserable; his overexcited system is wretched, soul and body, without *the constant strain* which the stimulus affords.

Here is a solution of the fact that has astonished thousands; how the unhappy drunkard, with all the certain consequences of his course staring him in the face, and amid the entreaties and arguments of distressed friends, and the solemn denunciations of holy writ sounding in his ears, and the sure prospect of an untimely grave, will still press on, and hold the destroyer still firmer to his lips. It is because nature shrieks at every pore, if I may be allowed the expression. Every nerve, every vein, every fibre pines, and groans, and aches for its accustomed stimulus. No substitute will do; no ransom can purchase relief; insatiate as the grave, every fibre cries, Give, give! The dictates of reason are drowned in the clamor of the senses. Thus the *temperate drinker, by persisting in the practice,* throws himself within the influence of *a law of his system,* of which he can no more control the development, nor resist the urgency, than he can that law which circulates the blood through his heart, or any other law peculiar to animal life. That law is the LAW OF STIMULATION, which is never unduly aroused, except by sinful indulgences; but when aroused, is dreadfully urgent. We will state a case strikingly exemplifying the influence of this law.

A gentleman, an acquaintance and friend of the writer, contracted the habit of drinking during his college course. He settled in the practice of the law in one of the villages of his native state. He soon became invested with offices of honor and profit, and although young, gave promise of shining brilliantly in the profession he had chosen. He was the pride of a large and respectable family, who witnessed his growing prospects with that satisfaction and delight which the prosperity of a beloved son and brother cannot fail to impart. In the midst of these circumstances the physician was one day called in haste to see him. He had fallen into a fit. His manly form lay stretched upon the carpet, while his features were distorted and purpled from the agony of the convulsions. After some days, however, he recovered, without having sustained any permanent injury. Being in company with his physician alone, soon after, he said to him, "I suspect, sir, you do not know the cause of my fit; and as I may have a return of it, when you will probably be called, I think it proper that you should be made acquainted with my habits of life." He then informed his physician, that for a number of years previous he had been in the daily use of ardent spirit, that the practice had grown upon him ever since he left college, and that he was conscious it injured him. However, it was not known even to his own family what quantity he used. His physician did not hesitate to inform him of the extreme danger to his life in persisting in the use of intoxicating drinks. He acknowledged his perfect conviction of the truth of all that was said, and resolved to abandon his wicked course.

Not many weeks after, he was seized with another fit; but owing to the absence of the family physician, he did not see him until some time after he had come out of it. The physician, however, who attended, informed him it was violent. After repeated assurances of his increasing danger, and the remonstrances of friends, who had now begun to learn the real cause of his fits, he renewed his promises and determination to reform, and entered upon a course of total abstinence, which he maintained for several months, and inspired many of his friends with pleasing hopes of his entire reform and the reëstablishment of his health. But, alas, in an unguarded moment, he dared to taste again the forbidden cup, and with this fled all his resolutions and restraints. From that time he drank more openly and freely. His fits returned with painful violence; friends remonstrated, entreated, pleaded, but all in vain. He thus continued his course of intemperance, with intervals of fits and sickness, about eight or ten months, and at length died *drunk* in his bed, where he had lain for two or three weeks in a continual state of intoxication.

The writer has stated this case in detail, to show the influence of *the law of stimulation,* or what in popular language is termed, "the appetite for spirituous liquors," when once it is awakened.

Here we have the instance of an individual, of a fine and cultivated intellect, with every thing on earth to render him happy, that could be comprised in wealth, friends, honor, and bright prospects. Ay, indeed, too, he professed an interest in the blood of the Saviour, and had communed with Christians at his table ; surrounded by those whom he tenderly loved, the wife of his bosom, and the dear pledges of her devotion. Yet, in spite of all these considerations, and the most sensible conviction of his fatal career, he continued to drink, and thus pressed downward to the gate of death and hell.

Now what was this? What giant's arm dragged this fair victim to an untimely grave? Was it for the want of motives and obligations to pursue an opposite course? No. Was it for the want of intellect and talents to appreciate those obligations? No. Was it trouble, arising from disappointed hopes and blasted prospects? Certainly, by those who knew him best, he was accounted a man who might have been happy. What was it, then, that urged this individual, with his eyes open upon the consequences, and in the face of every thing most dear, thus to sacrifice his *all* upon the altar of intemperance? It *was that law* of which we have spoken, enkindled into action by his tippling, and which once developed, he could no more control, *while persisting in his pernicious practice of drinking,* than he could have hurled the Andes from their base, or have plucked the moon from her orbit.

We say, then, that all persons who drink ardent spirit habitually, bring themselves inevitably under the influence of a law *peculiar to their natures,* which leads on to ruin.

Instances may indeed have occurred, in which individuals have used ardent spirit daily for a long course of years, and yet died without becoming drunkards; but it only proves that these have been constitutions that could *resist* the *speedy development* of the law in question. Where one individual is found with a constitution vigorous enough to resist the development of this law through a life of habitual drinking, thousands go down to a drunkard's grave, and a drunkard's retribution, from only a few years' indulgence.

We have thus briefly shown the *immense cost* of the use of alcoholic liquors. We have shown that they contain *no property that can impart substantial strength or nourishment* to the body; and that they are actually a POISON. We have shown that they *destroy* both *body* and *soul;* clouding the view of truth, and resisting the influences of the Holy Spirit. "No drunkard shall inherit the kingdom of God." We have shown that the *temperate use* of these liquors tends inevitably to the *intemperate use;* since those who drink them habitually, throw themselves within the influence of a *law of their natures,* which leads on directly to ruin.

In view of such considerations and such facts, who is so degraded, so enslaved to appetite, or the love of gain, that he will not lend his aid to the TEMPERANCE REFORM? Who will indulge in what he calls the temperate use, flattering himself that he can control his appetite, when thousands, who have boasted of *self-control,* have found themselves, ere they were aware, within the coil of a serpent whose touch is poison, and whose sting is death? O, who that regards his neighbor, his family, his own reputation, or his own soul, will in this day of light be found dallying with that which affords at best only *sensual* pleasure, and which *at the last biteth like a serpent, and stingeth like an adder?*

DEBATES OF CONSCIENCE

WITH

A DISTILLER, A WHOLESALE DEALER,

AND

A RETAILER.

BY HEMAN HUMPHREY, D.D.

PRESIDENT OF AMHERST COLLEGE.

DIALOGUE I.

AT THE DISTILLERY.—FIRST INTERVIEW.

DISTILLER. Good morning, Mr. Conscience; though I know you to be one of the earliest risers, especially of late, I hardly expected to meet you here at day-dawn.

CONSCIENCE. I am none too early, it seems, to find you at your vocation. But how are you going to dispose of this great black building?

DISTILLER. Why, I do not understand you.

CONSCIENCE. What are you doing with these boiling craters, and that hideous worm there?

DISTILLER. Pray explain yourself.

CONSCIENCE. Whose grain is that? and what is bread called in the Bible?

DISTILLER. More enigmatical still.

CONSCIENCE. To what market do you mean to send that long row of casks? and how many of them will it take, upon an average, to dig a drunkard's grave?

DISTILLER. Ah, I understand you now. I was hoping that I had quieted you on that score. But I perceive you have come upon the old errand. You intend to read me another lecture upon the sixth commandment. But what would you have me do?

CONSCIENCE. Put out these fires.

DISTILLER. Nay, but hear me. I entered into this business with your approbation. The neighbors all encouraged me. My brethren in the church said it would open a fine market for their rye, and corn, and cider; and even my minister, happening to come along when we were raising, took a little with us under the shade, and said he loved to see his people industrious and enterprising.

CONSCIENCE. "The times of this ignorance God winked at—but now commandeth all men everywhere to repent." In one part of your defence, at least, you are incorrect. It was not my *voice*, but my *silence*, if any thing, which gave consent; and I have always suspected there was some foul play in the matter, and that I was kept quiet for the time by certain deleterious opiates. Indeed, I distinctly recollect the morning bitters and evening toddy, which you were accustomed to give me; and though I thought but little of it then, I now see that it deadened all my sensibilities. This, I am aware, is no excuse. I ought to have resisted—I ought to have refused, and to have paralyzed the hand which put the cup to my lips. And when you struck the first stroke on this ground, I ought to have warned you off with the voice of seven thunders. That I did not then speak out, and do my duty, will cause me extreme regret and self-reproach to the latest hour of my life.

DISTILLER. But what, my dear Conscience, has made you all at once so much wiser, not only than your former self, but than hundreds of enlightened men in every community, whose piety was never doubted? I myself know, and have heard of not a few good Christians, including even deacons and elders, who still continue to manufacture ardent spirit, and think, or seem to think it right.

CONSCIENCE. And think it right! Ask their consciences. I should like to witness some of those interviews which take place in the night, and which make Christian distillers—

(what a solecism!)—so much more irritable than they used to be. I know one of the brotherhood, at least, whose conscience has been goading him these five years, and yet he perseveres.

DISTILLER. But if I stop, what will the people do? Half the farmers in town depend upon their rye and cider to pay their taxes, and even to support the Gospel.

CONSCIENCE. So, then, you are pouring out these streams of liquid death over the land, and burning up your own neighbors, to enable them to pay their taxes and support religion! Why don't you set up a coffin factory, to create a brisker demand for lumber, and so help the farmers to pay their taxes; and then spread the smallpox among the people, that they may die the faster, and thus increase your business, and give you a fair profit? It will not do. I tell you, that I can give you no peace till you put out these fires and destroy that worm.

DISTILLER. How can I? Here is all my living, especially since, as you know, my eldest son fell into bad habits, in spite of all the good advice I daily gave him, and squandered what might have afforded me a comfortable independence.

CONSCIENCE. Suppose you were now in Brazil, and the owner of a large establishment to fit out slave-traders with handcuffs for the coast of Africa, and could not change your business without considerable pecuniary sacrifice; would you make the sacrifice, or would you keep your fires and hammers still going?

DISTILLER. Why do you ask such puzzling questions? You know I don't like them at all, especially when my mind is occupied with other subjects. Leave me, at least till I can compose myself, I beseech you.

CONSCIENCE. Nay, but hear me through. Is it right for you to go on manufacturing fevers, dropsy, consumption, delirium tremens, and a host of other frightful diseases, because your property happens to be vested in a distillery? Is it consistent with the great law of love by which you profess to be governed? Will it bear examination in a dying hour? Shall I bid you look back upon it from the brink of eternity, that you may from such recollections gather holy courage for your pending conflict with the king of terrors? Will you bequeath this magazine of wrath and perdition to your only son not already ruined, and go out of the world rejoicing that you can leave the whole concern in the hands of one who is so trustworthy and so dear?

[Here the Distiller leaves abruptly, without answering a word.]

SECOND INTERVIEW.

Distiller. (Seeing Conscience approach, and beginning to tremble.) What, so soon and so early at your post again? I did hope for a short respite.

Conscience. O, I am distressed—I cannot hold my peace. I am pained at my very heart.

Distiller. Do be composed, I beseech you, and hear what I have to say. Since our last interview I have resolved to sell out, and I expect the purchaser on in a very few days.

Conscience. What will *he* do with the establishment when he gets it?

Distiller. You must ask him, and not me. But whatever he may do with it, *I* shall be clear.

Conscience. I wish I could be sure of that; but let us see. Though you will not make poison by the hundred barrels any longer yourself, you will sell this laboratory of death to another man, for the same horrid purpose. You will not, with your own hands, go on forging daggers for maniacs to use upon themselves and their friends, provided you can get some one to take your business at a fair price. You will no longer drag the car of Juggernaut over the bodies of prostrate devotees, if you can *sell out the privilege to good advantage!*

DISTILLER. Was ever any man's conscience so captious before? You seem determined not to be satisfied with any thing. But beware; by pushing matters in this way you will produce a violent "reaction." Even professors of religion will not bear it. For myself, I wish to treat you with all possible respect; but forbearance itself must have its limits.

CONSCIENCE. Possibly you may be able to hold me in check a little longer; but I am all the while gathering strength for an onset which you cannot withstand; and if you cannot bear these kind remonstrances now, how will you grapple with "the worm that never dies?"

DISTILLER. Enough, enough. I will obey your voice. But why so pale and deathlike?

CONSCIENCE. O, I am sick, I am almost suffocated. These tartarean fumes, these dreadful forebodings, these heart-rending sights, and above all, my horrid dreams, I cannot endure them. There comes our nearest neighbor, stealing across the lots, with his jug and half bushel of rye. What is his errand, and where is his hungry, shivering family? And see there too, that tattered, half-starved boy, just entering the yard with a bottle—who sent him here at this early hour? All these barrels—where are the wretched beings who are to consume this liquid fire, and to be consumed by it?

DISTILLER. Spare me, spare me, I beseech you. By going on at this rate a little longer you will make me as nervous as yourself.

CONSCIENCE. But I cannot close this interview till I have related one of the dreams to which I just alluded. It was only last night that I suffered in this way, more than tongue can tell. The whole terrific vision is written in letters of fire upon the tablet of my memory; and I feel it all the while burning deeper and deeper.

I thought I stood by a great river of melted lava, and while I was wondering from what mountain or vast abyss it came, suddenly the field of my vision was extended to the distance of several hundred miles, and I perceived that, instead of springing from a single source, this rolling torrent of fire was fed by numerous tributary streams, and these again by smaller rivulets. And what do you think I heard and beheld, as I stood petrified with astonishment and horror? There were hundreds of poor wretches struggling and just sinking in the merciless flood. As I contemplated the scene still more attentively, the confused noise of boisterous and profane merriment, mingled with loud shrieks of despair, saluted my ears. The hair of my head stood up—and looking this way and that way, I beheld crowds of men, women, and children, thronging down to the very margin of the river—some eagerly bowing down to slake their thirst with the consuming liquid, and others convulsively striving to hold them back. Some I saw actually pushing their neighbors headlong from the treacherous bank, and others encouraging them to plunge in, by holding up the fiery temptation to their view. To insure a sufficient depth of the river, so that destruction might be made doubly sure, I saw a great number of men, and some whom I knew to be members of the church, laboriously turning their respective contributions of the glowing and hissing liquid into the main channel. This was more than I could bear. I was in perfect torture. But when I expostulated with those who were nearest to the place where I stood, they coolly answered, *This is the way in which we get our living!*

But what shocked me more than all the rest, and curdled every drop of blood in my veins, was the sight which I had of this very distillery pouring out its tributary stream of fire! And O, it distracts, it maddens me to think of it. There you yourself stood feeding the torrent which had already swallowed up some of your own family, and threatened every moment to sweep you away! This last circumstance brought me from the bed, by one convulsive bound, into the middle of the room; and I awoke in an agony which I verily believe I could not have sustained for another moment.

Distiller. I will feed the torrent no longer. The fires of my distillery shall be put out. From this day, from this hour, I renounce the manufacture of ardent spirit for ever.

DIALOGUE II.

WHOLESALE DEALER'S COUNTING-ROOM.

Conscience. (Looking over the ledger with a serious air.) What is that last invoice from the West Indies?

Rum-Dealer. Only a few casks of fourth proof, for particular customers.

Conscience. And that domestic poison, via New Orleans; and on the next page, that large consignment, via Erie Canal?

Dealer. O, nothing but two small lots of prime whiskey, such as we have been selling these twenty years. But why these chiding inquiries? They disquiet me exceedingly. And to tell you the plain truth, I am more than half offended at this morbid inquisitiveness.

Conscience. Ah, I am afraid, as I have often told you, that this is a bad business; and the more I think of it, the more it troubles me.

Dealer. Why so? You are always preaching up industry as a Christian virtue, and my word for it, were I to neglect my business, and saunter about the hotels and steamboat wharves, as some do, you would fall into convulsions, as if I had committed the unpardonable sin.

Conscience. Such pettish quibbling is utterly unworthy

of your good sense and ordinary candor. You know, as well as I do, the great difference between industry in some safe and honest calling, and driving a business which carries poverty and ruin to thousands of families.

Dealer. *Honest* industry! This is more cruel still. You have known me too long to throw out such insinuations; and besides, it is notorious, that some of the first merchants in our city are engaged, far more extensively, in the same traffic.

Conscience. Be it so. "To their own Master they stand or fall." But if fair dealing consists in "doing as we would be done by," how can a man of your established mercantile and Christian reputation sustain himself, if he continues to deal in an article which he knows to be more destructive than all the plagues of Egypt?

Dealer. Do you intend, then, to make me answerable for all the mischief that is done by ardent spirit, in the whole state and nation? What I sell is a mere drop of the bucket, compared with the consumption of a single county. Where is the proof that the little which my respectable customers carry into the country, with their other groceries, ever does any harm? How do you know that it helps to make such a frightful host of drunkards and vagabonds? And if it did, whose fault would it be? I never gave nor sold a glass of whiskey to a tippler in my life. Let those who will drink to excess, and make brutes of themselves, answer for it.

Conscience. Yes, certainly *they* must answer for it; but will that excuse those who furnish the poison? Did you never hear of abettors and accessaries, as well as principals in crime? When Judas, in all the agony of remorse and despair, threw down the thirty pieces of silver before the chief priests and elders, exclaiming, *I have sinned, in that I have betrayed the innocent blood*—they coolly answered, *What is that to us? See thou to that.* And was it therefore nothing to them? Had they no hand in that cruel tragedy? Was it nothing to Pilate—nothing to Herod—nothing to the multitude who were consenting to the crucifixion of the Son of God—because they did not drive the nails and thrust the spear?

O, when I think of what you are doing to destroy the bodies and souls of men, I cannot rest. It terrifies me at all hours of the night. Often and often, when I am just losing myself in sleep, I am startled by the most frightful groans and unearthly imprecations, coming out of these hogsheads. And then, those long processions of rough-made coffins and beggared families, which I dream of, from nightfall till daybreak, they keep me all the while in a cold sweat, and I can no longer endure them.

DEALER. Neither can I. Something must be done. You have been out of your head more than half the time for this six months. I have tried all the ordinary remedies upon you without the least effect. Indeed, every new remedy seems only to aggravate the disease. O, what would not I give for the discovery of some anodyne which would lay these horrible phantasms. The case would be infinitely less trying, if I could sometimes persuade you, for a night or two, to let me occupy a different apartment from yourself; for when your spasms come on, one might as well try to sleep with embers in his bosom, as where you are.

CONSCIENCE. Would it mend the matter at all, if, instead of sometimes dreaming, I were to be always wide awake?

DEALER. Ah, there's the grand difficulty. For I find that when you do wake up, you are more troublesome than ever. *Then* you are always harping upon my being a professor of religion, and bringing up some text of Scripture, which might as well be let alone, and which you would not ring in my ears, if you had any regard to my peace, or even your own. More than fifty times, within a month, have you quoted, "*By their fruits ye shall know them.*" In fact, so uncharitable have you grown of late, that from the drift of some of your admonitions, a stranger would think me but little, if any, better than a murderer. And all because some vagabond or other may possibly happen to shorten his days by drinking a little of the identical spirit which passes through my hands.

CONSCIENCE. You do me bare justice when you say that I have often reproved you, and more earnestly of late than I formerly did. But my remonstrances have always been between you and me alone. If I have charged you with the guilt of hurrying men to the grave and to hell, by this vile traffic, it has not been upon the house-top. I cannot, it is true, help knowing how it grieves your brethren, gratifies the enemies of religion, and excites the scorn of drunkards themselves, to see your wharf covered with the fiery element; but I speak only in your own ear. To yourself I have wished to prove a faithful monitor, though I have sad misgivings, at times, even with regard to that. You will bear me witness, however, that I have sometimes trembled exceedingly, for fear that I should be compelled, at last, to carry the matter up by indictment to the tribunal of Eternal Justice.

To avoid this dreadful necessity, let me once more reason the case with you in few words. You know perfectly well, that ardent spirit kills its tens of thousands in the United States every year; and there is no more room to doubt that many of these lives are destroyed by the very liquor which you sell, than if you saw them staggering under it into the drunkard's grave. How then can you possibly throw off bloodguiltiness, with the light which you now enjoy? In faithfulness to your soul, and to Him whose vicegerent I am, I cannot say less than this, especially if you persist any longer in the horrible traffic?

DEALER. Pardon me, my dear Conscience, if, under the

excitement of the moment, I complained of your honest and continued importunity. Be assured, there is no friend in the world, with whom I am so desirous of maintaining a good understanding as with yourself. And for your relief and satisfaction, I now give you my solemn pledge, that I will close up this branch of my business as soon as possible. Indeed, I have commenced the process already. My last consignments are less, by more than one half, than were those of the preceding year; and I intend that, when another year comes about, my books shall speak still more decidedly in my favor.

CONSCIENCE. These resolutions would be perfectly satisfactory, if they were in the *present tense.* But if it was wrong to sell five hundred casks last year, how can it be right to sell two hundred this year, and one hundred next? If it is criminal to poison forty men at one time, how can it be innocent to poison twenty at another? If you may not throw a hundred firebrands into the city, how will you prove that you may throw one?

DEALER. Very true, very true—but let us wave this point for the present. It affects me very strangely.

CONSCIENCE. How long, then, will it take to dry up this fountain of death?

DEALER. Don't call it so, I beseech you; but I intend to be entirely out of the business in two or three years, at farthest.

CONSCIENCE. Two or three years! Can you, then, after all that has passed between us, persist two or three years longer in a contraband traffic? I verily thought, that when we had that long conference two or three months ago, you resolved to close the concern at once; and that, when we parted, I had as good as your promise, that you would. Surely, you cannot so soon have forgotten it.

DEALER. No, I remember that interview but too well; for I was never so unhappy in my life. I did almost resolve, and more than half promise, as you say. But after I had time to get a little composed, I thought you had pushed matters rather too far; and that I could convince you of it, at a proper time. I see, however, that the attempt would be fruitless. But as I am anxious for a compromise, let me ask whether, if I give away all the profits of this branch of my business to the Bible Society, and other religious institutions, till I can close it up, you will not be satisfied?

Conscience. Let me see. Five hundred dollars, or one hundred dollars, earned to promote the cause of religion by selling poison! By killing husbands, and fathers, and brothers, and torturing poor women and children! It smells of blood—and can God possibly accept of such an offering?

Dealer. So then, it seems, I must stop the sale at once, or entirely forfeit what little charity you have left.

Conscience. You must. Delay is death—death to the consumer at least; and how can you flatter yourself that it will not prove your own eternal death? My convictions are decisive, and be assured, I deal thus plainly because I love you, and cannot bear to become your everlasting tormentor.

DIALOGUE III.

AT THE RETAILER'S STAND.

Conscience. Do you know that little half-starved, barefooted child, that you just sent home with two quarts of rank poison?

(Retailer hums a tune to himself, and affects not to hear the question.)

Conscience. I see by the paper of this morning, that the furniture of Mr. M—— is to be sold under the hammer to-morrow. Have I not often seen him in your taproom?

Retailer. I am extremely busy just now, in bringing up our ledger.

CONSCIENCE. Have you heard how N—— abused his family, and turned them all into the street the other night, after being supplied by you with whiskey?

RETAILER. He is a *brute*, and ought to be confined in a dungeon six months at least, upon bread and water.

CONSCIENCE. Was not S——, who hung himself lately, one of your steady customers? and where do you think his soul is now fixed for eternity? You sold him rum that evening, not ten minutes before you went to the prayer-meeting, and had his money in your pocket—for you would not trust him—when you led in the exercises. I heard you ask him once, why he did not attend meeting, and send his children to the Sabbath-school; and I shall never forget his answer. "Come, you talk like a minister; but, after all, we are about of one mind—at least in some things. Let me have my jug and be going."

RETAILER. I know he was an impudent, hardened wretch; and though his death was extremely shocking, I am glad to be rid of him.

CONSCIENCE. Are you ready to meet him at the bar of God, and to say to the Judge, "He was my neighbor—I saw him going down the broad way, and I did every thing that a Christian could do to save him?"

RETAILER. (Aside. O that I could stifle the upbraidings of this cruel monitor.) You keep me in constant torment. This everlasting cant about *rank poison, and liquid fire, and blood, and murder*, is too much for even a Christian to put up with. Why, if any body but Conscience were to make such insinuations and charges, he would be indictable as a foul slanderer, before a court of justice.

CONSCIENCE. Is it *slander*, or is it *because I tell you the truth*, that your temper is so deeply ruffled under my remonstrances? Suppose I were to hold my peace, while your hands are becoming more and more deeply crimsoned with this bloody traffic. What would you say to me, when you come to meet that poor boy who just went out, and his drunken father, and broken-hearted mother, at the bar of God? Would you thank your conscience for having let you alone while there was space left for repentance?

RETAILER. Ah, had honest trader ever *such* a conscience to deal with before? Always just so uncompromising—always talking about the "golden rule"—always insisting upon a moral standard which nobody can live up to—always scenting poverty, murder, and suicide, in every glass of whiskey, though it were a mile off. The truth is, you are not fit to live in this world at all. Acting in conformity with your more than puritanical rules, would starve any man and his family to death.

CONSCIENCE. Well, here comes another customer—see the carbuncles! Will you fill his bottle with wrath, to be poured out without mixture, by and by, upon your own head? Do you not know that his pious wife is extremely ill, and suffering for want of every comfort, in their miserable cabin?

RETAILER. No, Mr. E——, go home and take care of your family. I am determined to harbor no more drunkards here.

CONSCIENCE. You mean to make a distinction then, do you, between harboring those who are already ruined, and helping to destroy such as are now respectable members of society. You will not hereafter tolerate a single *drunkard* on your premises; but—

RETAILER. Ah, I see what you are aiming at; and really, it is too much for any honest man, and still more for any Christian to bear. You know it is a long time since I have pretended to answer half your captious questions. There's no use in it. It only leads on to others still more impertinent and puzzling. If I am the hundredth part of that factor of Satan which you would make me, I ought to be dealt with, and cast out of the church at once; an why don't my good brethren see to it?

Conscience. That's a hard question, which they, perhaps, better know how to answer than I do.

Retailer. But have you forgotten, my good Conscience, that in retailing spirit, I am under the immediate eye and sanction of the laws. Mine is no contraband traffic, as you very well know. I hold a license from the rulers and fathers of the state, and have paid my money for it into the public treasury. Why do they continue to grant and sell licenses, if it is wrong for me to sell rum?

Conscience. Another hard question, which I leave them to answer as best they can. It is said, however, that public bodies have no soul, and if they have no soul, it is difficult to see how they can have any conscience; and if not, what should hinder them from selling licenses? But suppose the civil authorities should offer to sell you a license to keep a gambling-house, or a brothel, would you purchase such a license, and present it as a salvo to your conscience?

Retailer. I tell you once more, there is no use in trying to answer your questions; for say what I will, you have the art of turning every thing against me. It was not always so, as you must very distinctly remember. Formerly I could retail hogshead after hogshead of all kinds of spirits, and you slept as quietly as a child. But since you began to read these Reports and Tracts about drinking, and to attend Temperance meetings, I have scarcely had an hour's peace of my life. I feared that something like this would be the effect upon your nervous temperament, when you began; and you may recollect that I strongly objected to your troubling yourself with these new speculations. It now grieves me to think that I ever yielded to your importunity; and beware that you do not push me to extremities in this matter, for I have about come to the resolution that

I will have no more of these mischievous pamphlets, either about my store or tavern; and that your temperance agents may declaim to the winds and walls, if they please.

CONSCIENCE. I am amazed at your blindness and obstinacy. It is now from three to five years since I began to speak—though in a kind of indistinct undertone at first—against this bloody traffic. I have reasoned, I have remonstrated, and latterly I have threatened and implored with increasing earnestness. At times you have listened, and been convinced that the course which you are pursuing, in this day of light, is infamous, and utterly inconsistent with a Christian profession; but before your convictions and resolutions have time to ripen into action, the love of *money* regains its ascendency: and thus have you gone on *resolving, and relapsing, and re-resolving*—one hour at the preparatory lecture, and the next unloading whiskey at your door; one moment mourning over the prevalence of intemperance, and the next arranging your decanters to entice the simple; one day partaking of the cup of the Lord at his table, and the next offering the cup of devils to your neighbors; one day singing,

> " All that I have, and all I am,
> I consecrate to Thee,"

and the next, *for the sake of a little gain,* sacrificing your character, and polluting all you can induce to drink! O, how can I hold my peace? How can I let you alone? If you will persist, your blood, and the blood of those whom you thus entice and destroy, be upon your own head. Whether you will hear, or whether you will forbear, I shall not cease to remonstrate; and when I can do no more to reclaim you, I will sit down at your gate, in the bitterness of despair, and cry, *Murder!* MURDER!! MURDER!!!

RETAILER. (Pale and trembling.) " Go thy way for this time; when I have a convenient season, I will call for thee."

BARNES

ON THE

TRAFFIC IN ARDENT SPIRITS.

THERE are some great principles in regard to *our* country, which are settled, and which are never to be violated, so long as our liberties are safe. Among them are these: that every thing may be subjected to candid and most free discussion; that public opinion, enlightened and correct, may be turned against any course of evil conduct; that that public opinion is, under God, the prime source of security to our laws and to our morals; and that men may be induced, by an ample and liberal discussion, and by the voice of conscience and of reason, to abandon any course that is erroneous. We are to presume that we may approach any class of American citizens with the conviction that if they are *convinced* that they are wrong, and that their course of life leads to sap the foundation of morals and the liberties of their country, they will abandon it.

Our present proposition is, that THE MANUFACTURING AND VENDING OF ARDENT SPIRITS IS MORALLY WRONG, AND OUGHT TO BE FORTHWITH ABANDONED.

We mean by the proposition, that it is an employment which *violates the rules of morals that ought to regulate a man's business and conduct.* The doctrine proceeds on the supposition, that there is somewhere a correct standard of morals—a standard by which a man's whole conduct and course of life is to be tried; and that *this* business cannot be vindicated by a reference to that standard. Or, for example, we mean that it is man's duty to love God, and seek to honor him, and that this business cannot be vindicated by a reference to that standard. That it is man's duty to love his fellow-men, and seek to promote their welfare, and that this business cannot be vindicated by that standard. That it is man's duty to render a valuable compensation to his fellow-men in his transactions with them, and that this business cannot be vindicated by that standard. That every man is bound to pursue such a course of life as shall promote the welfare of the entire community in which he lives, as shall *not* tend to promote crime, and pauperism, and misery, and to make widows and orphans, and that this business cannot be vindicated by that standard. In one word, that by any rules of life that have been set up to regulate the conduct of men, whether in the Bible, in the necessary relations of the social compact, in the reason and conscience of Christians, and of other men, this business is incapable of vindication, and is to be regarded as immoral.

In this proposition, however, it is important to be understood. We mean to confine it simply to the business where it is sold as an article of *drink*. For to sell it as a medicine, with the same precaution as other poisons are sold, would be no more immoral than it is to sell arsenic. And to sell it for purposes of manufacture, where it is necessary for that purpose, is no more immoral than to sell any other article with that design. Between selling it for *these* purposes, and selling it as an article of drink, there is, as any one can see, the widest possible difference.

When we speak of this business as *immoral*, it is also important to guard the use of the word *immoral*. That word, with us, has come to have a definite and well understood signification. When we speak of an immoral man, we are commonly understood to attack the foundations of his character; to designate some gross vice of which he is guilty, and to speak of him as profane, or licentious, or profligate, or dishonest, or as unworthy of our confidence and respect. Now, we by no means intend to use the word in such a wide sense, when we say that this business is immoral. We do not mean to intimate that in no circumstances a man may be engaged in it and be worthy of our confidence, and be an honest man, or even a Christian; for our belief is, that many such men have been, and are still, unhappily engaged in this traffic. The time has been, when it was thought to be as reputable as any other employment. Men may not see the injurious tendency of their conduct. They may not be apprized of its consequences; or they may be ignorant of the proper rules by which human life is to be regulated. Thus, the slave-trade was long pursued, and duelling was deemed right, and bigamy was practised. But for a man to maintain that all these would be right *now*, and to practise them, would be a very different thing.

In this view of the subject, we do not of course speak of the dead, or offer any reflection on their conduct or character. Many men are unwilling to regard this traffic as wrong, because, by so doing, they would seem to convey a reflection on their parents, or friends, who may have been engaged in the same business. But nothing of this kind is intended. The great laws of morals are indeed unchanged: but the degrees of light and knowledge which men possess may be very different. We should not deem it right to apply *our* laws and knowledge, in judging of the laws of Sparta, which authorized theft; nor our laws to judge of the conduct of the Hindoo in exposing his father on the banks of the Ganges; nor our present views to determine on the morality of our fathers an hundred years ago in the slave-trade; nor our views of the marriage relation to condemn the conduct of Abraham, David, or Jacob. Man's conduct is to be estimated by the light which he has. They who sin without law, are to be judged without law; and they who sin in the law, are to be judged by the law. Your father might have been engaged in the traffic in ardent spirits. Whether he was innocent or not, is not now the question, and has been determined by a higher tribunal than any on earth. The question now is, whether *you* can pursue it with a good conscience; or whether, with all that you know of the effects of the traffic, it be right or wrong for you to pursue it.

With these necessary explanations, I proceed to PROVE that, in the sense in which it has been explained, the traffic is MORALLY WRONG.

In proving this proposition, I shall take for granted two or three points which are now conceded, and to establish which would lead me too far out of my way. The first is, that this is not an employment in which *the properties of the article are unknown.* The seller has as good an opportunity to be acquainted with the qualities of the article, and its effects, as the buyer. There is no concealment of its character and tendency; there can be no pretence that you were deceived in regard to those qualities, and that you were unintentionally engaged in the sale of an article which has turned out to be otherwise than you supposed it to be. For, alas, those properties are too well ascertained; and all who are engaged in this employment have ample opportunity to know what they are doing, and engage in it with their eyes open.

The *effects* of this traffic are well known. The public mind has been, with remarkable intensity, directed to this subject for ten years in this land, and the details have been laid before the American public. It is believed that no vice has ever been so faithfully guaged, and the details so well ascertained, as the vice of intemperance in this nation. It is far better understood than the extent of gambling, or piracy, or robbery, or the slave-trade. It is established now, beyond the possibility of debate, that ardent spirits is a poison, as certain, as deadly, and destructive, as any other poison. It may be more slow in its effects, but it is not the less certain. This is established by the testimony of all physicians and chemists who have expressed an opinion on the subject. It is not necessary for the welfare of man as an ordinary drink. This is proved by the like testimony, by the example of many thousands who abstain from it, and by the fact, that before its invention, the Roman soldier, the Scythian, and the Greek, were as hardy and long-lived as men have been since. Its direct tendency is to produce disease, poverty, crime, and death. Its use tends to corrupt the morals, to enfeeble the intellect, to produce indolence, wretchedness, and woe in the family circle; to shorten life, and to hurry to a loathsome grave; to spread a pall of grief over families and nations. It is ascertained to be the source of nine-tenths of all the pauperism, and nine-tenths of all the crimes in the land. It fills our streets with drunkards, our almshouses with loathsome wretches, our jails with poor criminals, and supplies our gibbets with victims. It costs the land in which we live more than 100,000,000 of dollars annually, and renders us no compensation but poverty, want, curses, loathsomeness, and tears.

In any single year in this Union, could the effects be gathered into one single grasp, they would present to the eye the following affecting details. An army of at least 300,000 drunkards—not made up of old men, of the feeble, but of those in early life; of our youth, of our men of talents and influence; an enlistment from the bar, the bench, the pulpit, the homes of the rich, and the firesides of piety; the abodes of the intelligent, as well as the places of obscurity, and the humble ranks—all reeling together to a drunkard's grave. With this army Napoleon would have overrun Europe. In the same group would be no less than 75,000 criminals, made such by the use of ardent spirits; criminals of every grade and dye, supported at the expense of the sober, and lost to morality, and industry, and hope; the source of lawsuits, and the fountain of no small part of the expenses of courts of justice. In the same group would be no less than 200,000 paupers, in a land abounding in all the wealth that the richest soil can give, and under all the facilities which the most favored spot under the whole heaven can furnish for acquiring a decent and an honest subsistence. Paupers, supported at the expense of the sober and the industrious, and creating no small part of our taxes, to pay for their indolence, and wretchedness, and crimes. And in the same group would be no less than 600 insane persons, made such by intemperance, in all the horrid and revolting forms of delirium—the conscience destroyed, the mind obliterated, and hope and happiness fled for ever. And in the same group there would be no less than 30,000 of our countrymen, who die annually, as the direct effect of the use of ardent spirit. Thirty thousand of our countrymen sinking to the most loathsome and dishonored of all graves, the grave of the drunkard. This is just a summary of the obvious and sure effects of this vice. The innumerable woes that it incidentally causes; the weeping and groans of the widow and the fatherless; the crimes and vices which it tends to introduce into abodes that would, but for this, be the abodes of peace, are not, and cannot be taken into the account.

Now, this state of things, if produced in any other way, would spread weeping and sackcloth over nations and continents. Any sweeping pestilence that could do this, would hold a nation in alarm, and diffuse, from one end of it to the other, trembling and horror. The world has never known any thing else like it. The father of mischief has never been able to invent any thing that should diffuse more widespread and dreadful evils.

It is agreed further, and well understood, that this is the *regular effect of the traffic, and manufacture, and use of this article.* It is not casual, incidental, irregular. It is uniform, certain, deadly, as the sirocco of the desert, or as the malaria of the Pontine marshes. It is not a periodical influence, returning at distant intervals; but it is a pestilence, breathing always—diffusing the poison when men sleep and when they wake, by day and by night, in seed-time and harvest—attending the manufacture and sale of the article *always.* The destroyer seeks his victim alike in every hogshead, and in every glass. He exempts no man from danger that uses it; and is always secure of prostrating the most vigorous frame, of clouding the most splendid intellect, of benumbing the most delicate moral feelings, of palsying the most eloquent tongue, of teaching those on whose lips listening senates hung, to mutter and babble with the drunkard, and of entombing the most brilliant talents and hopes of youth, wherever man can be induced to drink. The establishment of every distillery, and every dram-shop, and every grocery where it is sold, secures the certainty that many a man will thereby become a drunkard, and be a curse to himself and to the world. The traffic is not only occasionally and incidentally injurious, but it is like the generation before the flood in its effects, evil, and only evil continually.

Now the question is, whether this is an employment in which a moral man and a Christian man *ought* to be engaged. Is it such a business as his countrymen ought to approve? Is it such as his conscience and sober judgment approve? Is it such as his God and Judge will approve?

In examining this, let it be remembered, that the *reason* why this occupation is engaged in, and the sole reason, is, *to make money.* It is not because it is supposed that it will benefit mankind; nor is it because the man supposes that duty to his Creator requires it; nor is it because it is presumed that it will promote public health, or morals, or happiness; but it is engaged in and pursued solely as a means of livelihood or of wealth. And the question then is reduced to a very narrow compass: Is it *right* for a man, for the sake of gain, to be engaged in the sale of a poison—a poison attended with destruction to the property, health, happiness, peace, and salvation of his neighbors; producing mania, and poverty, and curses, and death, and woes innumerable to the land, and to the church of God? A question this, one would think, that might be very soon answered. In answering it, I invite attention to a few very obvious, but undeniable positions.

1. It is an employment which tends to *counteract the very design of the organization of society.* Society is organized on a benevolent principle. The structure of that organization is one of the best adapted instances of design, and of benevolence, anywhere to be found. It is on this principle that a lawful employment—an employment fitted to produce subsistence for a man and his family, will not interfere with the rights and happiness of others. It may be pursued without violating any of their rights, or infringing on their happiness in any way. Nay, it may not only not interfere with *their* rights and happiness, but it will tend to promote directly their welfare, by promoting the happiness of the whole. Or, for example, the employment of the farmer may be pursued, not only without interfering with the rights or privileges of the mechanic, the physician, or the merchant, but it will directly contribute to *their* welfare, and is indispensable to it. The employment of the physician not only contributes to the support of himself and family, but to the welfare of the whole community. It not only does *not* interfere with the rights and happiness of the farmer and the mechanic, but it tends directly to their advantage. The employment of the merchant in lawful traffic, not only contributes to his support, but is directly beneficial

to the whole agricultural part of the community; for, as has been well said, "the merchant is the friend of mankind." He injures no man, at the same time that he benefits himself; and he contributes to the welfare of the community, by promoting a healthful and desirable exchange of commodities in different parts of the land, and of various natures. The same is true of the mechanic, the mariner, the legislator, the bookmaker, the day-laborer, the schoolmaster, the lawyer, the clergyman.

Now, we maintain that the traffic in ardent spirits, as a drink, is a violation of this wise arrangement. It tends to sap the foundation of the whole economy. It is solely to benefit the trafficker, and it tends to evil, evil only, evil continually. If every man should act on this principle, society could not exist. If every man should choose an employment that should *necessarily* and *always* interfere with the peace, and happiness, and morals of others, it would at once break up the organization. If every manufacturer should erect a manufactory, as numerous as our distilleries and dram-shops, that should necessarily blight every farm, and produce *sterility* in its neighborhood, every farmer would regard it as an unlawful employment; and if pursued, the business of agriculture would end. If a physician could live only by diffusing disease and death, who would regard his as a moral employment? If a mariner could pursue his business from this port to Calcutta or Canton, only by importing the plague in every return voyage, who would deem it an honorable employment? If an apothecary could pursue his business only by killing nine persons out of ten of those with whom he had dealing, who would deem it a lawful business? If a man can get a living in his employment only by fitting out a privateer and preying upon the peaceful commerce of the world, who will deem it a lawful employment? If a man lives only to make a descent on the peaceful abodes of Africa, and to tear away parents from their weeping children, and husbands from their wives and homes, where is the man that will deem this a *moral* business? And why not? Does he not act on the same principle as the man who deals in ardent spirits—a desire to make money, and that only? The truth is, that in all these cases there would be a violation of the great fundamental law on which men must agree to live together in society—a violation of that great, noble, and benevolent law of our organization, by which an honest employment interferes with no other, but may tend to diffuse blessings in the whole circle of human engagements. And the traffic in ardent spirits is just as much a violation of this law, as in any of the cases specified.

2. Every man is bound to pursue such a business as to *render a valuable consideration* for that which he receives from others. A man who receives in trade the avails of the industry of others, is under obligation to restore that which will be of real value. He receives the fruit of toil; he receives that which is of value to himself; and common equity requires that he return a valuable consideration. Thus, the merchant renders to the farmer, in exchange for the growth of his farm, the productions of other climes; the manufacturer, that which is needful for the clothing or comfort of the agriculturist; the physician, the result of his professional skill. All these are valuable considerations, which are fair and honorable subjects of exchange. They are a mutual accommodation; they advance the interest of both parties. But it is not so with the dealer in ardent spirits. He obtains the property of his fellow-men, and what does he return? That which will tend to promote his real welfare? That which will make him a happier man? That which will benefit his family? That which diffuses learning and domestic comfort around his family circle? None of these things. He gives him that which will produce poverty, and want, and cursing, and tears, and death. He asked

an egg, and he receives a scorpion. He gives him that which is established and well known as a source of no good, but as tending to produce beggary and wretchedness. Now, if this were practised in any other business, it would be open fraud. If in any way you could palm upon a farmer that which is not only *worthless*, but mischievous—that which would certainly tend to ruin him and his family, *could there be* any doubt about the nature of this employment? It makes no difference here, that the man *supposes* that it is for his good; or that he applies for it. *You know* that it is *not* for his benefit, and you know—what is the only material point under this head—that it will tend to his ruin. Whatever *he* may think about it, or whatever *he* may desire, you are well advised that it is an article that will tend to sap the foundation of his morals and happiness, and conduce to the ruin of his estate, and his body, and his soul; and you know, therefore, that you are *not* rendering him any really valuable consideration for his property. The dealer may look on his gains in this matter—on his houses, or mortgages, or lands, obtained as the result of this business—with something like these reflections.

"This property has been gained from other men. It was theirs, honestly acquired, and was necessary to promote their own happiness and the happiness of their families. It has become mine by a traffic which has not only taken it away from them, but which has ruined their peace, corrupted their morals, sent woe and discord into their families, and consigned them perhaps to an early and most loathsome grave. This property has come from the hard earnings of other men; has passed into my hands without any valuable compensation rendered; but has been obtained only while I have been diffusing want, and woe, and death, through their abodes."

Let the men engaged in this traffic look on their property thus gained; let them survey the woe which has attended it; and then ask, as honest men, whether it is a moral employment.

3. A man is bound to pursue such a business as shall tend to *promote the welfare of the whole community.* This traffic does not. We have seen that an honorable and lawful employment conduces to the welfare of the whole social organization. But the welfare of the whole cannot be promoted by this traffic. *Somewhere* it must produce poverty, and idleness, and crime. Even granting, what cannot be established, that it may promote the happiness of a particular portion of the community, yet it must be at the expense of some other portion. You may export poison to Georgia, and the immediate effect may be to introduce money into Philadelphia, but the only important inquiry is, what will be the effect on the *whole body politic?* Will it do more good than evil on the whole? Will the money which you may receive here, be a compensation for all the evil which will be done there? Money a compensation for intemperance, and idleness, and crime, and the loss of the health, the happiness, and the souls of men?

Now we may easily determine this matter. The article thus exported will do as much evil *there* as it would if consumed *here.* It will spread just as much devastation somewhere, as it would if consumed in your own family, and among your own friends and neighbors. We have only to ask, what would be the effect if it were consumed in your own habitation, in your neighborhood, in your own city? Let all this poison, which is thus exported to spread woes and death somewhere, be concentrated and consumed where you might see it, and is there any man who will pretend that the paltry sum which he receives is a compensation for what he knows would be the effect of the consumption? You keep your own atmosphere pure, it may be, but you export the pestilence, and curses, and lamentation elsewhere, and receive a compensation for it. You sell disease, and death, and poverty, and nakedness, and tears to other families, to clothe and feed your own. And as the result of this current of moral poison and pollution which you may cause to flow into hundreds of other families, you may point to a splendid palace, or to gay apparel of your sons and daughters, and proclaim that the evil is hidden from your eyes. Families, and neighborhoods, and states, may groan and bleed somewhere, and thousands may die, but *your* gain is to be a compensation for it all. Is this an honorable traffic?

Suppose a man were to advertise consumptions, and fevers, and pleurisies, and leprosy, for gold, and could and would sell them; what would the community say to such a traffic? Suppose, for gain, he could transport them to distant places, and now strike down by a secret power a family in Maine, and now at St. Mary's, and now at Texas, and now at St. Louis; what would the community think of wealth gained in such a traffic? Suppose he could, with the same ease, diffuse profaneness, and insanity, and robberies, and murders, and suicides, and should advertise all these to be propagated through the land, and could prevail on men to buy the talismanic nostrum for gold—what would the community think of such a traffic as this? True, he might plead that it brought a vast influx of money—that it enriched the city, or the country—that the effects were not seen there; but what would be the public estimate of a man who would be willing to engage in such a traffic, and who would set up such a plea? Or suppose it were understood that a farmer from the interior had arrived in Philadelphia with a load of flour, nine-tenths of whose barrels contained a mixture, more or less, of arsenic, and should offer them for sale; what would be the feelings of this community at such a traffic? True, the man might plead that it would produce gain to his country; that they had taken care to remove it to another population; that his own family was secure. Can any words express the indignation which would be felt? Can any thing express the horror which all men would feel at such a transaction as this, and at the cold-blooded and inhuman guilt of the money-loving farmer? And yet we witness a thing like this every day, on our wharves, and in our ships, and our groceries, and our inns, and from our men of wealth, and our moral men, and our *professed Christians*—and a horror comes through the souls of men, when we dare to intimate that this is an immoral business.

4. A man is bound to pursue such a course of life as *not necessarily to increase the burdens and the taxes* of the community. The pauperism and crimes of this land grow out of this vice, as an overflowing fountain. Three-fourths of the taxes for prisons, and houses of refuge, and alms-houses, would be cut off, but for this traffic and the attendant vices. Nine-tenths of the crimes of the country, and of the expenses of litigation for crime, would be prevented by arresting it. Of 653 who were in one year committed to the house of correction in Boston, 453 were drunkards. Of 3,000 persons admitted to the workhouse in Salem, Mass., 2,900 were brought there directly or indirectly by intemperance. Of 592 male adults in the almshouse in New York, not 20, says the superintendent, can be called sober; and of 601 women, not as many as 50. Only three instances of murder in the space of fifteen years, in New York, occurred, that could not be traced to ardent spirit as the cause. In Philadelphia, ten. This is the legitimate, regular effect of the business. It tends to poverty, crime, and woe, and greatly to increase the taxes and burdens of the community.

What is done then in this traffic? You are filling our almshouses, and jails, and penitentiaries, with victims loathsome and burdensome to the community. You are engaged in a business which is compelling your fellow-citizens to pay taxes to support the victims of your employment. You are filling up these abodes of wretchedness and guilt, and then asking your fellow-citizens to pay enormous taxes indirectly to support this traffic. For, if every place where ardent spirits can be obtained, were closed in this city and its suburbs, how long might your splendid palaces for the poor be almost untenanted piles; how soon would your jails disgorge their inmates, and be no more filled; how soon would the habitations of guilt and infamy in every city become the abodes of contentment and peace; and how soon would reeling loathsomeness and want cease to assail your doors with importunate pleadings for charity.

Now we have only to ask our fellow-citizens, what right they have to pursue an employment tending thus to burden the community with taxes, and to endanger the dwellings of their fellow-men, and to send to my door, and to every other man's door, hordes of beggars loathsome to the sight; or to compel the virtuous to seek out their wives and children, amidst the squalidness of poverty, and the cold of winter, and the pinchings of hunger, to supply their wants? Could impartial justice be done in the world, an end would soon be put to the traffic in ardent spirits. Were every man bound to alleviate all the wretchedness which his business creates, to support all the poor which his traffic causes, an end would soon be made of this employment. But alas, you can diffuse this poison for gain, and then call on your industrious and virtuous countrymen to alleviate the wretchedness, to tax themselves to build granite prisons for the inmates which your business has made; and splendid palaces, at an enormous expense, to extend a shelter and a home for those whom your employment has turned from their own habitations. Is this a moral employment? Would it be well to obtain a living in this way in any other business?

5. The business is *inconsistent with the law of God,*

which requires us to love our neighbor as ourselves. A sufficient proof of this would be a fact which no one could deny, that no man yet, probably, ever undertook the business, or pursued it from that motive. Its defence is not, and cannot be put on that ground. No man in the community believes that a continuance in it is required by a regard to the welfare of his neighbor. Every one knows that his welfare does not require it; and that it would be conferring an inestimable blessing on other men, if the traffic was abandoned. The single, sole object is gain; and the sole question is, whether the love of gain is a sufficient motive for continuing that which works no good, but constant ill to your neighbor.

There is another law of God which has an important bearing on this subject. It is that golden rule of the New Testament, which commends itself to the conscience of all men, to do to others as you would wish them to do to you. You may easily conceive of your having a son, who was in danger of becoming a drunkard. Your hope might centre in him. He might be the stay of your age. He may be inclined to dissipation; and it may have required all your vigilance, and prayers, and tears, and authority, to keep him in the ways of soberness. The simple question now is, what would you wish a neighbor to do in such a case? Would it be the desire of your heart, that he should open a fountain of poison at your next door; that he should, for gain, be willing to put a cup into the hands of your son, and entice him to the ways of intemperance? Would you be pleased if he would listen to no remonstrance of yours, if he should even disregard your entreaties and your tears, and coolly see, for the love of gold, ruin coming into your family, and your prop taken from beneath you, and your gray hairs coming down with sorrow to the grave? And yet to many such a son may you sell the poison; to many a father whose children are clothed in rags; to many a man whose wife sits weeping amidst poverty and want, and dreading to hear the tread and the voice of the husband of her youth, once her protector, who now comes to convert his own habitation into a hell. And there are not a few men of fair standing in society who are engaged in this; and not a few—O tell it not in Gath—who claim the honored name of Christian, and who profess to bear the image of Him who went about doing good. Can such be a *moral* business?

6. The traffic is *a violation of that law which requires a man to honor God.* Whether ye eat, or drink, or whatsoever ye do, do all to the glory of God. And yet is this a business which was ever engaged in, or ever pursued, with a desire to honor God? Is it an employment over which a man will pray? Can he ask the God of heaven to give him success? Let him, then, in imagination, follow what he sells to its direct result; let him attend it to its final distribution of poverty, and woes, and crimes, and death, and then kneel before heaven's eternal King, and render thanksgiving for this success? Alas, it cannot be. Man pursues it not from a desire to honor God. And can the man who is engaged in a business on which he cannot implore the blessing of heaven; who is obliged to conceal all thoughts of it if he ever prays; who never engaged in it with a desire to glorify God, or to meet his approbation, can *he* be engaged in a business which is lawful and right?

I might dwell further on these points. But I am now prepared to ask, with emphasis, whether an employment that has been attended with so many ills to the bodies and souls of men; with so much woe and crime; whose results are evil, and only evil continually; an employment which cannot be pursued without tending to destroy the very purposes of the organization of society; without violating the rule which requires us to render a valuable consideration in business; without violating the rule which requires a man to promote the welfare of the whole of the community; which promotes pauperism and crime, and imposes heavy burdens on your fellow-citizens; which is opposed equally to the love of man and the law of God—*whether this is a moral, or an immoral employment?*

The question is submitted. If moral, it should be driven on with all the power of American energy; with all the aids of wealth, and all the might of steam, and all the facilities of railroads and canals; for our country and the church calls the man to the honorable employment. But if it be immoral and wrong, it should be abandoned on the spot. Not another gallon should ever pass from your store, if it be evil, only evil, and that continually.

We are prepared now to examine a few of the OBJECTIONS to this doctrine.

1. The first is, that the traffic is not condemned in the Bible. To this the answer is very obvious. The article was then unknown. Nor was it known until 600 years after the Bible was completed. This mode of extending and perpetuating depravity in the world was not suggested by the father of evil, until it was too late to make a formal law against it in the Bible, or to fortify the argument of human depravity from this source. It is neither in the Bible, nor in any other code of laws, the custom to specify crimes which do not exist. How remarkable in a code of laws would have been such a declaration as the trafficker demands, "Thou shalt not deal in ardent spirits," hundreds of years before the article was known. The world would have stood in amazement, and would have been perplexed and confounded by an unmeaning statute. But further, it is not the practice in the Bible, or in any other book of laws, to specify each shade and degree of wrong. Had it been, there could have been no end of legislation, and no end to books of law. I ask the dealer in ardent spirits,

where is there a formal prohibition of piracy, or bigamy, or kidnapping, or suicide, or duelling, or the sale of obscene books and paintings? And yet does any man doubt that these are immoral? Does he believe that the Bible will countenance them? Will he engage in them, because they are not specified formally, and with technical precision, in the Scriptures? The truth is, that the Bible has laid down great principles of conduct, which on all these subjects can be easily applied, which *are* applied, and which, under the guidance of equal honesty, may be as easily applied to the traffic of which I am speaking. Still further, the Bible *has* forbidden it in principle, and with all the precision which can be demanded. A man cannot pursue the business, as has been shown, without violating its great principles. He cannot do justly in it; he cannot show mercy by it; he cannot seek to alleviate human woes by it; he cannot do as he would wish to be done unto; he cannot pursue it to glorify God. The great principles of the Bible, the spirit of the Bible, and a thousand texts of the Bible are pointed against it; and every step the trafficker takes, he infringes on the spirit and bearing of some declaration of God. And still further, it is *his* business to make out the propriety of the employment, not ours to make out the case against him. Here is the rule—for him to judge. By this he is to be tried; and unless he can find in the volume a rule that will justify him in a business for gain that scatters inevitable woes and death; that accomplishes more destruction than all the chariots of war and the desolations of gunpowder on the field of blood; that sends more human beings to the grave, than fire, and flood, and pestilence, and faminc, altogether; that heaps on human society more burdens than all other causes combined; that sends armies on armies, in a form more appalling, and infinitely more loathsome than Napoleon's "food for cannon," to the grave: unless he can find some prophecy, or some principle, or some declaration, that will justify these, the Bible is against him, and he knows it. As well might he search for a principle to authorize him to plant a Bohon Upas on every man's farm, and in the heart of every city and hamlet.

2. A second plea is, "If I do not do it, others will; the traffic will go on." Then, I answer, *let* others do it, and on them, not on you, be the responsibility. But it is said, perhaps, if it is not in your hands—the hands of the respectable and the pious—it will be in the hands of the unprincipled and the profligate. I answer, THERE LET IT BE. There, if anywhere, it should be. There, if these principles are correct, is its appropriate place. And if that were done, intemperance would soon cease to curse the land. *It is just because it is upheld by the rich, and the reputable, and by professed Christians, that the reform drags so heavily.* The business has never found its proper level. And O that the dealers in it would kindly forego this plea of benevolence, and feel themselves released from this obligation. But is this a correct principle of conduct? Is this the rule which heaven has given, or which conscience gives, to direct the doings of man? Have I a right to do all which I know other men will do? Other men will commit murder. Have I a right to do it? Other men will commit adultery. Have I a right to do it? Other men will curse, and swear, and steal. Have you a right to do it? Other men will prey on unoffending Africa, and bear human sinews across the ocean to be sold. Have you a right to do it? The traffic in human flesh will go on; ships will be fitted out from American ports; and American hands will bear a part of the price of the tears and groans of enslaved men. And why should not you participate with them, on the same principle?

3. A third excuse is, that the traffic is the source of gain to the country. Now this is known to be not so. More

than 100,000,000 of dollars would be necessary to repair to this land the annual loss in this business. Is it no loss that 300,000 men are drunkards, and are the slaves of indolence and want? Is it no loss to the nation that 30,000 each year go to the grave? Is there no loss in the expense of supporting 75,000 criminals, and nine-tenths of the paupers in the land? Is it no loss that bad debts are made, and men are made unable and unwilling to pay their debts? Whence are *your* bad debts? Whence, but directly or indirectly from this business? From the indolence, and want of principle, and want of attention, which intemperance produces?

4. The man who is engaged in this business says, perhaps, "I have inherited it, and it is the source of my gain; and what shall I do?" I answer, beg, dig—do any thing *but* this. It would be a glorious martyrdom *to starve*, contrasted with obtaining a livelihood by such an employment. In this land, assuredly, men cannot plead that there are no honorable sources of livelihood open before them. Besides, from whom do we hear this plea? As often as otherwise from the man that rolls in wealth; that lives in a palace; that clothes his family in the attire of princes and of courts; and that moves in the circles of fashion and splendor. O how cheering is *consistent* pleading; how lovely the expressions of perfect honesty! This business may be abandoned without difficulty. The only question is, whether the love of man, and the dictates of conscience, and the fear of God, shall prevail over the love of that polluted gold which this traffic in the lives and souls of men shall introduce into your dwelling.

During a warmly contested election in the city of New York, it is stated in the daily papers that numerous applications were made for *pistols* to those who kept them for sale. It is added that the application was extensively denied, on the ground of the apprehension that they were intended for bloodshed in the excitement of the contest. This was a noble instance of principle. But on the plea of the dealer in ardent spirits, why should they have been withheld? The dealer in fire-arms might have plead as the trafficker in poison does: "This is my business. I obtain a livelihood by it. *I am not responsible for what will be done with the fire-arms.* True, the people are agitated. I have every reason to believe that application is made with a purpose to take life. True, blood may flow and useful lives may be lost. But *I* am not responsible. If they take life, they are answerable. The excitement is a favorable opportunity to dispose of my stock on hand, and it is a part of my business to avail myself of all favorable circumstances in the community to make money." Who would not have been struck with the cold-blooded and inhuman avarice of such a man? And yet there was not *half* the moral certainty that those fire-arms would have been used for purposes of blood, that there is that ardent spirits will be employed to produce crime, and poverty, and death.

I have no time to notice other objections. Nor need I. I have stated the *principle* of all. I just add here, that the excuses which are set up for this traffic will apply just as well to any other business as this, and will fully vindicate any other employment, if they are to be sustained. Apply these excuses to the case of a bookseller. The question might be suggested, whether it was a moral or an immoral business to deal in infidel, profligate, and obscene pictures and books. True, it might be alleged that they did evil, and only evil continually. It might be said that neither the love of God or man would prompt to it. He might be pointed to the fact, that they *always* tended to corrupt the morals of youth; to blight the hopes of parents; to fill up houses of infamy; to blot out the hopes of heaven; and to sink men to hell. But then he might with commendable coolness add, "This traffic is not condemned in the Bible. If *I* do not engage in it, others will. It contributes to my livelihood; to the support of the press; to the promotion of business; and I am not responsible for *their* reading the books, nor for their desire for them. I am pursuing the way in which my fathers walked before me, and it is *my living, and I will do it.*" Wherein does this plea differ from that of the trafficker in ardent spirits? Alas, we have learned how to estimate its force in regard to other sins; but we shrink from its application in regard to this wide-spread business, that employs so much of the time and the wealth of the people of this land.

Here I close. The path of duty and of safety is plain. These evils may be corrected. A virtuous and an independent people may rise in their majesty and correct them all. I call on all whom I now address, to exert their influence in this cause; to abandon all connection with the traffic; and to become the firm, and warm, and thorough-going advocates of the temperance reformation. Your country calls you to it. Every man who loves her welfare, should pursue no half-way measures; should tread no vacillating course in this great and glorious reformation.

But more especially may I call on *young men*, and ask *their* patronage in this cause. For they are in danger; and they are the source of our hopes, and they are our strength. I appeal to them by their hopes of happiness; by their prospects of long life; by their desire of property and health; by their wish for reputation; and by the fact that by abstinence, strict abstinence alone, are they safe from the crimes, and loathsomeness, and grave of the drunkard. Young men, I beseech you to regard the liberties of your country; the purity of the churches; your own usefulness; and the honor of your family—the feelings of a father, a mother, and a sister. And I conjure you to take this stand by a reference to your own immortal welfare; by a regard to that heaven which a drunkard enters not—and by a fear of that hell which is his own appropriate, eternal home.

Again I appeal to my fellow professing Christians; the ministers of religion, the officers and members of the pure church of God. The pulpit should speak, in tones deep, and solemn, and constant, and reverberating through the land. The watchmen should see eye to eye. Of every officer and member of a church it should be known where he may be found. We want no vacillating counsels; no time-serving apologies; no coldness, no reluctance, no shrinking back in this cause. Every church of Christ, the world over, should be, in very deed, an organization of pure temperance under the headship and patronage of Jesus Christ, the friend and the model of purity. Members of the church of God most pure, bear it in mind, that intemperance in our land, and the world over, stands in the way of the Gospel. It opposes the progress of the reign of Christ in every village and hamlet; in every city; and at every corner of the street. It stands in the way of revivals of religion, and of the glories of the millennial morn. Every drunkard opposes the millennium; every dram-drinker stands in the way of it; every dram-seller stands in the way of it. Let the sentiment be heard, and echoed, and reëchoed, all along the hills, and vales, and streams of the land, *that the conversion of a man who habitually uses ardent spirits is all but hopeless.* And let this sentiment be followed up with that other melancholy truth, that the money wasted in this business—now a curse to all nations—nay, the money wasted in one year in this land for it, would place a Bible in every family on the earth, and establish a school in every village; and that the talent which intemperance consigns each year to infamy and eternal perdition, would be sufficient to bear the Gospel over sea and land—to polar snows, and to the sands of a burning sun. The pulpit must speak out. And the press must speak. And you, fellow-Christians, are summoned by the God of purity to take your stand, and cause your influence to be felt.

THE FOOLS' PENCE.

Have you ever seen a London gin-shop? There is perhaps no statelier shop in the magnificent chief city of England. No expense seems to be spared in the building and the furnishing of a gin-shop.

Not many years ago a gin-shop was a mean-looking, and by no means a spacious place, with a few small bottles, not bigger than a doctor's largest vials, in the dusty window. But now, however poor many of the working classes may be, it seems to be their pleasure to squander their little remaining money upon a number of these palaces, as if they were determined that the persons whom they employ to sell them poison should dwell in the midst of luxury and splendor. I do not mean to say, that we have a right to throw all the blame upon the master or the mistress of a gin-shop. For my part, I should not like to keep one, and be obliged to get rich upon the money of the poor infatuated creatures who will ruin both soul and body in gin-drinking; but the master of the gin-shop may be heard to say, "I don't force the people to drink; they will have gin, and if I do not sell to them somebody else will." The story of "The Fools' Pence," which follows, is worth attending to.

A little mean-looking man sat talking to Mrs. Crowder, the mistress of the Punch-bowl: "Why, Mrs. Crowder," said he, "I should hardly know you again. Really, I must say you have things in the first style. What an elegant paper; what noble chairs; what a pair of fire-screens; all so bright and so fresh; and yourself so well, and looking so well!"

Mrs. Crowder had dropped languidly into an arm-chair, and sat sighing and smiling with affectation, not turning a deaf ear to her visitor, but taking in with her eyes a full view of what passed in the shop; having drawn aside the curtain of rose-colored silk, which sometimes covered the window in the wall between the shop and the parlor.

"Why, you see, Mr. Berriman," she replied, "our business is a thriving one, and we don't love to neglect it, for one must work hard for an honest livelihood; and then you see, my two girls, Letitia and Lucy, were about to leave their boarding-school; so Mr. Crowder and I wished to make the old place as genteel and fashionable as we could; and what with new stone copings to the windows, and new French window-frames to the first floor, and a little paint, and a little papering, Mr. Berriman, we begin to look tolerable. I must say too, Mr. Crowder has laid out a deal of money in fitting up the shop, and in filling his cellars."

"Well, ma'am," continued Mr. Berriman, "I don't know where you find the needful for all these improvements. For my part, I can only say, our trade seems quite at a stand-still. There's my wife always begging for money to pay for this or that little necessary article, but I part from every penny with a pang. Dear Mrs. Crowder, how do you manage?"

Mrs. Crowder simpered, and raising her eyes, and looking with a glance of smiling contempt towards the crowd of customers in the shop, "The fools' pence—'tis THE FOOLS' PENCE that does it for us," she said.

Perhaps it was owing to the door being just then opened and left ajar by Miss Lucy, who had been serving in the bar, that the words of Mrs. Crowder were heard by a man named George Manly, who stood at the upper end of the counter. He turned his eyes upon the customers who were standing near him, and saw pale, sunken cheeks, inflamed eyes, and ragged garments. He turned them upon the stately apartment in which they were assembled; he saw that it had been fitted up at no trifling cost; he stared through the partly open doorway into the parlor, and saw looking-glasses, and pictures, and gilding, and fine furniture, and a rich carpet, and Miss Lucy, in a silk gown, sitting down to her piano-forte: and he thought within himself, how strange it is, by what a curious process it is, that all this wretchedness on my left hand is made to turn into all this rich finery on my right!

"Well, sir, and what's for you?"

These words were spoken in the same shrill voice which had made the "fools' pence" ring in his ears.

George Manly was still in deep thought, and with the end of his rule—for he was a carpenter—he had been making a calculation, drawing the figures in the little puddles of gin upon the counter. He looked up and saw Mrs. Crowder herself as gay as her daughters, with a cap and colored ribbons flying off her head, and a pair of gold earrings almost touching her plump shoulders. "A glass of gin, ma'am, is what I was waiting for to-night, but I think I've paid the last '*fools' pence*' I shall put down on this counter for many a long day."

George Manly hastened home. His wife and his two little girls were sitting at work. They were thin and pale, really for want of food. The room looked very cheerless, and their fire was so small that its warmth was scarcely felt; yet the commonest observer must have been struck by the neatness and cleanliness of the apartment and every thing about it.

"This is indeed a treat, girls, to have dear father home so soon to-night," said Susan Manly, looking up at her husband as he stood before the table, turning his eyes first upon one and then upon another of the little party: then throwing himself into a chair, and smiling, he said,

"Well, children, a'n't you glad to see me? May not those busy little fingers stop a moment, just while you jump up and throw your arms about your father's neck, and kiss him?"

"O yes, we have time for that," said one of the girls, as they both sprang up to kiss their father.

"But we have no time to lose, dear father," said Sally, pressing her cheek to his, and speaking in a kind of coaxing whisper close to his ear, "for these shirts are the last of the dozen we have been making for Mr. Farley, in the Corn-market."

"And as no work can be done to-morrow," added Betsy gravely, who stood with her little hand in her father's, "we are all working as hard as we can; for mother has promised to take them home on Monday afternoon."

"Either your eyes are very weak to-night, dear wife," said George, "or you have been crying. I'm afraid you work too hard by candlelight."

Susan smiled, and said, "*Working* does not hurt my eyes," and as she spoke, she turned her head and beckoned with her finger to her little boy.

"Why, John, what's this that I see?" said his father. "What, you in the corner! Come out, and tell me what you have been doing."

"Nay, never mind it, dear husband; John will be very good, I hope, and we had better say no more about what is past."

"Yes, but I must know," said he, drawing John close to him. "Come, tell me what has been the matter."

John was a plain-spoken boy, and had a straight-forward way of speaking the truth. He came up to his father, and looked full in his face, and said, "The baker came for his money to-night, and would not leave the loaves without mother paid for them; and though he was cross and rough to mother, he said it was not her fault, and that he was sure you had been drinking away all the money; and when he was gone, mother cried over her work, but she did not say any thing. I did not know she was crying, till I saw her tears fall, drop, drop, on her hands; and then I said bad words, and mother sent me to stand in the corner."

"And now, John, you may bring me some coal," said Susan; "there's a fine lump in the coal-box."

"But first tell me what your bad words were, John," said his father; "not swearing, I hope?"

"No," said John, coloring, but speaking as bluntly as before, "I said that you were a bad man. I said, bad father."

"And they were bad words, I am sure," said Susan, very calmly; "but you are forgiven, and so you may get me the coal."

George looked at the face of his wife, and as he met the tender gaze of her mild eyes now turned to him, he felt the tears rise in his own. He rose up, and as he put the money into his wife's hands, he said, "There are my week's wages. Come, come, hold out both hands, for you have not got all yet. Well, now you have every farthing. Keep the whole, and lay it out to the best advantage, as you always do. I hope this will be a beginning of better doings on my part, and happier days on yours; and now put on your bonnet, and I'll walk with you to pay the baker, and buy a bushel or two of coal, or any thing else you may be in want of; and when we come back I'll read a chapter of the Bible to you and the girls, while you get on with the needle-work."

Susan went up stairs to put on her bonnet and shawl, and she remained a little longer, to kneel down on the spot where she had often knelt almost heart-broken in prayer—prayer that her heavenly Father would turn her husband's heart, first to his Saviour, and then to his wife and children; and that, in the meantime, he would give her patience. She knelt down this time to pour out her heart in thanksgiving and praise. The pleasant tones of her husband's voice called her from her knees.

George Manly told his wife that evening, after the children were gone to bed, that when he saw what the pence of the poor could do towards keeping up a fine house, and dressing out the landlord's wife and daughters; and when he thought of his own hard-working, uncomplaining Susan, and his children in want, and almost in rags, while he was sitting drinking, and drinking, night after night, more like a beast than a man, destroying his own manly strength, and the fine health God had given him, he was so struck with sorrow and shame, that he seemed to come to himself at last. He made his determination, from that hour, never again to put the intoxicating glass to his lips, and he hoped he made it in dependence upon God for grace and strength to keep it.

It was more than a year after Mrs. Crowder, of the Punch-bowl, had first missed a regular customer from her house, and when she had forgotten to express her wonder as to what could have become of the good-looking carpenter that generally spent his earnings there, and drank and spent his money so freely—

"There, get on as fast as you can, dears; run, girls, and don't stop for me, your beautiful dresses will be quite spoilt; never mind me, for my levantine is a French silk, and won't spot."

These words were screamed out as loud as her haste would permit, by Mrs. Crowder, who was accompanying her daughters, one Sunday evening, to the tea-gardens.

She was answered by Miss Lucy, "You know, ma, we can't run, for our shoes are so tight."

"Then turn into one of these houses, dears," said the mother, who was bustling forward as fast as she could.

"No, indeed," replied the other daughter, who found time to curl her lip with disdain, notwithstanding her haste and her distress, "I'll not set a foot in such filthy hovels."

"Well, dears, here is a comfortable, tidy place," cried the mother at length, as they hastened forward; "here I'll enter, nor will I stir till the rain is over; come in, girls, come in. You might eat off these boards, they are so clean."

The rain was now coming down in torrents, and the two young ladies gladly followed their mother's example, and entered the neat and cleanly dwelling. Their long hair hung dangling about their ears, their crape bonnets had been screened in vain by their fringed parasols, and the skirts of their silk gowns were draggled with mud. They all three began to stamp upon the floor of the room into which they had entered with very little ceremony; but the good-natured mistress of the house felt more for their disaster than for her floor, and came forward at once to console and assist them. She brought forth clean cloths from the dresser-drawer, and she and her two daughters set to work to wipe off, with quick and delicate care, the rain-drops and mud-splashes from the silken dresses of the three fine ladies. The crape hats and the parasols were carefully dried at a safe distance from the fire, and a comb was offered to arrange the uncurled hair, such a white and delicately clean comb as may seldom be seen upon a poor woman's toilet.

When all had been done that could be done, and, as Miss Lucy said, "they began to look themselves again," Mrs. Crowder, who was lolling back at her ease in a large and comfortable arm-chair, and amusing herself by taking a good stare at every thing and every one in the room, suddenly started forward, and cried out, addressing herself to the master of the house, upon whose Bible and at whose face she had been last fixing her gaze, "Why, my good man, we are old friends: I know your face, I'm certain; still, there is some change in you, though I can't exactly say what it is."

"I used to be in ragged clothes, and out of health," said George Manly, smiling, as he looked up from his Bible; "I am now, blessed be God for it, comfortably clad, and in excellent health."

"But how is it," said Mrs. Crowder, "that we never catch a sight of you now?"

"Madam," said he, "I'm sure I wish well to you and all people; nay, I have reason to thank you, for words of yours were the first means of opening my eyes to my own foolish and sinful course. You seem to thrive—so do we. My wife and children were half-naked and half-starved only this time last year. Look at them, if you please, now; for, so far as sweet, contented looks go, and decent raiment befitting their station, I'll match them with any man's wife and children. And now, madam, I tell you, as you told a friend of yours one day last year, that ''tis the FOOLS' PENCE which have done all this for us.' The fools' pence! I ought to say, the pence earned by honest industry, and spent in such a manner that I can ask the blessing of God upon the pence."

When Mrs. Crowder and her daughters were gone, George Manly sat without speaking for some considerable time. He was deep in thought, and his gentle, pious wife felt that she knew on what subject he had been thinking so deeply; for when he woke up from his fit of thought, a deep sigh stole from his lips, and he brushed away the tears which had filled his eyes.

"Susan," he said, "what can I render to the Lord for all his goodness to me? From what a fearful depth of ruin have I been snatched! Once I met some of my old companions, who so set upon me to draw me to drink with them, that I thought Satan must have urged them on. Another time, I went walking on, and found myself at the door of the poison-shop, without knowing how I got there; but God gave me strength to turn instantly away, and not linger a moment to dally with temptation.

"I could not help thinking, as I was reading this holy book, when that showy dame came in from whose hand I so often took the poisonous cup, how much I owed to God for saving me from ruin, and giving me that peace and satisfaction in religion which I now enjoy; and making me, I hope, a blessing to you all. O, what a love was the love of Christ to poor sinners! He gave his own blood as our precious ransom; he came to save us from our sins, that we may serve him in newness of life."

The above history, which is taken from a Tract of the Religious Tract Society in London, has its counterpart in the case of multitudes in our own country. Let him who would not shorten his days, and make his family wretched, and ruin his own soul, resolve with George Manly, "*never again to put the intoxicating glass to his lips*;" and like him, let him go humbly and with childlike confidence to God for strength to keep his resolution, and for grace to pardon all his sins, through the blood and righteousness of Christ. Then shall he have peace of mind, and be a blessing in his day; and when this brief life is ended, he shall enter into eternal joy.

PUBLISHED BY THE AMERICAN TRACT SOCIETY.

THE

POOR MAN'S HOUSE REPAIRED;

OR,

THE WRETCHED MADE HAPPY.

A NARRATIVE OF FACTS.

For fifteen years of my married life I was as miserable as any woman could be. Our house was the picture of wretchedness externally, and it looked still more wretched within. The windows were patched, the walls shattered, the furniture defaced and broken, and every thing was going to ruins.

It had not always been so: once my home was happy, and I used to take much pleasure and some pride in hearing the neighbors say, "How neat and trim neighbor N——'s house always looks!" But they could not say so long.

One thing after another changed. Our table was no longer spread with comfortable food, nor surrounded with cheerful faces; but there were scanty meals, sour looks, and loud and angry words; while, do the best I could, I was not able to conceal the tatters of my own and my children's clothing. My husband is a mechanic; his employment is good, and he might have made his family as happy as any family in the place; but he was in the habit of taking ardent spirit every day. *He* thought it did him good; *I* knew it did not, for I found him every day more and more unkind. Our comforts, one by one, were stripped away, till at last I saw myself the wife of a confirmed drunkard.

I well remember, one evening, I was sitting by the fire, mending my poor boy's tattered jacket. My heart was very sad. I had been thinking of the happy evenings I had spent with my husband before our marriage; of the few pleasant years that succeeded; of the misery that then came; of the misery yet to come; and for me there seemed no ray of hope or comfort. My husband was a terror to his family, and a nuisance to the neighborhood; my children were idle, ragged, and disobedient; myself a heart-broken wife and wretched mother. While I thought of all this, I could no longer retain my composure, but, dropping my work, I leaned my head upon my hand and wept bitterly. My husband had been absent all day, and I was now expecting him home every minute. It was growing late, so I wiped away my tears as well as I could, and put the embers together, to make my fireside look as inviting as possible. But I dreaded my husband's return—his sharp voice and bitter words pained me to the heart, and rougher treatment than all this I often experienced from him who had once been to me all that I could wish.

At length the door opened, and Robert entered. I saw by his flushed countenance and angry expression that I had better remain silent; so, with a sinking heart, I placed a chair for him by the fire, and continued my work without speaking.

Robert broke silence, and in a sharp tone said, "What

on earth do you sit there for, at work on that dirty rag? Why don't you give me something to eat?" and snatching the work roughly from my hands, he threw it into the fire. I sprang forward to rescue my poor child's garment, and so quick were my movements, that I saved it from much injury. But while I was shaking the ashes from it, my husband again snatched it from my hands, and with a terrible oath, defying me to touch it, once more threw it into the fire. I was afraid to attempt to save it; so I turned away, with bitter feelings to see my labor all lost, and my destitute child made still more destitute by its father's hand. But, as patiently and kindly as I could, I set before Robert the supper I had prepared for him. It did not look very inviting, to be sure; but I could offer nothing more. He swore he would not taste a particle. I now reproached him for not having provided any thing better for myself and children. But this was no time for reproach. Robert's anger rose to the highest pitch. He dashed the cup and plate I had placed for him to the floor, and seizing me roughly by the arm, he opened the door, and forcing me from the dwelling, bid me enter again, if I dared. The night was cold and windy. I was thinly dressed, and even ill. But I forbore to take refuge under a neighbor's roof. My heart was too sad and desolate to admit of human consolation. At this sorrowful moment I remembered that

> "Earth hath no sorrow that heaven cannot heal;"

so, falling almost unconsciously upon my knees, I prayed that God would comfort my stricken heart; that my sins might be pardoned; that I might be enabled to repose all my griefs in the bosom of that gracious One who has kindly promised to give the heavy-laden rest. I then prayed for my miserable husband, that God would have mercy upon him, and deliver him from his dreadful delusion before it was too late. I prayed, too, for my poor children, with all the fervor of a mother's soul. This was the first prayer I had offered for years; for I had been an impenitent woman. Had I prayed sooner, I might have saved myself much sorrow and distress. But as it was, I arose from my knees with feelings far less hopeless and bitter. I then crept back to the house, and on looking in at the window, I found that Robert had fallen asleep; so I opened the door quietly, without disturbing his heavy slumbers, and laid myself down to rest.

The events of this evening were no uncommon events to me. Each succeeding day brought but the same rough treatment, the same wretchedness and want. Robert grew worse and worse. He not only destroyed all our peace, but brought noise and discord into the whole neighborhood, till at last, for the sake of quiet, he was taken to the house of correction. I never can forget that dreadful night when he was carried away. He came home shockingly intoxicated. The little children crept into the farthest corner of the house to shield themselves from his fury. He threatened every thing with destruction. I was in danger of my life, and ran for safety into the nearest house, where a poor widow lived. Robert followed—we fastened the door—he swore he would set fire to the building, and burn it over our heads. But some one passing by heard the uproar, and went for the town officers. Several of them came, just as my infatuated husband was pelting the window with stones. They took him away by force, while he was uttering the most shocking oaths. I sat down and wept with shame and vexation. My little Jane put her arm round my neck, and said, "Don't cry, ma—he has gone—wicked pa has gone, and I hope he will never come back—he is so cross, and beats us so." I hardly knew what to say in answer to my little girl, but I felt that it was a dreadful thing to have my children speak so of him whom I would gladly have taught them to love and honor.

I determined, now my husband was away, to support my family by my own work; for wretched as my home was, I could not bear to leave it and come upon the town. I could not earn much, for my health was feeble, but I managed, by depriving myself of several meals, to save enough to mend my poor neighbor's window.

But Robert longed to regain his liberty. He resolved that he would do better, and upon promising orderly conduct, was permitted to return to his family. Badly as he had treated me, I was glad to see him back again. He looked humble, and spoke to me kindly. He kissed the younger children, too, and for a while every thing went on smoothly. To me it seemed like the dawning of better days, and when Robert one evening brought home some new shoes for our oldest boy, and a new gown for my little Jane, I actually wept for joy, and Jane said, her "wicked pa had come back very good."

But these bright days were not to last. Darker ones came, darker than I had ever known before, or perhaps they seemed darker, from the transient sunshine that had gleamed upon us. I again heard my children crying for food, when I had no food to give them. I was again often turned from my dwelling, or, if I offered any resistance, was forced to receive harsh words and cruel blows. But it is in vain to tell all I suffered. Many have gone through the same fiery trial, and will feel that a recital of my woes is but a recital of what they too have borne.

There was one privilege, the want of which I at this time felt deeply. The village church was within sight of our door. I used to hear the bell ring, and see the children of the neighborhood go by, neatly dressed, to the Sabbath-school; but I had no gown, nor bonnet, nor shawl fit to wear, and my children were still more destitute than myself. So we were obliged to spend the Sabbath in sadness at home, while Robert, if the day was fine, would profane it by going on the water to fish, or would linger with his companions round the door of the grogshop—not to enter, it is true; for the dram-seller, with his wife and children, dressed very fine, and were accustomed to attend church; and but for that dreadful shop, I might have gone there too.

Our minister was one of those who thought it his duty to "reason on temperance," as well as "righteousness," and "judgment to come;" and through his exertions, and the exertions of other good men, a reform had commenced, which gave great encouragement to the friends of human happiness and virtue. Temperance-meetings were held once a month in different parts of the town, and in spite of much opposition, and many prophecies to the contrary, the cause went on.

I heard much said about these meetings, and resolved to attend the next; so, when the evening came, I borrowed a cloak and bonnet of one of the neighbors, and hastened to the church. The prayers I there heard did my wounded spirit good, and the plain, impressive language of the minister spoke to my very heart. I resolved to persuade my husband, if possible, to go with me when there should be another meeting.

A circumstance occurred about this time that quite destroyed my remaining courage, and almost caused me to give Robert up for lost. We lived in a small, shabby-looking house, a part of which he rented to a very poor family. They could not pay the rent immediately upon its being due. It was in the depth of winter, and the poor woman had a little infant, not more than two weeks old. But Robert's heart was shut to all kind feelings. One very stormy day he drove the whole family out of doors, and they were obliged to seek some other dwelling. It was too much for the poor woman in her feeble state. She caught a severe cold, and died in a few days. After this heartless act, my faith quite failed me, and I felt as if nothing could recall my husband to a sense of duty. But I little knew the workings of his mind. He seemed to return a little to his senses, when he saw that his cruelty had probably caused the death of the poor woman, and rendered a large family of helpless children motherless. His countenance became more dark and gloomy, and he scarcely raised his eyes to notice any one.

Things were in this state, when one day our minister called, as he was visiting the people of his parish. I was very glad to see him, and told him all my griefs freely. He gave me what consolation he could, and informed me that there was another temperance-meeting in the evening, which he hoped I would attend; "and," added he, "bring your husband along with you, if you can persuade him to come."

When Robert came home to supper, I was surprised and delighted to find him sober; so I told him of the minister's visit, and the meeting in the evening. He seemed pleased that the minister had called, and even asked me how things looked about the room, "for," said he, "we don't look quite so stylish here as we once did, Mary."

"No, Robert," said I, with a sigh, as I surveyed the wretched apartment; "but if you would attend the temperance-meeting, and hear what the minister says about saving money, I think it would soon look much better here, and the boys might have better jackets, and I might have a better gown. Oh, Robert"—

I would have said more, but my eyes filled with tears, and I could not. Robert hung down his head, and looked ashamed. He knew he had spent, for rum, money enough to feed and clothe his family well. I thought he had half a mind to tell me he would go with me. When I had cleared away the supper, and sent the children to bed, I put on my bonnet, and said, "I will just step into neighbor Warren's, and borrow Nancy's cloak."

"Have not you any cloak of your own?" said he.

"No," I replied, "I have been without one a long time."

Robert said no more, but when I came back with the cloak, and said to him, "Will you go with me?" he said, in a tone which seemed as if he were trying to suppress kinder feelings, "Go along, Mary, and don't be always fretting about me." I was grieved, but said nothing, and proceeded to the meeting alone, praying that Robert might think better of it, and come. The services were even more interesting than they had been at the preceding meeting. The minister said every thing to convince, and I felt a distressing anxiety, that I could not control, to have my husband hear all that was said. Judge, then, of my surprise and pleasure, when, a short time after I had returned home, Robert entered, and said, "Guess where I have been, Mary."

"Not to meeting, Robert."

"Yes, Mary, to meeting. I took up my hat after you had gone, thinking that I would go down to the shop; for I felt uneasy, and wanted something to suppress my disagreeable thoughts. But as I passed by the meeting-house, it was so well lighted up, and the bell was ringing, and the people going in, I thought perhaps I had better go in too; and I am glad I did. Wife, I do believe the minister is right. I know that hard drinking has been the ruin of myself and family, and while the minister was speaking, I thought I would try to break away from my bad habits."

"O, Robert, *will you try?*" I exclaimed, while my heart beat with pleasure to hear him thus speak.

"'Tis hard work, Mary, harder than you think for."

"I know it is hard, my dear husband; but only think of the happiness it would bring to us all—of the ruin from which it will save our little boys—the agony from which it will save your poor wife. O, Robert, if you have one spark of love remaining in your bosom for any of us"—

I could not go on; but leaning my hands upon my husband's shoulder, I sobbed aloud.

Robert seemed affected, and said, in a doubtful tone, "Perhaps I might leave it off by degrees."

"O no, Robert, no," I answered, "that will never do. Don't you remember how particular the minister was to say, '*Leave it off at once?*' You will never do it by degrees."

Robert looked steadily into the fire, and did not say one word more. When not under the influence of strong drink, he is a man of good sense, and I thought it better to leave him to his own reflections. I know not what passed through his mind. The kinder and better feelings of other days seemed to be awakened from their slumber, or rather, He from whom "all just thoughts and holy desires proceed," was influencing his determination. As for myself, I longed in secret to pour out my soul to God. So I went into the bedroom, where my poor children were fast asleep; and after seeing that they were well covered up, I kissed each one of them, and knelt down by their side to offer up my prayer. I prayed as I had never done before. I seemed, through my Redeemer, to gain a nearer and bolder access to the throne of grace. My heart was filled with deep gratitude, penitence, humility, and joy; and from that hour I have dared to hope myself a child of God. O that blessed, blessed night. It caused joy among the angels in heaven, over the reconciliation of one soul to God—over the desire of another soul to return to the path of duty. It caused joy on earth, in our poor, humble dwelling—joy in the bosom of the long-afflicted wife—joy that her own soul was trusting in Christ—joy that her husband was purposing to forsake his wretched way, and turn into a happier, better path.

The next day, before Robert went out, I encouraged him all I could to persevere. I brought to his remembrance as much of the lecture as I could, so that it might be fresh in his mind. He left me in good spirits, and promised to see me again at night a sober man. But O, what an anxious day was it for me! I dreaded, and yet longed for evening to come, and my heart beat as I heard his footstep at the door. But he had kept his word—he had not tasted a drop of spirit during the day. He had seen, too, the minister and several members of the Temperance Society. In consequence of the meeting on the last evening, many new names were added to the temperance list, and they had promised, in case of entire abstinence till the next meeting, to receive his. I could scarcely believe my senses when I heard my husband speak thus, and the prospect of his becoming a sober man seemed too delightful to be ever realized. For a time, I rejoiced with trembling; but when, day after day, I saw him return orderly and quiet, my courage revived, and I felt that he *would persevere.*

At length the evening came round for the next meeting, and my husband and myself went, O so happy! and put our names to the pledge. What a different prospect did our home now present. I could not keep my countenance for joy, when the neighbors came in to congratulate me on the change. I could now dress my children neat and comfortable, and send them to the Sabbath-school. I went myself with my husband constantly to church, and on making known my wish to our minister, publicly professed my faith in the Saviour of sinners. Thus happily did the winter and summer pass away. One day in autumn, as the minister was passing by, my husband was in the road in front of the house.

The minister remarked, "I am glad, Robert, to see your *house repaired* and looking so well."

"Thank you, sir; why, it does look some better." As the minister was about to pass on, Robert added, "Mr. G., I have not drank a drop of rum for one year, come next Monday. So you see the effect upon my house. I used to work hard before, and spent about all I earned for rum, to drink myself, or to give away. Many a time I have been at my work on a Sunday, and earned a dollar or more in the course of the day, and taken the money, and then laid out the whole in rum. Now I can clothe my family well, and have something to lay out upon my house. Last summer, my boy and I saved sixty dollars besides supporting the family."

Sixty dollars saved! But who can tell the value of the happy days and nights of this year; or the worth of a kind, sober, industrious husband and father, compared with a cross, cruel, and drunken one? Ask the wife; what would she tell you? Ask the children; what would be their answer?

Some of my husband's former wicked companions felt piqued and envious that Robert was free from their degrading habit. They saw him thriving, respected, and happy. His life and prospects were a continued reflection upon theirs. They longed to see him fall, and determined, if possible, to effect his ruin. As he was quietly returning home one evening, he passed by the shop which he was once so much in the habit of frequenting. They accosted him: by taunts and jeers which he had not firmness enough to resist, they drew him into their company. Once there, they thought him within their power. When they could not induce him to violate his pledge by taking rum, they called him a "cold-water man;" "a white-livered coward;" "priest-ridden;" "afraid of his minister," and many other titles of reproach. They then told him he had not promised to drink no wine; and, after much persuasion, they induced him to take a glass. But in this glass they had mingled the poison. Once stimulated, he called for more and yet more, till these wretches had the pleasure of seeing him who had so long stood firm, reeling from the shop, to mar at once all that was pleasant and peaceful at home. When my husband did not return at supper-time, I felt rather anxious, but thought he might be delayed, as he sometimes is; so I put his supper to the fire and sat down to my knitting-work, while one of the boys read to me from his Sabbath-school book.

We were thus employed when my deluded husband entered. O the agony of that moment! Had he been brought to me a corpse, I could not have been more shocked. Had those wicked men that thus seduced my husband entered my house and done the same things that they caused him to do, they might have been indicted for the outrage. In the morning Robert had come to himself; but he saw in the broken furniture, in the distrustful looks of the children, in the swollen eyes and distressed countenance of his wife, more than he cared to know. There was a mixture of remorse and obstinacy in his looks, and when he left me for the morning, instead of his usual "Good-morning, Mary," he shut the door roughly after him and hurried away.

When evening came again, Robert returned to the shop, and asked for a glass of rum. He wanted something to stifle the keen reproaches of conscience. The dram-seller knew my husband, knew of his reform, that from being a nuisance to the town, he had become an orderly and respectable citizen; and now that he had been seduced from the right way, instead of denying him the cause of all our former misery—instead of a little friendly advice—with his *usual courteous smile*, he put the fatal glass into his hand.

For a time my poor Robert continued in a very bad way. He mingled again with his profane and wicked associates; he was ashamed to see his minister, and took no notice of him when he passed; hung down his head when he met any of his temperance friends, and seemed to be fast returning to his former miserable habits.

But he was not thus to become the dupe of wicked and designing men. His wife's prayers and tears were not thus to be of no avail. On a sudden he awoke from his delusion. He had lived a whole year without rum; and though exposed to all weathers, he knew his health had been better, his head clearer, his nerves firmer, his purse heavier, and his home happier. He called one evening to see the President of the Temperance Society; confessed his weakness in yielding to temptation; asked the forgiveness of the Society; requested to have his name, which had been erased from the temperance list, renewed; and promised never again to violate the pledge. Since that night my husband has continued a perfectly temperate man. No temptation has ever led him again to violate his pledge.

I have been induced to give this history of his reform to the world, in order, if possible, to persuade others to follow his example, to show them *how* quiet and plenty were restored to a wretched dwelling, virtue and respectability to a ruined family, and the *poor man's house repaired.*

A clergyman, worthy of all confidence, and acquainted with the writer of the above, and the circumstances detailed, testifies, that the case is "literally and faithfully described."

JAMIE;

OR,

A VOICE FROM IRELAND FOR TEMPERANCE.

A TRUE NARRATIVE.

BY PROFESSOR EDGAR,

OF BELFAST.

In a populous and civilized district of Ulster lived Jamie, a day-laborer; a fellow of right good sense and practical talent, carpenter and mason, shoemaker and blacksmith, and aught else the case required. The variety of his powers had nearly ruined him. On all hands he was in requisition, and everywhere he was a favorite—kindness flowing to him in its common channel, spirituous liquor. Wherever he went, he was *treated.* This was too much for flesh and blood, and Jamie became, in the style of the world's false charity, "fond of the drop." His cash flew to the spirit-shop, and brought neither health nor happiness in return. The neighbors called him—alas, for such lullabies to conscience!—an honest, good-hearted fellow, who did nobody any harm but himself. While, however, they tempted, and flattered, and deceived, their victim was posting to ruin.

But, while moderate drinkers were training him to drunkenness, God was raising up the Temperance Society as an ark of safety to him from the flood of their temptations. One of the publications of the Ulster Temperance

Society fell into his hands, and he read it, for he was of an inquiring spirit, and a blessing attended it. What, said he, in amazement, can this be true?—distilled spirits of no more use to any man in health than arsenic or opium? "Distilled spirits are too tempting, and dangerous, and violently intoxicating, to be used as a common beverage at all!" O, thought he, that at least is true. "Distilled spirits are in their very nature injurious to the human constitution; and every man who indulges even in their moderate use, injures himself in proportion to the quantity which he consumes." Jamie was astonished, and well he might be; but Jamie was conscientious, and though he had the manhood to confess, what few moderate drinkers will, that he liked a glass, yet, because he had still a conscience, notwithstanding the searing it had got from the fiery drink, he said to himself, "I must, at least, *try* whether these wonderful statements respecting distilled spirits be true." James *tried*, and the effects were delightful. In a very short time he found, from happy experience, that his health was better from the change; that his purse was better; that soul and body, the whole man of him was far better, in all respects, since he renounced the maddening draught.

His duty was now clear before him—to *abstain* from the raging drink which, in time past, had been emptying his pocket, destroying his character, and bringing down his body to the grave, and his soul to hell. He did his duty in the right way for doing duty—*at once*, and *right on*.

He saw, however, that something more was incumbent on him than merely doing his duty in this particular—he must, for the good of others, let it be known, without ostentation, that his duty was done. Abstaining, he said to himself, has done me good; the banishment of spirituous liquors would do my country good; what is every man's duty is my duty; and therefore, in love to my brethren, I'll freely give the blessing which to me has been so freely given. Union is strength, thought he: separate efforts are a rope of sand; united, they are the cable which holds the mighty ship. He resolved to establish a Temperance Society.

For this purpose, he supplied himself *immediately* with a number of Tracts on temperance; for Jamie knew that when self-interest or passion come in, second thoughts are not always best; and forthwith he commenced travelling around, reading them, at spare hours throughout the neighborhood, wherever he could find half-a-dozen people to listen to him. He was a good reader, and very soon found that his reading was not without effect; for in a short time he heard of a decent woman telling her neighbor to send for Jamie to the wake which was to be held in her house, if she wished to save her whiskey, and have peace and quietness; for, said she, he came to the wake in my house, and read and talked about temperance, till both the whiskey and the people seemed either persuaded or frightened, for hardly one had the courage to put to his lips what Jamie called, indeed too truly, "the accursed thing."

Jamie, however, soon found to his cost that he had commenced a very great and a very sore work. The spirit-sellers, four of whom were at a single cross-roads in his neighborhood, he expected to be against him, and drunkards he expected would be against him too; but he soon found that his chief opponents lay in quite another quarter. Sensible people soon began to see that spirit-sellers are drones on the community, doing no good, but much harm: and, besides, one of them having first allowed a temperance meeting to be held in his barn, conscientiously shut up his spirit-shop, and joined the Temperance Society, being convinced that spirit-selling is poison-selling, and that each spirit-shop might justly have on its sign-board, "Beggars made here." Of the drunkards, some indeed did call him hard names, and impute to him base motives; but from among even these, lost as they seemed to be to all hope, he was, by God's grace, enabled to reclaim some, as brands snatched from the burning, while others of them said to him, in the bitterness of their reflecting moments, Go on, Jamie, your work is God's work. Had you commenced but a little sooner, what a blessing might your Society have been to us; but alas, it is all over with us now!

What at first surprised Jamie much was, that the fathers or husbands of these very drunkards were his most bitter opponents. He went to them with a glad heart, expecting that they would hear with delight of a plan by which drunkards, in great numbers, have been reclaimed, and by which the temperate can be effectually secured against temptation; but his heart sunk when he found, not that they received him coldly, for to such receptions he was accustomed, but that they, as well as others who boast much of being "temperate enough already," lost all temper at the very sound of temperance.

Some of these neighbors of Jamie were regular in attendance on public worship, orthodox and strict, which gave them an influence in the neighborhood. Jamie, therefore, was anxious to enlist them on the side of temperance. Yet he could not but know, and very seriously consider, that whether, in market or fair, these same men either bought or sold, there could be no such thing as a *dry* bargain; that at *churns*, and wakes, and funerals, and marriages, and such like, they always pushed round the bottle cheerily; that they held it churlish to refuse either to give or take a treat; that at their evening tea-parties it was not uncommon for six or eight gallons of spirituous liquor to be consumed by a few neighbors, men and women, in a single night; that in every house which their minister visited, the bottle was put to his mouth; and that as the natural consequence of all this and far more, not only was the crime of drunkenness, whether in minister or private layman, treated with much false charity, and called by many soft names, but drunkenness was spreading its ravages through many families, and bringing down many heads in sorrow to the grave.

Jamie was indeed charitable, but he was unable to persuade himself that, amid such universal drinking, all the objections to his Temperance Society arose merely from ignorance, or prejudice, or conscience; and therefore, when people were telling him, as they often did, that they cared not a rush about spirituous liquor, "they could either drink it or let it alone," he used sometimes to reply, "Oh, I know well enough that you can drink it; what I want to know is, whether you can let it alone:" and at other times he would tell them Dean Swift's story of the three men who called for whiskey in a spirit-shop: I want a glass, said the first, for I'm very hot; I want a glass, said the second, for I'm very cold; let me have a glass, said the third, because I like it!

As Jamie's opponents were no match for him in argument, they tried the plans usually resorted to when the wisdom and the spirit by which truth speaks cannot be resisted. For a while they tried ridicule. That, however, neither satisfied their own consciences nor frightened Jamie, for Jamie could stand a laugh, what many a man can't do who has stood grape-shot. Then they circulated reports about his having got drunk on different occasions, and having been caught drinking in secret; and some believed them, being of the same mind with the distiller, who asserted it to be mere humbug that any man could live without whiskey, and that wherever the croaking cold water society men did not drink in the daytime, they made up for it by drinking at night. These evil reports, however, fell dead after a little, and nobody was vile enough to take them up again; and though attempts were made to circulate the lie, that Jamie had grown weak and sickly since he gave up drinking, yet every body who looked him in the face saw, that though he had neither a purple nose nor whiskey blossoms on his chin, yet he was stronger and healthier than ever; and that he could say, what every member of the Temperance Society, whether temperate or intemperate formerly, can say with truth, after abstaining for a single month from distilled spirits, that in every sense of the word he is better for the change.

Foiled thus in all their attempts, the opponents of Jamie and of temperance rallied strong for one last charge ; and as it was against Jamie's weak side—who has not a weak side?—they already chuckled in triumph. Jamie had thrown away his glass for ever, but his pipe stuck firm between his teeth still. The time was, when he was strong and well without tobacco, and when the taste of tobacco was disgusting and sickening to him ; but respectable people were smoking, and chewing, and snuffing around him, and when he went to the wake, the funeral, or the evening gathering, "Why," thought he, "should I be singular, and not take a whiff like the rest?" He chose smoking, probably, because he considered it to be the most *genteel* way of being dirty and disgusting; and, according to the general law of habits, being most inveterate where the article used was at first most nauseous, he soon became so confirmed a smoker that one-half of what he smoked would have kept him decently clothed.

The lovers of strong drink, therefore, thought that they had Jamie on the hip completely, when they told him that his only reason for giving up whiskey was, that he could not afford to buy both it and tobacco; and promised, though with no sincerity, that they would quit drinking if he would quit smoking.

The reproach stuck like a burr to Jamie's conscience. He asked himself again and again, Is my use of tobacco a stumbling-block in the way of any? Does it do injury to the great cause which has all my heart? He read, he thought, and read and thought again; and the more he read and thought, the more was he convinced that the habitual use of tobacco in any of its forms is useless ; is wasteful of time and money; is dirty; is offensive to others, and a breach of Christian charity; is a bad example to the simple and young; is a temptation to drunkenness, and injurious to health. He resolved to renounce it, and flung the old black pipe from him to lift it again no more. Thus Jamie was conqueror still; and his victory was one which Alexander, the conqueror of the world, could not gain. Jamie gained a victory over himself, and he that ruleth over his own spirit is better than he that taketh a city; but Alexander, who wept because he had not other worlds besides his own to subdue, died as a fool dieth, and sleeps in a drunkard's grave.

Jamie learned an important lesson in his victory, which will be of use to him as long as he lives. Whatever bad habit, he says, has got hold upon you, *break it off at once.* Would you pull your child out of the fire cautiously and gradually; or would you out with him at once? So let it be with every thing wrong. Don't prepare for ceasing from sin to-morrow, or next year, but cease from it *now.* Do so yourself; go right up to your neighbor without fear, and in love tell him to do the same, having this assurance on your mind continually, that *what ought to be done, can be done.*

Jamie seemed from the commencement, to have taken for his motto, Expect great things, work for them, and you shall have them. Work as though all depended on self; pray as knowing all to depend upon God. He knew his place, and modestly kept it; yet when opportunity offered for dropping a word on behalf of temperance, in the ear either of clergyman or layman, whatever his rank, he did what conscience told him was right towards a neighbor and a brother. Jamie's pockets and hat were filled with tracts, which, as the most suitable plan for his shallow purse, and perhaps, too, for securing a reading of them, he generally lent, and sometimes gave away, to all who promised to read.

Let it not be supposed that amidst such active benevolence he neglected his own business. No; Jamie had not learned in vain the apostle's maxim, "Let him labor, working with his hands the thing which is good, that he may have to give to him that needeth." It was nothing for him to start off half a dozen miles of an evening after his work was finished, to procure some new tracts, or attend a temperance-meeting, or read and talk kindly to some poor drunkard, whose wife had sent him a hint that her husband would be glad to see him; or else to procure the services of some clergyman to address the next meeting of his Temperance Society. Jamie is one of those who imagine that the business of a minister of the Gospel is not finished when he has preached a couple of discourses on the Sabbath; he really presumes to say, that both minister and layman should be "instant in season and out of season," and like their great Master, going about continually doing good. He does not set up for a preacher, nevertheless, but confines himself to his own proper sphere. He applied to ministers to address his meetings, and though some few of them refused, telling him significantly that they preach the Gospel, even when Jamie did ask in his simplicity, if Paul forgot his resolution to know nothing but Christ and him crucified, when he reasoned of righteousness, *temperance*, and judgment to come; yet to the honor of the ministry around him be it told, that whenever he got up a meeting, a minister was at Jamie's service to address it.

Though, as a body, Jamie's Temperance Society was most steady, yet a few, and only a few, fell. It would be harsh to say that some were glad at their fall; at least many temptations were thrown in their way; and when they fell, a shout of triumph was raised against the Temperance Society. Such trials as these only urged Jamie on with fresh vigor.

Suppose, he used to say, that every drunkard should return again to drunkenness and ruin; would not this be another proof that truth, and honor, and principle, are all as nothing before the drunken appetite? Would not this be a louder and a stronger call to save the young, to stop young sons and daughters, now safe, from filling the place of drunken parents when they are gone? What ruins these poor wretches? he would ask. Is it the mere *abuse* of a good and wholesome thing? No. Distilled spirits are tempting, deceitful, and too violently intoxicating to be at all habitually used with safety; and as four hundred of the ablest doctors now living have established, and unnumbered facts prove, they are unwholesome and injurious to body and soul. Let every man, then, for his own sake abstain; and for the sake of others too, especially such as are near and dear to him, O let him abstain for ever.

Who, he would ask, give currency and influence to the absurd fooleries which are circulated respecting the marvellous excellences of spirituous liquors, while common-sense tells that they are of no more use to a man than to a cow or horse? Not drunkards, surely; for, on such a subject at least, they would not be believed. Who give support and respectability to spirit-shops, and the whole spirit-trade? Drunkards surely could make nothing respectable, and no spirit-seller would put on his sign-board, "The drunkard's spirit-shop." Again, he would put it to men's consciences to answer, who give respectability and permanence to all the *treatings* and other customs by which each successive generation of drunkards is trained? There was no getting over the undeniable fact, that moderate spirit-drinkers must bear the responsibility of all this; and the more the matter was canvassed, the more clearly was it seen, that the only way in which drunkenness can be put down is the very way which Jamie and the Temperance Society proposed—*the union of the temperate in refraining from intoxicating drinks, and promoting temperance.*

To *parents* Jamie addressed himself with unwearied and anxious importunity. Would you object, he would say to them, when other arguments had failed—would you object to your son becoming a member when going away from you to live, perhaps, amidst the temptations of a large town? Would you be afraid, lest keeping him away from the temptations of the bottle would make him an easier prey to the solicitations of the strange woman, whose house is the way to death, and whose steps take hold on hell? He met with none, whether spirit-sellers or spirit-drinkers, who were able to resist this appeal; and from this, as well as other causes, the young formed a large and zealous portion of Jamie's Society. The young he was particularly anxious to enlist in his cause, not merely because youth is the time of truth, and of open, warm hearts, and in an especial manner God's time, but because he believed spirit-drinking parents to be the great agents in making their children drunkards.

A case which happened in his own neighborhood, gave him a melancholy confirmation of this opinion. A respectable moderate drinker, who only now and then exceeded his single tumbler of punch, had seven daughters, whom he was in the habit of treating to a little glass of punch each day after dinner. He, of course, considered it good, and they were soon taught to consider it so too. They began first to like their one glass; then they began to like two glasses much better; one glass called for another, till, in the end, they found, according to the adage, that though one glass of spirits is too much for any one, two glasses are quite too little. Right onward they went to drunkenness and crime; for, alas, it was too true in their case, as in all others, that any one may be ruined who can be persuaded to drink intoxicating liquors. With the help of whiskey, as the murderer said, a man can do any thing; so, at least, it was with these poor girls; they are living with broken character, virtue and all lost. There is, however, one exception, the youngest; and how did she escape? She was too young when her father died to be influenced by her father's example; and her father, with the character of a moderate, regular man, died sitting at table with his tumbler of punch before him.

Principally through the prudent and laborious exertions of Jamie, a great moral reformation has been effected throughout an extensive district; three hundred names are enrolled on the list of his Temperance Society; wives and sisters are blessing him for husbands and brothers reformed: the standard of public sentiment in regard to temperance has been nobly raised; people don't talk now as formerly of a man's being *somewhat elevated* or *tipsy*, or merely *overtaken*, when he is drunk, for they have learned to call things by their right names, and not practise imposture by slang phrases. Public resolutions have been passed against giving spirituous liquor at wakes or funerals, churns, ploughing-matches, or evening parties; men and women can go to market and fair, buy and sell, and yet never think of *treating* or being *treated* with spirits; and what still more fully exhibits the extent of the reformation, it has reached, in some cases, even the most degraded victims of iniquity, some of whom at least are now consistent members of the Temperance Society.

Arguing on the subject of temperance has, in a good degree, ceased in the neighborhood; and though a number of the old or ill-disposed appear decidedly resolved to have their glass, whatever the consequences, in the spirit of the fellow who told his doctor that he loved his glass, and did not care a fig for his liver, yet the young and conscientious are becoming more hearty in the cause of Jamie and temperance.

Nothing gladdened Jamie's heart more than the success which crowned his efforts in the Sabbath-school, of which he is superintendent. Spirit-drinking he not only knew to be a barrier against the progress of the Gospel, in preventing drunkards from hearing it, and grieving away the Spirit of God from the moderate drinker, but he felt it to be peculiarly injurious to the young, in often swallowing up that money which should be spent in their education, and in withholding from many even the poor pittance which should cover their nakedness in the Sabbath-school and the house of God.

As, therefore, the children of the poor had wrung out so much of the bitter dregs of spirit-drinking, he was anxious that Temperance Societies, the sworn foes of spirit-drinking, should, with their earliest, warmest efforts, return blessings to them for years of sorrow, oppression, and wrong. Sabbath-school teachers, too, he saw to be among God's choicest instruments in the work of reform. Young, yet serious, active, and benevolent, possessed of the confidence of their scholars and their parents, and from their own character, and their connection with a noble system of Christian enterprise, exercising a mighty moral influence, wide as the world, what could they not do for the regeneration of the public mind, especially of that mind which shall be all active, in good or ill, when the present generation are mouldering in the grave.

He commenced, therefore, the work of reformation in his own Sabbath-school, and he commenced in the right way, by communicating information, and bringing both teachers and scholars to think and apply the truth for themselves. He wished none, he said, to join his ranks against the great enemy, but volunteers; he wished for no influence over any one, but the influence of truth, and no bond upon any but the bond of an enlightened conscience. He introduced a proposal for each teacher in rotation to read an interesting extract to the scholars on some suitable subject, and temperance of course was not excluded. The mere hearing of the principles of Temperance Societies was sufficient to make converts of some of the teachers; for what can be more rational than abstaining from intoxicating drinks and promoting temperance? but it was not so with others.

Freethinkers may talk as they please about a man having no more control over his belief than over the hue of his skin or the height of his stature, still it is a simple fact of Jamie's experience, that it is mighty hard to convince a man who does not wish to be convinced; and that, when anybody first resolves to continue to drink, he is then marvellously fertile in objections against the Temperance Society.

One of the teachers especially, who had been at different times *overtaken* by the bottle coming from the market or fair, was so opposed to temperance, that when his turn for reading on the subject came, he had still some excuse; and Jamie, without in any way wounding his feelings, was prepared with an extract to read for him, till at length, finding him softening down under the influence of truth and love, he, on one morning of his turn for reading, put an extract into his hand, and said kindly, Just go out for a little and read it over by yourself, and that will prepare you for reading it nicely to the children. He did so, and came in and read it as one who felt its power. Jamie saw that his heart was full, he knew that *now* is the time for doing good, and not to-morrow, and therefore rising up and proposing that a Temperance Society should be formed in the school, he put his own name to the usual declaration, *We resolve to refrain from intoxicating drinks, and promote temperance.*

The next man who stepped forward was the self-same teacher who had so long opposed. "Children," said he, "spirituous liquor is a bad thing; it has done me harm; it is doing harm to every thing good, and to show that I hate it and renounce it, I put down my name." The other teachers followed; the elder children followed the noble example of their teachers, and as a proof that they knew and felt what they did, when after school-hours on next Candlemas-day, the master of a day-school which some of them attended, brought forth whiskey to treat the scholars according to custom, the noble little temperance heroes rose, as if by concert, and marched out of the room.

While thus Jamie urged on the good work of reforming

others, his own soul knew the blessings of the promise, "He that watereth others, shall be watered also himself." After renouncing whiskey, he felt a sweetness and power in God's word which he had never known before. He almost doubted whether it could be the same old Bible that he used to read. He had been abusing God's mercy by indulging in sin in time past, as if in expectation that sovereign grace would some moment descend in a miracle and drag him to holiness and heaven; but now he saw clearly that God is sincere in all his promises, and that the gracious invitations of the Gospel mean just what they say.

His first duty, he saw clearly, was to give his own self to the Lord. To that God of love who asked his heart, he gave it. He heard God in his word saying, "Believe on the Lord Jesus Christ, and thou shalt be saved;" and he took God at his word, and obeyed his command. From what he knew to be sin, he ceased at once; and what God told him was duty, he did at once, as God enabled him, without stopping to calculate consequences, for he left them with his Maker. He knew that no one goes to heaven or hell alone, the influence of the most humble being necessarily exerted either for good or ill; and as though travailing in birth for immortal souls, he was each day, by his conversation and example, saying to his neighbor, Come with us, and we will do you good. The more heartily and fully he obeyed God, the better he liked God's service; and the more extensive acquaintance he obtained of the great salvation of the Gospel, the more strongly did he feel himself drawn by a Saviour's love to accept, to adorn, and propagate it. Though beyond middle life, he had never celebrated his Saviour's love at the Lord's table. Now, however, he saw it to be his duty and privilege; and those whose hearts are set on winning souls, can conceive with what holy joy a worthy young minister, whose church Jamie had lately joined, saw him sitting down to commemorate with his fellow-Christians the dying love of the great Redeemer.

"Not unto us, O Lord, not unto us, but unto thy name give glory, for thy mercy, and for thy truth's sake."

I knew a man by the name of D——, who was a very skilful, robust, and prosperous blacksmith, and a man of more than ordinary intelligence. He yielded to the temptation to which his trade exposed him, till he became habitually intemperate, and actually a nuisance to the neighborhood. The innkeeper, who was also a storekeeper, on whom he depended for his daily supplies of strong drink, amounting, it is believed, to little less than a barrel and a half annually, at length hired him to abstain for one year, by giving him his note of hand of ten dollars. He immediately became a calm and peaceable man. His health, and appetite, and business returned to him. And he would tell you that the innkeeper had done him the greatest kindness he had ever received. "I was undone," said he. "Now I enjoy myself and my family, and the best farm in the town would not tempt me to return to the use of ardent spirits." The poor man kept his resolution till the end of the eleventh month, which it seems he had mistaken for the end of the year, and then ventured to indulge a little; and alas, when I saw him last, he was dragging his legs along, supported by two of his companions, who I feared were pursuing the same miserable course to destruction, and seemed to be lending him their sympathy; and he was one of the most loathsome and degraded human beings my eyes ever beheld. I should not be surprised to know that he is now with the dead. May my latter end not be like his.

A respectable merchant in P——, having long observed that a farmer, with whom he often traded, was in the habit of using ardent spirits to great excess, offered one day to give him fifty dollars, if he would drink no more for ten years; except so much as his physician should think necessary for his health. The farmer agreed to the proposition, and the bargain was confirmed in writing. It was not long before he felt unwell, applied to his physician, and bitters were prescribed. He had scarcely begun to use them, when he found that his appetite for ardent spirits was returning with almost irresistible violence. He foresaw the evil that would probably ensue, threw away his bitters, and dashed his bottle to pieces. He drunk no more ardent spirits till the ten years had expired, when he called on the merchant, and informed him that the conditions of the obligation had been, on his part, fulfilled. "Of course, then," said the merchant, "you want your money." "No," he replied, "I cannot take it. I have saved far more than my fifty dollars in my bills at your store, and I have made ten times that sum by attention to my business." The merchant has long since gone to his rest. The farmer still lives, has a large estate, and a fine family around him, and is a respectable and worthy citizen; for, till this day, he drinks no ardent spirits.

DECLARATION OF THIRTY-EIGHT PHYSICIANS.

"The undersigned, physicians of Cincinnati, feel it their duty to express their decided opinion in opposition to the habitual, as well as occasional use of ardent spirits. They are convinced, from all their observation and experience, that ardent spirits are not only *unnecessary*, but absolutely *injurious* in a healthy state of the system; that they produce many, and aggravate most of the diseases to which the human frame is liable; that they are unnecessary in relieving the effects of cold and fatigue, which are best relieved by rest and food; that their use in families, in the form of bitters, toddy, punch, etc., is decidedly pernicious, perverting the appetite, and undermining the constitution; that they are equally as poisonous as opium or arsenic, operating sometimes more slowly, but with equal certainty."

THE

WONDERFUL ESCAPE.

In the town where I reside were twelve young men who were accustomed, early in life, to meet together for indulgence in drinking and all manner of excess. In the course of time, some of them engaged in business; but their habits of intemperance were so entwined with their very existence, that they became bankrupts or insolvents. Eight of them died under the age of forty, without a hope beyond the grave, victims of intemperance. Three others are still living in the most abject poverty. Two of these had formerly moved in very respectable circles, but now they are in the most miserable state of poverty and disgrace.

One more, the last of the twelve, the worst of all, remains to be accounted for. He was a sort of ringleader; and being in the wine and spirit trade, his business was to take the head of the table at convivial parties, and sit up whole nights drinking and inducing others to do the same, never going to bed sober. He was an infidel, a blasphemer, a disciple of Tom Paine, both in principle and practice, yet he was a good-natured man, and would do any body a kindness. At length he left the town, and went to reside at a distance, where, for a time, he refrained from drinking, was married, and every thing seemed prosperous around him; but instead of being thankful to God for his mercy, and watching against his besetting sin, he gave way to his old propensity, and brought misery on his family and friends.

One dark night, being in the neighborhood of Dudley, he had been drinking to excess, wandered out of the house, and staggered among the coalpits, exposed to fall into them, and be lost. He proceeded on till he fell, and rolled down the bank of the canal; but God, who is rich in mercy, had caused a stone to lie directly in his path, and the poor drunkard was stopped from rolling over into the water, where, by one turn more, he would have sunk into eternal ruin. His senses returned for a moment; he saw that if he attempted to stand, he would fall headlong into the canal, and crawled back again into the road. But this miraculous preservation had no effect upon him; he merely called it a lucky escape.

Once, after having indulged in many days of intemperance, being come a little to his senses, he began to reason with himself upon his folly—surrounded with blessings, yet abusing the whole—and in an angry, passionate manner, he muttered, "O, it 's no use for me to repent; my sins are too great to be forgiven." He had no sooner uttered these words, than a voice seemed to say, with strong emphasis, "If thou wilt forsake thy sins, they shall be forgiven." The poor man started at what he believed to be real sound, and turned round, but saw no one, and said to himself, "I have been drinking till I am going mad." He stood paralyzed, not knowing what to think, till relieved by a flood of tears, and then exclaimed, "Surely, this is the voice of mercy, once more calling me to repentance." He fell on his knees, and half suffocated by his feelings, cried out, "God be merciful to me a sinner." The poor wretch was broken-hearted; and now his besetting sin appeared more horrible than ever; but it must be conquered, or he must perish. Then commenced a contest more terrible than that of conflicting armies; the soul was at stake; an impetuous torrent was to be turned into an opposite course. He now began to search the Bible, which he had once despised. Here he saw that crimson and scarlet sins could be blotted out, and made white as snow; that the grace of God was sufficient. He refrained from intemperance, commenced family prayer, and hope again revived; but his deadly foe still pursued him, and he was again overcome.

Now his disgrace and sinfulness appeared worse than ever, and with melancholy feeling he cried out, in anguish of spirit, that he was doomed to eternal misery, and it was useless to try to avert his fate. His cruel enemy took this opportunity to suggest to his mind that he had so disgraced himself, that it would be better to get rid of his life at once—frequently the end of drunkards. The razor was in his hand: but the Spirit of the Lord interposed, and the weapon fell to the ground. Still his enemy pursued him, and seemed to have new power over his sin of intemperance. He would sometimes refrain for days and weeks, and then again he was as bad as ever. Hope seemed now to be lost; especially one day, when, after having been brought into great weakness through intemperance, death appeared to be very near, and his awful state more terrific than ever. Not a moment was to be lost; he cast himself once more at the footstool of his long-insulted Creator, and with an intensity of agony cried out, "What profit is there in my blood when I go down to the pit? Shall the dust praise thee? Shall it declare thy truth? Hear, O Lord, and have mercy upon me; Lord, be thou my helper." He sunk down exhausted; he could say no more. That prayer was heard; and a voice from heaven seemed to reply, "I will help thee; I have seen thy struggles, and I will now say to thine enemy, 'Hitherto thou hast come—but no further.'"

A physician was consulted as to the probability or possibility of medicine being rendered effectual to stop the disposition to intemperance. The poor man would have suffered the amputation of all his limbs, could so severe a method have freed him from his deadly habit, which, like a vulture, had fastened upon his very vitals. Eagerly did he begin to take the simple medicine prescribed—a preparation of steel—with earnest prayer to God for help in this last struggle for life; but faith and prayer proved the best of remedies; he persevered, and conquered; and be it said to the honor and glory of the Lord God Almighty, who sent his angel to whisper in the poor man's ear, "I will help thee," that from the latter end of September, 1816, to the present hour, nearly twenty years, *not so much as a spoonful of spirituous liquor, or wine of any description, has ever passed the surface of that man's tongue.*

The above account of his own experience, was given by Mr. Hall, a merchant of Maidstone, Kent, at the anniversary of the British and Foreign Temperance Society, May, 1836.

Mr. Hall stated, in conclusion, that he had since been aiming to be useful to his fellow-men, and had written a Tract, the object of which was to call drunkards, and all sinners to repentance, of which more than one hundred thousand copies had been circulated. See Tract No. 349.

Has the reader a relative, friend, or neighbor, who drinks his daily drams, and is plunging into that awful gulf which yearly swallows up its thousands of victims? Let the above history suggest a duty, and encourage to its performance. This is not a solitary instance of victory obtained over powerful and raging appetite. There is evidence that tens of thousands of persons in the United States, who were once intemperate, have become sober, useful citizens; and not a few of them ardent Christians. And this has been effected, not by despising and reproaching them, but chiefly through the divine blessing on *the kind personal influence of friends*, excited by no other motive than Christian benevolence and love of their fellow-men. The self-despair of the intemperate man arises, in a great measure, from the conviction that he is an outcast from public respect and sympathy. He is moved by the language of kindness; and if suitably warned of his danger, and pointed to the way of escape, may be saved from ruin. Persuade him to refrain till reason resumes her sway, and the burning desire for stimulus has subsided. A few months will generally effect this great change. In his sober hours he often weeps over his folly, his ear is open to the voice of friendship, and he will yield to kind remonstrance—perhaps consent to place himself under the care of a temperate physician. *Go to him when alone*, with tenderness and love. Offer him such aid as is needed by himself or family. Give him the above history, in view of which none need despair. Bring him, if possible, to the house of God. Go to him again and again, till you obtain his pledge, to abstinence. Follow him with kindness. Support him in the struggle. Induce him *utterly to abandon all that can intoxicate, as his only safety;* wholly to refrain from the *place* and the *company* where intoxicating drinks are used; and in dependence on Christ, humbly to offer the prayer, "Hold thou me up, and I shall be safe." Interest yourself in his welfare, and persevere till you gain the glorious triumph—the conquest of an *immortal mind*, that may diffuse blessings on every side in this life, and be a star in the Redeemer's crown of glory for ever.

PUBLISHED BY THE AMERICAN TRACT SOCIETY.

THE
EVENTFUL TWELVE HOURS;
OR,
THE DESTITUTION AND WRETCHEDNESS
OF
A DRUNKARD.

"It is a sorrowful heart," said I to myself, as I raked over the dying embers upon the hearth, to throw a transient gleam of light over my dreary cottage—"it is a sorrowful heart that never rejoices; and though I am somewhat in debt at the *Blue Moon*, and the landlady of the *Stag* has over and over again said she'd never trust me, still she has not yet refused me, only at first. Many 's the shilling I have paid them both, to be sure," said I, rising involuntarily and going to the cupboard: "I had better take a mouthful before I go out, for it's no use to wait any longer for Mary's return."

Just at this moment the eldest of my two children inquired in a piteous tone, "if that was mother." "Your mother? no," said I; "and what if it was, what then?" "Because, father," continued the child, "I thought perhaps she had brought a loaf of bread home, for I am so hungry." "Hungry, child," said I; "then why did you not ask me before you went to bed?" "Because, father, I knew there was no bread. When mother sent me to get a loaf this morning at the grocer's, Mrs. Mason said our last month's bill had not yet been settled, and she could not trust any more; and so we have only had a few potatoes. When mother went out to look for work, she promised to bring a loaf home very early." "Why, Jane," said I, "this is a new story—what, is there nothing at all in the house?" "No, father, nothing; and that is not all, father; mother cried this morning about it when she went out; and though she never uses bad words, said something about cursed drink: she said she should be back before dark, and it has now been dark a long time, and hark, how it rains."

The fire flickered up a little, and at this moment the latch of the door clicked; I peeped up through the gloom, a pang of conscious shame stealing through my frame; but it was not my wife, as I of course supposed—it was Mrs. Mason. I was surprised and confused. "Where is your wife, James?" said she, in a mild, firm tone. "Is that mother?" said my child again, in a rather sleepy tone; "I am so glad you are come, I am so hungry." "That child," said I, "has gone to bed without her supper to-night," fumbling about at the same time upon the mantel-piece for a bit of candle, which I could not find. "Yes," said Mrs. Mason, very gravely, "and without its dinner too, I fear; but where is your wife, James? for I am come to see whether she brought any thing home with her for herself and family; for I could not feel comfortable after I had refused your child a loaf this morning, just as I know the refusal was." I now stammered out something about "sorry," and "ashamed," and "bad times." "But where *is* your wife, James?" "She is, perhaps, at neighbor Wright's," said I, briskly, glad to catch an opportunity of a minute's retreat from my present awkward position; "I'll just step and see. Jane, get up, child." "No, James," said Mrs. Mason, in a tone not to be misunderstood; "no, James, I wish she was sitting by their comfortable fireside; I called in there just now, as I came along, to pay a little bill, and they spoke very kindly of your wife, and hoped she might be enabled to rub through this winter—but I will call again in half an hour: Mary will have come home, I hope, by that time."

The door closed upon her, and I remained in a kind of half stupor; my month's unpaid bill, my public-house scores, my destitute home; these and a thousand things connected with my situation, kept me musing in no very comfortable frame of mind, when the latch again clicked, the door opened, and through the half gleam of one flickering flame, I just caught the glimpse of a form, that in the next instant, cold and wet, sunk lifeless in my arms. It was Mary. As she sunk down upon me, she just said, with a shudder, "Cold." Shall I stop to tell you of the agony of my mind? Shall I endeavor to relate a portion of the thoughts that chased each other with a comet's rapidity through my brain; the remembrance of our past comforts, and our happiness too? Recovering after the lapse of an instant, I called, "Jane, Jane, get up, and make haste; your mother is come home, and is very ill and faint; get a light"—she was quickly at my side—"get a light," for the little unfriendly flame had ceased to burn.

"But where are you, mother?" said Jane. "Jane, child," said I, angrily, "your mother is here; get a light directly." "We haven't a bit of candle, father." "Then get some wood out of the back room—break up some little bits—O, do make haste." "We haven't a bit of wood, father." "Child, child—" "Yes, father, but we haven't any." My poor wife at this moment gave a kind of sob, and with a slight struggle, as if for breath, sunk heavier in my arms. I tried to hold her up in an easier posture, calling to her in a tender manner, "Mary, my dear Mary;" but my sensations and my conscience almost choked me. In this moment of anguish and perplexity, my wife, for aught I knew, dead in my arms—without light, without fuel, without food, without credit, Mrs. Mason returned. Jane had managed to make the fire burn up, just so as to disclose our wretched situation. "Your wife ill?" said Mrs. Mason, hastily stepping forward—"very ill, I fear, James, and wet and cold—run hastily, James," reaching herself a broken chair, "and call in Mrs. Wright, and place your wife on my lap." This I immediately did, and as I opened the door to go out, I heard Mrs. Mason ask Jane to get a light—and shame made me secretly rejoice, that I had escaped the humiliation, for the present, of confessing that we had not even a bit of a candle in the house.

Mrs. Wright was preparing for supper: they were regular and early folks, and my heart sunk within me when, in my hurry, I unceremoniously opened the door—I mean the contrast I saw between their cottage and my own; a clean cloth was laid, with spoons, and basins, and white, clean plates, and knives and forks, with every other necessary comfort. Wright was sitting with his back towards the fire, with a candle in one hand and a book in the other, reading to his wife, who was leaning forward, and just in the act of taking a pot off the hanger, in which it would be easy to guess, was something warm for supper. The fire and candle gave a cheerful light, and every thing looked "comfortable." "My wife is taken very ill," said I, "and Mrs. Mason, who has just stepped in, begged me to call in your help." "Mrs. Mason at your house now?" said Mrs. Wright; "come, Wright, reach me my cloak, and let us make haste and go." We were all at the door, when Mrs.

Wright said, "What, come to fetch us without a lantern? and ours is at the glazier's. What are we to do?" "The distance is very short," I said. "Yes," said Wright, "but long enough for an accident; how I do like necessaries;" adding, in an undertone, as he pulled his wife along, something about "enough for *tavern debts*, but nothing to buy *necessaries*."

On opening my cottage door, I called out—for no one was in the room—"Mrs. Mason, are you up stairs? how is Mary? here is Mrs. Wright; shall I come up?" No one answered, and Mrs. Wright passed me, going softly up stairs, saying, in a low tone, as she ascended, "James, you had better make up a good fire, and get some water heated as fast as you can." Again I was aghast. "Get some water heated," said I; and the wretchedness of our bedless bed and furnitureless room crossed my mind at the same time. Mrs. Mason, at this moment, leaned over the banisters, and said, in a soft voice, "James, fetch the doctor, and lose no time; make haste, for life may depend on it." My wretchedness seemed now complete; the very fire of delirium and confusion seemed to seize upon my brain; and hastily calling out to Jane to attend upon Mr. Wright, I snatched up my hat, and pushed by my neighbor without heeding some inquiries he had begun about the necessaries that were then so much required.

It rained, and was very dark; the road to the doctor's was not the best, and he lived rather more than a mile off; it was impossible to proceed faster than a slow, cautious walk. I was now alone, and, in much bitterness of spirit, began to upbraid myself, and those companions of my folly who had led me on to habits that had first disgraced, and then brought me to severe ruin. With what vivid brightness did the first year of our marriage, its comforts and its hopes, again pass before me; and when my mind led me on through all its changing scenes, up to the moment when Mrs. Mason, in her low, subdued tone of voice, called to me to fetch the doctor, and to mind I lost no time; I could only realize my wife as dying, and myself the cruel tyrant who had, by neglect, ill usage, and partial starvation, brought her to an untimely end.

When I entered the doctor's house, "Is that you, James King?" said he, sharply; "do you want me?" "Yes, sir," said I; "my wife is very ill, and Mrs. Mason, who called in just at the time she was taken, desired me to come and to request your attendance upon her. I am afraid, sir, it is no little affair." "Mrs. Mason, Mrs. Mason," said the doctor; "I am inclined to think Mrs. Mason has better drugs in her shop for your wife's complaint, than my shop affords, and I expect I shall have to tell her so." I hung down my head with shame; I understood what he meant. He then moved towards the door, putting on his greatcoat as he walked along. "But stop," said he, just as we got to the outer door, "how did you come—no lantern?" "I can carry your lantern before you, sir," said I. "Yes," said he, "and *I* may bring it back." "But I will return with you, sir; my wife will most likely want some medicine." "Yes, James," said he, "and if she does, I shall want the money longer still." I had no word to reply, it was no time to begin being independent. The doctor's large glass lantern was brought, and our journey back was quickly performed. I should have thought a great deal of giving 7*s.* 6*d.* for such a lantern, if I had really required just such an one; yet I had paid as many pounds on my scores, and thought nothing at all about it.

On getting home, I found that somehow it had been managed to make up a good fire, and the tea-kettle was boiling, and Mrs. Mason was just making a little tea. "How is Mary?" said I, hardly daring to look Mrs. Mason in the face. "Well, Mrs. Mason," said the doctor, "pray what is the matter?" and as the doctor spoke, Mrs. Mason took up the jug of tea she had made, conversed with the doctor in an undertone for half a minute, and both walked up stairs, leaving me again to reflection, in fact, taking no notice of me. I sunk down heavily upon the chair that was beside the fire, in a state of exhaustion, and while I was wondering where all this would end, was aroused by the cry of "James, James, the doctor says your wife must put her feet into warm water; so bring up some directly, James, in a large pan or bucket, or any thing that is handy; pray, make haste;" and before I could reply, for I doubted whether there was either, the door was shut, and again I was placed in a new difficulty. However, I found an old leaky pail and an old broken pan; so I set the pail into the pan to catch the leakage, and together, they did tolerably well; but I felt considerable shame as I handed this lumbering affair up stairs, well knowing it would call forth some remark.

I had just again seated myself at the fire, when the doctor, in no very gentle tone, called out, "James, here, man, take this paper to my office; Mr. Armstrong will give you some physic for your wife, and then it will be twice given, for I suppose you will never pay for it." I stared at him, or rather paused and hesitated—who could tell why? was it the taunts I was thus obliged to endure; or was it bodily exhaustion? I had eaten all the food my poor Mary had put into my basket for my breakfast; and, as it appeared, all she had in the world; yet I had managed to borrow sixpence at noon, intending to buy me a loaf and cheese, and half a pint of beer for my dinner; but venturing upon half a pint of beer first, I called for another; and, becoming thirsty, for a pint; and so my dinner and my afternoon's work were both lost together. It must now have been nearly ten o'clock, and I had tasted no food, as I said before, since breakfast. I felt faint, and well I might; however, with a heavy step and a heavier heart, taking up the doctor's lantern, and looking round upon the empty wretchedness before me, I again set out for the doctor's. And did I not also think over neighbor Wright's comfortable, cheerful room, and his boiling pot; while I, who had that day spent a borrowed sixpence upon beer, had not even a crust of bread for myself or family? And did I forget the pence, and then the shillings, and then the pounds I had paid at public-houses; selling, and pawning my bed from under me, and my clothes from off my back, and all to gain misery and want, and lose my good name?

Mr. Armstrong was a kind-hearted young man, and soon prepared the medicines, and by kind and cheerful hopes concerning my poor Mary, and a little civil conversation, raised my spirits, and I walked back somewhat lighter of heart; but I was thoroughly wet, and the cold rain pierced my very marrow, for I was wearing summer clothing in the winter season—I had no other. Cold and wet, exhausted and miserable, I once more lifted the latch of my own cottage door. The candle was dimly burning. My fears arose, and my heart sunk within me: "Is Mary worse?" said I. "She is no better," said Mr. Wright, who was sitting over the dying embers—"no better—heavy work, James."

I placed the medicine upon the table, and sat down, exhausted and wretched. Whose situation so low, could he have known all, that would not have pitied me? Wright rose, and carried the medicines up stairs; and in another minute all was the stillness of death. I could have borne any thing but this—at least I so felt—but under this oppressive stillness, my feelings gave way in torrents of tears, and every moment brought a fresh accusation against myself for my past doings; and again I looked around me, as well as my tearful eyes and dimly-lighted room would allow, and contrasted all with John Wright's. "So comfortable," said I, involuntarily. Indistinct sounds and cautious steppings were now heard above; and while I was raising myself up to listen, in order to catch, if possible, something that would acquaint me with the state of my poor Mary, the bedroom door opened, and down came Wright and his wife, the latter carefully lighting the doctor, Mrs. Mason being close behind him. I tried to recover myself a little, and to assume something like the appearance of courage; and in a half-choked, coughing voice, said, "How is my poor wife, sir?" The doctor, with a severity of manner, and imitating my manner of speaking, replied, "You should have coughed sooner, James;" then turning to Mrs. Mason, said, "Remember, *quiet* is the best medicine *now;* indeed, it is food and medicine in her present state; don't teaze her about any thing; at half past, mind—and again at twelve, until the pain subsides, when sleep will follow."

I shrunk back at the words "half past," which reminded me that I had not even a twenty-shilling clock in the house.

"James," said the doctor, "have you no time in the house?" "No, I suppose not," he answered himself. "Well, then, you must guess at it; oh dear, bad work indeed. Come, James, put that bit of candle into the lantern; I hope it does not rain now."

Wright opened the door, and I walked out with the lantern, the doctor following, and, buttoning his coat closely round him, remarked upon the darkness of the night. I walked on with an unsteady step, feeling as if every yard of ground I strode over would be the last. But, urged on by my situation, I reached the doctor's house without any remark from him upon my wearied step, and pulled his bell in rather a hasty manner.

"You are in a hurry, James," said he, "you forget the time of night; a gentle pull would have waked the attendant without disturbing my family. *My* family are very regular, James, and I make it a rule never to disturb them when it can be avoided; perhaps you think such things of no consequence: regularity, James, and sobriety, are two very principal things in a family."

By this time the attendant appeared, and, giving him the lantern and thanking the doctor for his kind attention, I left the door to return home. The door closed, and my situation was a very painful one; the sudden change from light to utter darkness obliged me to stand still a few minutes before I could venture to move, but a world of sensations ran through my mind, and distracted me more than ever; the weakness of my body prevented my checking its sensations; and, could I have weighed in the balance of reason, to say nothing of religion, at this moment, all foolish, sinful pleasures—falsely so called—of drinking, with the distress of mind and weariness of body I then endured, and had endured on this one single night, how light would they have seemed. Yes, even if I had not included the loss of positive property and health.

Once again, then, I reached my home. All was still; but soon Mrs. Mason came down. Before I could speak, she said, "Mary is better, James; she has fallen into a nice sleep." She spoke kindly, and looked kindly. I tried to answer her, but my feelings choked me; and seeing my effort to suppress them, she continued, "God has dealt very mercifully, James, towards you, in so blessing the means that have been used; but you have had no supper; you will find some nice warm soup by the side of the fire there; Mrs. Wright sent it in for you, by her husband, when she returned home: come, James, eat it while it is warm, it will do you good; your little girl and boy have both had some, and they are now warm in bed and fast asleep."

"Mr. and Mrs. Wright are very kind," I added, "and you are kind; what should I have done but for you and them?"

"Done, James?" said she mildly; "done, James? see how God orders his dispensations; 'in the midst of wrath he remembers mercy,' and I trust he has purposes of mercy in this event towards you and your family; but beware, James, for the Bible expressly says, 'My son, despise not the chastening of the Lord;' and again, 'whom the Lord loveth, he chasteneth.' But eat your supper; I will step up stairs and see if your wife is still sleeping, and if she is, I will come down and chat a little with you."

As she went softly up stairs my eyes followed her, and I said to myself, This is one of your religious ones, is it, that I have so often joined in jeering at? Surely I ate my supper with a thankful heart, and was much strengthened by it. Mrs. Mason soon returned, and stepping into the back room, where Jane lay, and her little brother, brought out three or four billets of wood, and a cheerful fire was soon made; so that with my warm, nourishing supper, the cheerful fire, and Mrs. Mason's mild and cheerful countenance and manner, I regained my spirits, and a considerable portion of my strength. After a little pause, she said,

"James, when Mary recovers, if it should please God to order it so, great care will be required lest she should relapse. You would not wish to lose her, James; she has, I believe, been a kind and affectionate wife to you, and a tender mother to your children. When you were first married every thing went well with you, and it was a remark I often made of you as a neighbor, that you wanted nothing but the true fear of God in your heart, and faith in our blessed Saviour, to make you a pattern to all around you. I used often to say a few words to Mary, and she always received them meekly, but I seldom saw you, and your manner never gave me any encouragement to talk to you on religious subjects. James, experience has enabled me to make one remark, that *absence from divine worship*, as a regular or customary thing, is an almost unerring sign of the absence of religion from the heart; and it is indeed seldom that I have seen you in your place on the Sabbath-day. The Sabbath is a blessed day when it is spent aright." So leaving me, she again went up stairs, remarking that Mr. Wright had been home to her house, to explain the cause of her absence, (and as I tolerably well guessed, this partly explained the mystery of fire and candle, and tea and sugar, and bread,) adding, "Mrs. Wright will come in at daylight, and will stay with Mary, and that will allow me to attend to my morning's business: you know, James, the Bible says, 'diligent in business, fervent in spirit, serving the Lord.'"

I longed to go and see my poor Mary, but I was not asked, and I supposed it right that it should be so. I now thought of my poor children; and going into their room, I felt distressed to find them so badly provided with bed-clothes. I kissed them, and secretly prayed, in a kind of way, that I might be spared to care more for them than I had lately done. I sat down, and began to reflect upon all the circumstances of the past day, and of this eventful night; but I soon fell into a sound sleep, which continued until Mrs. Mason awoke me, informing me that it was nearly daylight, and reminded me of her intentions to return home to her duties as soon as Mrs. Wright should arrive. "And why wait for Mrs. Wright, madam?" said I; "surely I can attend upon Mary now, or at least until Mrs. Wright does come." "It is very natural," said Mrs. Mason, "that you should desire to attend upon your wife, and think yourself capable of doing so; but my most particular directions from the doctor were, not to allow you to see your wife, if I could prevent you, until he had seen her once more; and you may remember, James, in how grave a manner he directed she might not in any way be teazed, nor—but, James, to deal honestly with you, and rightly as I consider it, whatever may be your future conduct to your wife, your behavior to her for these last three years has not been quite kind; and as grief and depression have very much to do with her present illness, we are all of opinion that you had better refrain from going to see her until she is more composed. You have bruised, James; seek now to heal."

I was touched with the reproof; I was, perhaps, more touched by the manner. Mrs. Mason was one who sought to win souls: she won my esteem and confidence, and I felt that if Mrs. Mason could talk to me thus, I had still something to lose. I went to call Mrs. Wright. On my return, Mrs. Mason was up stairs, but she had placed nearly a whole loaf and a piece of butter on the table, and some tea and sugar, and the kettle was singing by the fireside. These were times of deep thought to me. On Mrs. Wright's arrival, I thanked her for her great kindness, and hoped better times were in store. "Yes," she replied, "better times may be in store for you; I hope they are; you have certainly bought your corn at a very dear market lately, but you *may* find a better one to go to yet." Mrs. Mason now appeared, and ready to go home; the morning had just fully dawned. "Come, James," said she, "you must go with me; I want to send back a few things to Mary; and mind, you must not leave the house to-day after your return, and your little girl ought to be sent to account for your absence from work—that is, James, if—"

"If, madam?" said I quickly; "if what?"

"Yes, James, if you think you can maintain a new character, and desire really to become again, what I well remember you once was, a respectable man; yes, James, a respectable man; for remember, that word is the just right of every man who acts as every man ought to do. The word seems to surprise you: it is a sad mistake that seems insensibly to have crept into common acceptance in these days, that respectability must mean something belonging rather to riches and rank, than honesty and uprightness of character; respectability is as much the birthright of yourself as of young 'squire Mills; indeed, I may say that on this point, you both started in life exactly equal: his father was indeed respectable in every sense of the word; and your father was certainly nothing behind him; both faithfully discharged the duties of that station 'into which it pleased God to call them,' and this I consider, from the king to the cottager, is to be *respectable;* but, James, the young 'squire is as respectable a man, I am happy to say, as his father was, and why should not you become as respectable as yours? I have lived to see many changes, but the change I most mourn over, is the change of principle in my neighbors. Their respectability seems to be exchanged for finer clothes and fewer fireside, fewer home comforts; and I happen also to know, that if very much of the grain that has been made into poisonous beer and whiskey had been made into good wholesome bread, both you and I, James, should have been better off, I think, than we are now, for I have had my struggles as well as you; so have many others. I have worked early and late, taking care of *the pence,* to maintain my respectability; yet, let me again repeat it, your father and mother were respectable to the day of their death, and many in this village would gladly see their only child following their footsteps, and seeking the same inheritance they now possess 'in mansions in the skies.' But the road leads down hill to vice and folly, and I might add, the gulf of ruin lies at the bottom; you may be far down it; I fear you are, yet there is a hand that even now beckons to you, and says, 'Turn, turn, I have no pleasure in the death of him that dieth; wherefore turn and live:' but, James, you are not ignorant of your Bible."

I tried to conceal my emotions, for it was a very long time since I had heard such words as these. My Bible and the house of God had been long entirely neglected. Mrs. Mason perceived that I was affected, and moving towards the door, said, "Yes, James, it is a slippery, down-hill path that leads to ruin, and many there be that walk therein. Heaven may be said to lie upward, yet 'its ways are ways of pleasantness, and all its paths are peace.' But come, it is broad daylight, and I must hasten home."

As we passed neighbor Wright's cottage, I had not forgotten the comfort that was within, and I said secretly, "I'll see what's to be done." The arrival of Mrs. Mason at home seemed to give to all the liveliest pleasure and satisfaction; and their inquiries after my poor wife were made with a kindliness of manner that surprised me. "They respect-her," said I to myself; they took little notice of me, yet treated me with more civility than I had a right to expect. Mrs. Mason soon put up a few little things and directed me to give them to Mrs. Wright, and weighing me a pound of bacon, and putting a large loaf and half a pound of cheese into the basket with it, with some soap and candles, said, "I shall charge *these* to your bill, James. Patty, go into the garden and cut James a couple of nice cabbages; I dare say he will know what to do with them." Having had this unexpected provision made me for the day, and receiving parting words of encouragement from this kind friend, I returned home. I found my children up and washed, and breakfast ready. Mrs. Wright had kindly done this. Jane looked cheerful, and my little Harry came edging towards me, as if he did not know what to make of all this. "Mother's so ill, Jane says, father—is she; is she, father?" looking up in my face as I sat down, "is she?"

"She is better now, my boy," I said.

"Better, father? who made her ill? *you* didn't make her ill, did you, father?—nice bread, father—did mother bring this nice bread home, father? speak, father, you don't speak."

I could not trust myself to answer; so I rose, for I was much affected at the thought that Mrs. Mason had cared for these babes and their mother, but I had neglected them, and foolishly squandered away their comforts and even their necessary bread.

Mrs. Wright went home; but returned soon after we had finished breakfast; and by the time I had put things a little to rights, the doctor called. His "Well, James," filled me with no very pleasing sensations. "I hope we shall have a change, eh, James?" and passing on, went up stairs. Ah, thought I, I hope so too, for I know what you mean. He soon came down; said my wife might get up if she liked, taking a little care, and, "after to-day, give her a pill every noon for dinner off a loin of mutton, eh, James?

A few more broiled pills for *her*, and a pint less of liquor for *you*, and your old father and mother would soon come to life again. *Your* savings' bank is at the tavern, and the landlady of the Stag keeps your accounts, I believe, eh, James? I shall charge you nothing for this." This was the doctor. I received his reproofs humbly, and certainly thought, you have been very kind, but I also thought, you are not Mrs. Mason.

Soon after this, my poor Mary came down stairs, and I at once confessed my sorrow for my past conduct, and my determination to *drink no more;* and, to conclude, my wife slowly recovered, and, I may add, I recovered also; but I was very far down the hill, and consequently found it a long and hard tug to get up again; but Mrs. Mason encouraged me, Mrs. Wright helped me, the doctor cheered me, Mr. Armstrong praised me, our kind minister instructed me, my wife assisted me, and, as a crowning point of all, the blessing of God rested on me. I worked hard, I prayed in my family, I paid my debts, I clothed my children, I redeemed my bed, I mended my windows, I planted my garden and sold garden stuff, instead of buying; I bought me a wheelbarrow, I mended my chairs and table, I got me a clock; and now here I am, but never shall I forget John Wright or his wife, how long soever I may remember my other kind friends, and most of all, Mrs. Mason. But there were no temperance societies in those days, or I think I should have been reclaimed sooner.

THE

LOST MECHANIC RESTORED.

NEAR the close of 1831, says Mr. C——, of Hartford, Conn., I was requested by a pious and benevolent lady, to take into my employ a young man who had become intemperate. I objected that the influence of such a man would be injurious to my other workmen, and especially my apprentices. But the kind-hearted lady urged her request, saying that he was willing to come under an engagement not to drink at all, and to conform strictly to all the regulations of the establishment; that she received him into her family when a boy, and felt a deep interest in his welfare; that he had learned a trade, and was an excellent workman; had become hopefully pious, and united with one of our churches; had married a very worthy young woman, but his intemperance had blasted his fair prospects. He was now sensible of his danger; and she believed his salvation for this, if not for a future world, would turn on my decision.

I consented to make the trial; and he came, binding himself, by a written contract, to receive no part of his wages into his own hands, and to forfeit whatever should be due to him, in case he became intoxicated. He succeeded remarkably in my business, was industrious and faithful, and strictly temperate and regular in all his habits.

But in the summer of 1832, he was by some means induced to taste again an intoxicating drink, and a fit of drunken insanity ensued, which continued about a fortnight. Knowing that his wife had some money, he gave her no peace, day nor night, till he got possession of it. He then took the boat for New York, spent the money, and after bartering some of his clothes, returned, a most destitute and wretched object.

After he had become sober and rational once more, I happened to meet him in the street, and asked him why he did not come to work as usual. With a voice trembling and suppressed, and with a look of grief, self-reproach, and despair that I shall never forget, he said, "I can never come into your shop again. I have not only violated my contract with you, but I have treated you with the basest ingratitude, proved myself unworthy of your confidence, and destroyed the last hope of my reformation."

I assured him of my increased desire for his welfare; he returned to his employment, and his attention to business evinced the sincerity of his confessions.

But not more than three months had elapsed before he was taken again in the toils of his old deceiver; and at this time he was so furious and unmanageable, that he was arrested and committed to the workhouse. He was soon released, and engaged once more in my business. He continued for about two months, when he fell again; and after a frenzy of a week, came to me and begged me to take him to the workhouse, as the only means by which he should get sober. He remained there a few days, and then returned to his work.

Such was his history: a few months sober, industrious, and obliging in my shop; kind, attentive, and affectionate in his family; then a week furiously drunk, absent from my shop, violent and abusive in his family; then at the workhouse; and then sober, and at home again.

He had already been excommunicated from the church for his intemperance, had become a terror to his wife, who frequently sent for me to protect her from his violence, and seemed to be utterly abandoned.

In the month of May, 1833, he was again missing; and no one, not even his wife, knew what had become of him. But in the course of the summer she received a letter from him, in which he said he had got employment, and wished her, without informing me where he was, to come and live with him. She accordingly removed to his new residence, and I heard nothing from either of them.

About two years and a half after this, he came into my shop one day; but how changed. Instead of the bloated, wild, and despairing countenance that once marked him as a drunkard, he now wore an aspect of cheerfulness and health, of manliness and self-respect. I approached, took him by the hand, and said, "Well, ——, how do you do?" "*I am well*," said he, shaking my hand most cordially. "Yes," said I, "well in more respects than one." "*Yes, I am*," was his emphatic reply. "*It is now more than two years since I have tasted a drop of any thing that can intoxicate.*" He began by abstaining from ardent spirits only; "But," said he, "I soon found that what you had so often told me was true; that I could not reform but by abstaining from all that can intoxicate. I have done so, and you see the result."

I then inquired after the health of his wife and child: his reply was, "They are well and happy." I asked him if "his wife made him any trouble" now. "Trouble," said he, "no; and never did make any: it was I that made the trouble. You told me so, and I knew it at the time. *But what could I do?* So long as I remained here, I could not turn a corner in your streets without passing a grog-shop. I could not go to my meals without coming in contact with some associate who would try to entice me to drink with him; and even the keepers of these shops would try every artifice to induce me to drink; for they knew that if they could get me to taste once, I should never know when to stop, and they would be sure to get a good bill against me.

"I have now come," said he, "to tell you why I left you. It was because I knew that I should die if I did not leave off drinking, and I saw distinctly that I could never leave off while I remained in Hartford. My only hope was, in going where liquor was not to be had."

About two years and a half after this, he applied to me for further employment, as the business he was following had failed. I told him there was no man whom I should rather employ, but I could not think of having him encounter again the temptations which he had so miraculously escaped. He very pleasantly replied, "I am a man now, and do not believe I have any thing more to fear from the temptations of the city than you have."

I told him that I had confidence in the firmness of his purpose, but feared to see it put to the test. Yet, as he was out of business, I consented; and no man that I ever employed did better, or was more deserving of confidence and respect. He continued with me till spring, when he proposed to take his work into the country, so that he could be with his family: the arrangement was made, and I employ him still.

On the fourth of July last, (1839,) the Sunday-schools in the town where he resides made arrangements for a celebration, and I was invited to be present and address them. As I looked upon the audience, the first countenance that met my eye was that of this very man, *at the head of his Sunday-school class.* The sight almost overwhelmed me. Instead of a loathsome, drunken maniac—a terror to his family and a curse to society, whose very presence was odious, and his example pestilential—he was then, in the expressive language of Scripture, "clothed, and in his right mind;" and was devoted to the heavenly work of guiding children to Christ and salvation. He had made a public profession of religion, which he was daily honoring by a life of Christian meekness and sobriety.

O, who can comprehend the tide of domestic joy, of social happiness, and of Christian consolation which flows through the heart of this man and his family, in consequence of this change in his habits?

Now, what was the cause of this surprising change? What wrought this wonderful transformation in this individual? The whole story is told in one short line. *He went where intoxicating liquor was not sold.* Had he remained in this city, he would probably long since have been laid in the drunkard's grave.

PUBLISHED BY THE AMERICAN TRACT SOCIETY.

REFORMATION OF DRUNKARDS.

Truly we live in an age of wonders. Under peculiar influences, hundreds and thousands of once hopeless drunkards are becoming sober men—yet the work of reform has but commenced. It is computed that there are in the land no less than five hundred thousand habitual inebriates. The condition of each individual calls for sympathy and aid, that he may become a sober man, and through the blessing of God, gain eternal life.

For drunkenness there is and can be no apology; but the condition of the drunkard is often pitiable in the extreme. However gradual, or respectable, may have been his progress in the descent called *temperate drinking*, the appetite now *is formed* within him—the drunkard's appetite. Wretched man! He feels what not faintly resembles the gnawing of "the worm that never dies." He asks for help. There are times when he would give worlds to be reformed. Every drunkard's life, could it be written, would tell this in letters of fire. He struggles to resist the temptation, causes himself to be shut up in prison, throws himself on board a temperance ship for a distant voyage, seeks new alliances and new employments, wrestles, agonizes, but all in vain. He rises to-day but to fall to-morrow; and amid disappointment and reproach, poverty and degradation, he says, "Let me alone, I cannot live," and plunges headlong to destruction.

Who will come to his rescue? Who will aid in the deliverance of thousands of thousands from this debasing thraldom of sin and Satan? Our aid they must have.

Their *number* demands it. Half a million, chiefly adults, often heads of families, having each a wife and children, making miserable a million and a half of relatives and friends. They pass, too, in rapid succession. Ten years is the measure of a generation, and if nothing is done to save them, in the next forty years two millions may be swept into eternity.

Their personal degradation and suffering require it. What would we not do to pull a neighbor out of the water, or out of the fire, or to deliver him from Algerine captivity, or wrest him from the hand of a pirate or midnight assassin? But what captivity, what pirate, what murderer so cruel as Alcohol?

Their *families* plead for it. The innocent and the helpless, the lambs, in the paw of the tiger, and that tiger a husband and father. Amid hungering and thirsting, cold and nakedness, humiliation and shame, sufferings which no pen can describe, they ask for aid.

The good of the community demands it. While they live as they do, they are only a moth and a curse. The moment they are reformed, society is relieved of its greatest burden. The poor-house and the jail become almost tenantless.

The practicability of a sudden and complete reform of every drunkard in the land calls for it. This, science has denied. Religion has only said, "With man it is impossible, but not with God; for with God all things are possible." But science yields to experiment, and religion marches on joyful in the footsteps of Providence. Thousands among us say, "How it has been done, we know not. One thing we know, that whereas once we were drunkards, now we are sober men."

But above all, *the salvation of the soul* makes it indispensable. Temperance is not religion. Outward reformation is not religion; but by this reform a great obstacle is removed, and thousands of these miserable men may be brought into the kingdom of God. The strong chain that has been thrown around them by the "prince of the power of the air," is broken. They may be approached as they never could be before. Conviction of sin is fastened upon their conscience. Gratitude inspires their bosoms. Good men are, of choice, their companions. The dram-shop is exchanged for the house of God. A Bible is purchased. Their little ones they bring to the door of the Sabbath-school. They flee affrighted from the pit; and, through grace, many lift up their hands imploringly to heaven, as the only refuge for the outcast, the home for the weary. This has been the operation of the reform in England. Of thirty-five thousand reformed drunkards in that country, fifty-six hundred have become members of Christian churches, having hope in God and joy in the Holy Ghost. So it has been in Scotland; many there now sing of grace and glory. So it manifestly is in America, and so will it be more and more around the world, as ministers and Christians meet them in kindness and lead them to the waters of salvation.

But what can we do? How can we aid the poor unfortunate drunkard? This is the question.

All can do a little. Some can do much. Every man can get out of the way of his reform; cease setting him an example which proves his ruin; cease selling him an article which is death to the soul; discountenance the drinking usages of society, and those licensed and unlicensed dram-shops which darken the land. Every man can speak an encouraging word to the wretched inebriate; tell him of what is doing in the land, allure him and go with him to the temperance-meeting, and urge him to sign the pledge; and when he has signed, comfort and strengthen him, give him employment, give him clothing; and if he falls, raise him up, and if he falls seven times, raise him up and forgive him.

Try it, Christian brother. I know your heart beats in gratitude to God for what he has done; that he has raised up a new instrumentality for rescuing thousands of our race from the lowest degradation. It is a token of good for our country and the world. Enter into this field of labor. "You know the grace of our Lord Jesus Christ; that though he was rich, yet for our sakes he became poor, that we through his poverty might become rich." Go imitate his example; become poor, if need be, to save the lost. "Go out into the highways and hedges, and compel them to come in."

Try it, Christian philanthropist. "It is good neither to eat flesh, nor to drink wine, nor any thing whereby thy brother stumbleth, or is offended, or made weak." Sacrifices make the world happy, and God glorious.

Try it, Christian female. It is work for your sex. Woman is the greatest sufferer from intemperance: driven by it from her home; made an outcast from all the comforts of domestic love, while her babes cry for bread, and she has no relief. Lost men will listen to your words of kindness, be cheered by your benefactions, encouraged by your smiles.

Try it, young men. Have you no companions early

palsied, withered, and scathed by alcoholic fires, treading now on the verge of the drunkard's grave? Go after them in their misery. Go, thanking God that you are not as they are. Go, believing that you may save them; that they will receive you thankfully; that they must have your help, or be lost. Go, and be strong in this work. The movements of Providence call you to effort for the unfortunate and wretched, that you may pull them out of the fire. What you do in the blessed work, do quickly. O, if it be in your power to save one young man, do it quickly. Run and speak to that young man. He will thank you for it. His father will thank you. His mother will thank you. His sisters will thank you. His immortal soul, rescued and saved, will love you for ever.

TO THE POOR UNFORTUNATE DRUNKARD.

My Friend and Brother—You are poor and wretched. A horrid appetite hurries you on in the road to ruin. Abroad you are despised. Home is a desolation. A heart-broken wife weeps over you, yet does not forsake you. She hopes, she waits for your reform and for better days. Conscience bids you stop. But appetite, companions, and custom say, *One glass more.* That is a fatal glass. You rise but to fall again, and you feel that you can never reform. But you CAN REFORM. Thousands and thousands around you have reformed, and would not for worlds go back to drinking. They are happy at home; respected abroad; well dressed; well employed; have no thirst for the dreadful cup. They feel for you. They say, "Come thou with us, and we will do thee good." Come *sign the pledge*, the pledge of total abstinence. In this is your only hope. This is a certain cure. Touch not, taste not, handle not rum, brandy, whiskey, wine, cider, beer, or any thing that intoxicates, and you will be a new man, a happy man. Begin now. Try it now in the strength of the Lord. From this good hour resolve that none of these accursed drinks shall ever enter your lips. The struggle may be severe, but it will soon be over. Say then, "Come life, come death, by the help of God I will be free."

PUBLISHED BY THE AMERICAN TRACT SOCIETY.

TOM STARBOARD

AND

JACK HALYARD.

A NAUTICAL TEMPERANCE DIALOGUE.

JACK. Halloo, shipmate; what cheer? Mayhap, however, you don't choose to remember an old crony.

TOM. Why, Jack, is that you? Well, I must say, that if you hadn't hailed me I should have sailed by without knowing you. How you're altered! Who would have supposed that this weather-beaten hulk was my old messmate Jack Halyard, with whom I've soaked many a hard biscuit, and weathered many a tough gale on old Ocean? and then you used to be as trim in your rigging as the Alert herself; but now it's as full of ends as the old Wilmington brig that we used to crack so many jokes about at Barbadoes. Give me another grip, my hearty, and tell me how you come on.

Jack. Bad enough, Tom—bad enough. I'm very glad, however, to overhaul you again, and to find you so merry, and looking so fat and hearty. The world must have gone well with you, Tom.

Tom. You may well say that, Jack, and no mistake. The world has gone well with me. My appetite is good, my sleep sound; and I always take care to have a shot in the locker, and let alone a snug little sum in the seamen's savings-bank, that I've stowed away for squally times, or when I get old, so as to be independent of hospitals and retreats, and all that sort of thing. And what's more to the purpose, Jack, I try to have a clean conscience—the most comfortable of all; don't you think so?

Jack. Why yes, Tom, I do think that a clean conscience must be a very comfortable thing for a man to have. But I can't brag much of mine now-a-days; it gives me a deal of trouble sometimes.

Tom. Ah, that's bad, Jack—very bad. But come, let me hear something about you since we parted, some four years or so ago. Where have you last been, in what craft, etc.? Give me a long yarn: you used to be a famous hand at spinning long yarns, you know, Jack. Don't you remember how angry old copper-nosed Grimes used to get when the larboard watch turned in, and, instead of sleeping, we made you go ahead with the story you were on, which made him wish us all at Davy Jones' locker? Ha, ha, ha.

JACK. O yes, Tom, I remember it all very well; but—

TOM. And then, don't you recollect how we used to skylark in the lee scuppers with those jolly fellows, Buntline and Reeftackle, until the Luff had to hail, and send a Middy with his *compliments* to the *gentlemen* of the larboard watch, and to say, that if *quite agreeable to them*, less noise would be desirable? I say, Jack, you seem to have forgotten all these funny times in the Alert. Cheer up, man; don't be downhearted. Give me your flipper again; and if you are really in trouble, you may be sure, that as long as your old messmate Tom Starboard has a shot in the locker, or a drop of blood in his veins, he'll stand by Jack Halyard—aye, aye, to the last.

JACK. Thank you, Tom—thank you. You were always an honest fellow, and meant what you said; so let us steer for the sign of "The Jolly Tar," round the corner, and over a bowl of hot flip we'll talk over old times, and—

TOM. Avast there, Jack—avast, my hearty. None of your hot flip, or cold flip, or any other kind of flip for me. "The burnt child dreads the fire," as the old proverb says; and I am the child that was once pretty well scorched: but now I give it a wide berth. If you will come with me to my quiet boarding-house, "THE SAILOR'S HOME," I will be very glad to crack a joke with you; but you won't catch me in any such place as "The Jolly Tar," I can tell you. I mind what the old Philadelphia Quaker said to his son, who, as he was once coming out of a house of ill-fame, spied old Broadbrim heaving in sight, and immediately wore ship. The old chap, however, who always kept his weather-eye open, had had a squint of young graceless, and so up helm and hard after he cracked, and following him in, hailed him with, "Ah, Obadiah, Obadiah, thee should never be ashamed of *coming out*—thee should always be ashamed of *going in*." No, no, Jack, I side with friend Broadbrim: I won't enter such places.

JACK. Well, I don't know, Tom, but that you are about half right. I think, myself, that "The Jolly Tar" is not what it's cracked up to be. I am sure that neither the landlord nor the landlady look half as kindly on me as they did when I first came in, with plenty of money in my pocket. Indeed, they have been pretty rough within the last few days, and tell me that I must ship, as they want my advance towards the score run up, of the most of which I am sure I know nothing; but it's always the way.

TOM. Yes, Jack, it's always the way with such folks. The poor tar is welcomed and made much of as long as his pockets are well lined; but let them begin to lighten, and then the smiles begin to slacken off; and when the rhino is all gone, poor Jack, who was held up as such a great man, is frowned upon, and at last kicked out of doors: or if, mayhap, they have let him run up a score, he is hastily shipped off, perhaps half naked, and the advance is grabbed by the hard-hearted landlord, who made poor Jack worse than a brute with his maddening poison. Oh, Jack, how my heart has bled at witnessing the cruel impositions practised upon our poor brother sailors by these harpies. But come, I want to hear all about my old messmate. If I am not greatly out of my reckoning, grog is at the bottom of all your troubles, and long faces, and sighs, and groans. Cheer up, Jack, and unbosom yourself to your old friend and pitcher.

JACK. Well, Tom, as I know you to be a sincere fellow, I will unbosom myself. You were never nearer your right latitude than when you said that grog was at the bottom of my troubles. Yes, grog has pretty nearly used up poor Jack Halyard. A few years ago I was a light-hearted, happy fellow, and only drank because others did—not that I liked the taste particularly in those days, but I did it for good-fellowship, as it was called; and moreover, I did not like to seem odd; and when I shipped on board the man-of-war, where it was served out to us twice a day, I soon became fond of it. And you know we both used to long for the sun to get above the fore-yard, and for the afternoon middle watch, that we might splice the main-brace. Sure I am that it was *there* I first took a liking to the stuff; and O, Tom, don't you think the government will have much to answer for, in putting temptation in the way of us poor sailors? Instead of being our protector, it is our seducer. Our blood will stick in its skirts.

TOM. Yes, Jack, I think that Uncle Sam has a great deal to answer for on that tack; and I can say, too, that the love of rum that I acquired in the government service had pretty nearly fixed my flint, both for this world and the next. But still, Jack, it wont do for seamen to drink grog because the government supplies it, and think to excuse themselves by blaming it. No, no; that is a poor excuse. Men who brave the dangers of the mighty deep, as our class do, and face death in every form with unshrinking courage, ought to be able to resist such a temptation. It will be a poor reason to hand in to the Almighty when the angel summons all hands before his dread tribunal, in palliation of our drunkenness and the sins committed by us when under the influence of liquor, that the government, instead of comforting us, and fortifying us against heat and cold, etc., with coffee, and tea, and other wholesome small stores, poisoned our bodies and souls with vile rum. No, indeed, Jack, that will avail us naught in that awful day; and it will be poor consolation *in the drunkard's hell*, to blame the government. But go on.

JACK. Well, when the Alert's cruise was up, and we were paid off, about a dozen of us went to lodge with old Peter Hardheart, at the sign of the Foul Anchor; and as we had plenty of money, we thought we would have a regular blow-out. So Peter got a fiddler and some other unmentionable requisites for a jig, and we had a set-to in firstrate style. Why, our great frolic at Santa Martha, when Paddy Chips, the Irish carpenter, danced away his watch, and jacket, and tarpaulin, and nearly all his toggery, you know, and next morning came scudding along the beach towards the Alert, as she lay moored near shore, and crept on board on all-fours, like a half-drowned monkey, along the best bower, wouldn't have made a nose to it. Well, next morning I had a pretty smart touch of the horrors, and felt rather muddy about the head; but old Peter soon set us agoing again, and we kept it up for three days and three nights, carriage-riding, and dancing, and drinking, and theatre-going, etc.; and we thought the world was too little for us: when all at once old Hardheart took a round turn on us with, "I'll tell you what it is, you drunken swabs, I'll not have such goings-on in my house—my house is a decent house—you must all ship; yes, ship's the word. I must have the advance—you're more than a month's wages apiece in my debt." Tom, I was sober in an instant. My conscience smote me. In three days I had squandered the wages of a three years' cruise, and had not a dollar left to take to my poor old mother in the country, whom I had intended to go to see after the frolic was over, and give all my money to. O Tom, what a poor, pitiful, sneaking wretch I felt that I was. The two letters that I had received from her during my absence—so kind, so affectionate, and so full of fervent prayers to God that her poor boy might be preserved from the temptations that beset the sailor, and be brought safely back to her widowed arms—rushed to my remembrance, and overwhelmed me with grief; and I—I, who ought to have denied myself even innocent gratification until I had ministered to her wants, had forgotten the best of mothers, and had spent all of my hard earnings with the vilest of the vile.

TOM. Poor Jack, my heart bleeds for you; but cheer up, and go on.

JACK. Well, to shorten a long story, I was the next day bundled, when about three sheets in the wind, on board a merchantman, with an empty chest, although it was winter, old Hardheart nabbing the whole of my advance; and for two or three days, Tom, I suffered awfully from the horrors. I thought I was already in the hell to which the wicked who don't repent must go. Awake, asleep, at the helm, on the yard, in the storm, in the calm, everywhere I was haunted with the remembrance of my ingratitude to my poor dear mother—to her who had watched over me in helpless infancy and childhood; who had prayed over and for me so much; who had pinched herself to give me a snug outfit when I first went to sea; and who I knew had strained her poor old eyes in watching for the loved form of her Jack—for the papers must have apprised her of the arrival of the Alert two days after we got in. But, dear old woman, she watched in vain; Jack had forgotten his best friend; he had herded with beasts, and had became a beast himself. O Tom, what a miserable wretch I was. I sometimes tried to read in the Bible that she had given me, but it seemed as if every verse was a fiery scorpion stinging me for my crimes and ingratitude. As the ship in which I was, sailed under the temperance clause, I could get no liquor on board, and I determined to shun the accursed thing ever after; to turn over a new leaf in my log-book of life; to save my money; and to become a steady, sober lad, so that I might after a while be made a mate, and then a master, and have a shot in the locker for my dear old mother. These good resolutions lasted as long as I had no liquor; but you will see that they vanished like smoke when I came ashore, on the return of the vessel. As the wind was light in the bay in coming up, we were boarded by several boats from sailor boarding-houses, and among the rest by old Hardheart. When I saw him I fairly gritted my teeth with rage, for I had not forgotten how he treated me before; but he came up to me in so kind a manner, and inquired so affectionately after my health, and seemed to feel such a real interest in me, that I swallowed all his blarney and coaxing, and at last agreed to stop with him again for the night that I would be in the city, intending, the moment that we should be paid off next day, to steer straight for my old mother, if, mayhap, my cruelty had not broken her heart; and moreover, determining not to drink a drop of liquor in his house.

Tom. Dear Jack, I trust that you were able to keep that resolution.

Jack. You shall hear, Tom. When we got to old Peter's, I found, as usual, a good many people in the house; and the old woman and the girls were rejoiced to see me again, as they made out. The old woman at once proposed that we should celebrate my safe return in the big punch-bowl; but Peter said, "No, Jack has turned cold-water man, and he can't drink; but we'll drink for him." I observed that Peter sneered whilst he said this, and so did all the rest, and it galled me a good deal. While the punch was brewing, some of the men whispered, "*White-liver*"—"*poor sneak*"—"*no sailor;*" and after the punch had passed round amongst them once or twice, I thought I would just take *one swig*, to show them that I was not the poor sneak they took me for, and no more. But, Tom, that one swig sealed my doom: THE DANGER'S ALWAYS IN THE FIRST GLASS. The men cheered, and said they knew I was a man, and a *real seaman*, by the cut of my jib, and that I was too good for the Temperance Society; and the girls cast sheep's-eyes at me, and said that I was just the chap to run away with a woman's heart, and that my eyes were not made for the good of my soul, and such-like foolish and wicked talk. My weak head could not stand the punch, nor my vain heart the flattery, and I was soon regularly used up. Instead of having a dollar to take home to my poor old mother, I found myself, in a few days, the second time penniless; was forced to ship again; got back; the same scenes were acted over; and here I am, the miserable wretch that you see me—light in purse, sick in body, and tormented in mind; the past a curse, the future despair.

TOM. Well, Jack, I must say, that your case is hard enough. But don't despair, my boy. Many a poor fellow who has hung to a plank in mid-ocean until he thought it was surely all over with him, has been picked up and saved. The same kind Providence who has watched over us, and preserved us in so many dangers, will not desert us. What we have to do is, to turn from every evil way, and humbly trusting in the merits of Christ our Saviour, look up to him for mercy, repent of all sin, and resolve, in his strength, to fear and obey him in future. And I trust, Jack, that all will yet be well with you; and I rejoice that I have wherewithal to give you a lift towards fitting you out, and heading you off towards your old mother.

JACK. A thousand thanks, Tom—a thousand thanks. "A friend in need is a friend indeed." You have lightened my mind of a heavy cargo of care by your kind offer, made with the frankness of a sailor, and which I most gratefully accept. And now that I have finished my long and mournful yarn, it is your turn; and to tell the truth, Tom, I am exceedingly anxious to hear all about you. So heave ahead.

TOM. Well, Jack, here goes. You know when we left the Alert we had plenty of rhino in our pockets. So I intended to steer straight for my native village, in the state of Pennsylvania, where I had left my old father and a sweet, dear little sister, three years before, to cheer their hearts with a sight of their sailor-boy, and to make them comfortable with the cash. Unfortunately, as I passed through Philadelphia, I went with some wild fellows to the theatre—to so many the gateway to hell—and having grog enough aboard to make me pretty crank and foolish, I soon found myself in the third tier among the painted fire-ships; and as the proverb says, "When the wine is in, the wit is out," so I was led as the simple one of Scripture, "like an ox to the slaughter." Truly, Jack, "her house is the way to hell, going down to the chambers of death." The consequences you may readily imagine. I was made to drink until I was quite insensible; was robbed of all my money, and then turned out of doors into the cold street. When I came to myself it was nearly sunrise, and I could not imagine how I had got there. My head swam, my bones ached, and I felt as if it was "blue Monday" with me. I staggered off, not knowing where I was or whither I went, for half an hour or more, when I sat down on a flight of steps, and fell asleep. When I awoke, all the horrors of my situation rushed upon my mind; and O, Jack, I felt the raging hell in my bosom that you did when Hardheart first shipped you off. How sunk and degraded in my own eyes. I determined, however, upon going home, as the distance was short—only fifteen miles—and a bitter journey it was, Jack. I thought on my madness and folly, and wondered, with the poor ignorant Indian, why people would put an enemy into their mouths to steal away their brains. Instead of going to meet my dear father and sweet little sister with a joyous face and a pocket full of money, with which to make their hearts sing for joy, I was returning, like the prodigal son, from feeding upon husks with swine—poor, and with a heavy heart and a gnawing conscience. O the hell, Jack, of a bad conscience. It is the beginning of the existence of the worm that never dies, and of the fire that is never quenched. It is a foretaste of that eternal hell prepared for those who persist in violating God's holy laws. Well, I reached home at last, and a sad home I found it. The sand of my dear father's glass was almost run out—the poor old man was about slipping his cable. But O, Jack, how happy he looked; and so calm and resigned to the will of his heavenly Father, as he said—ready to set sail on the great voyage of eternity, or to stay and weather more of the rough gales of adversity in this life, just as God pleased. He held out his thin, white hand to me, and welcomed his boy, and thanked the Lord that he had given him a sight of me before his eyes were sealed in death. My poor sister hung weeping on my neck. But, Jack, bad as I then felt, I felt a thousand times worse when my dear old father beckoned me to him, and laying his hand on my head, prayed that God—his God, the Friend who had stood by him in every gale and tempest of life, and proved true to him till the last—would bless his dear boy Thomas, and take him into his especial keeping, and lead him to the blessed Jesus; and finally, when the voyage of life was over, that we all three might join the dear mother who had gone before us, at the right hand of the throne of God, to bless and praise his holy name for ever. He then put Susan's hand into mine, and blessed us both again, and said, "Thomas, I leave this dear, precious girl with you; watch over her, cherish and protect her, and be to her both father and brother. May the great God bless you, my dear children, and make you his. I have but little time to say more, for the icy hand of death is on me; my Saviour beckons, and I must away. Come, Lord Jesus." With these words the glorified spirit of my beloved father winged its flight to mansions in the skies—to that "rest prepared for the people of God;" and I was left with my weeping sister, almost stupefied with grief. Three days after, the clods of the valley covered the mortal remains of my honored parent, and then poor Sue and I felt that we were all in all to each other. I told her of all my troubles, and that I had robbed her by my vileness; but the dear girl kissed me, and said, "Dear brother, do not mourn on my account; I am young and healthy, and can easily support myself by my needle; but mourn on your own account—mourn over your sins, and your ingratitude to the great Being who has upheld you and preserved you in so many dangers, known and unknown, on the mighty deep. And promise me, dear brother, that you will never touch another drop of liquor again; it will be the first step towards reformation."

Jack. Poor dear girl. Of course, Tom, you promised?

Tom. Aye, aye, Jack, I did promise; and what's more, I kept my promise. But you must know how I was able to do it. Before I left the village a great Temperance-meeting was held there, and several of the friends of the cause delivered addresses, in which they showed so clearly and conclusively the great evils resulting from the use of spirituous liquors, that nearly every body in the village signed the pledge of total abstinence—at least, all of the respectable part of the community, and even a good many sots who had been given up as incorrigible. O Jack, if you had heard the awful accounts they gave of broken-hearted wives and beggared children; of the widows and orphans made by rum; of the misery and degradation attendant upon it; of the crimes committed under its influence—robbery, murder, suicide—leading to the penitentiary, the gallows, and death, it would have made your blood freeze in your veins. And these accounts were all true, Jack, for many of the horrible scenes had taken place about the neighborhood.

JACK. I don't doubt it at all, Tom. And moreover, I believe that not one half of the misery caused by rum—no, not the thousandth part, is ever known by the public. Many an injured wife and suffering and ruined child have concealed the history of their woes from the eye and ear of the world, and buried their sorrows deep in their own bosoms.

TOM. True, Jack, or breathed them only to their God, whose ear is always open to the cry of the afflicted, and whose hand is always ready to aid them. Well, I signed the pledge, which I am sure has a great effect in restraining one when tempted to swerve; for what man of honorable feelings would wilfully violate his word and promise? and a few weeks after, having fixed my sister comfortably with a pious milliner, I went to Philadelphia, and there shipped with a temperance captain for a South American port. O Jack, what a blessed voyage that was to me. On the first day out, all hands were called aft to the break of the quarter-deck, when the captain, who was a pious man, told us in a few words, that it was his practice to have "family worship" every morning and evening in the cabin, and he hoped that all his men would cheerfully unite with him. The captain was so kind in his manner, and appeared to be so sincere, and as he seemed, moreover, to regard us as human beings with immortal souls, and not as brute beasts, out of whose muscles and sinews he cared only to get plenty of work, we all willingly consented. So at sundown all hands were mustered in the cabin, except the man at the helm, as the weather was mild and the ship under easy sail; and the captain prayed fervently that God would give us a safe and pleasant passage, and bring us all to think of our souls. He then read a portion of Scripture, which he explained to us, and after singing a couple of hymns we were dismissed.

JACK. Ah, Tom, good captains make good crews, all the world over; and I'll warrant there was neither knocking down nor mutiny aboard of that vessel.

TOM. No, Jack; there was nothing but peace, and quietness, and good order; every man knew his place and did his duty; and the captain was like a father to us. He had a spare quadrant, which each of us used in turn in taking the daily observation, under his own eye; and he taught us how to work our reckoning; so that in the course of the voyage some of us got to know a good deal about navigation. And, Jack, I had good evidence of the value of religion also, particularly when we encountered the equinoctial gale in the southern tropic, and were near going down. Then it was, Jack, when we had lost our foretopmast, and our maintopsail and most of our other sails had been blown into ribbons; when the sea had carried away nearly all our bulwarks, and swept the decks clear of caboose, longboat, etc.; and the pumps were constantly going—at one time to the tune of more than a thousand strokes an hour—to keep the vessel free; and the axes were at hand, ready to cut away the masts when the worst should come—that our captain was calm and collected. He seemed to be as patient and submissive to the will of God, as if he had been *born* a Christian; and he gave many a kind word of encouragement to his men. What a difference there must have been between him and the vulgar, bullying man that Sam Bowsprit once sailed with, who was a wolf when there was no danger, and a sheep when there was; but it is always so with your bullies, whether in the cabin or the forecastle. To return to my story: in two or three days the gale spent its fury, and we reached our port in safety. One day while in port, in rummaging my chest, I discovered at the bottom a little package neatly tied up, which, upon opening, I found to contain two small books, called, "James' Anxious Inquirer after Salvation," and "Baxter's Call to the Unconverted;" with a few touching lines from my dear sister, earnestly beseeching me to look to my soul, and to read my Bible and these little books, and never to forget my God. Jack, this went to my heart like an arrow. It brought fresh to my mind the death-bed scene of my dear father, and I fell upon my knees, and, for the first time, *really* prayed to God. Yes, Jack, I then prayed indeed. I felt my ingratitude to God to some extent, and I began to see what a sinner I had been. I at once commenced reading my Bible and the little books, that I might learn more of my lost condition, and how to flee from the wrath to come. In the course of a day or two the captain observed that I was uneasy in my mind, and called me to him to ask if he could do any thing to aid me. I frankly told him all my trouble, and he at once pointed me to "the Lamb of God, who takes away the sin of the world." He then gradually and clearly unfolded to me the great gospel plan of redemption; and kneeling down together, he prayed most fervently for me. After a few days of deep solicitude and constant prayer to Almighty God, he, in his infinite mercy, shed light upon my soul, and I felt that Christ had died for me—*even me.* O Jack, then it was that I first tasted true joy—that joy which the world cannot give, and which the world cannot take away; that peace of mind which passeth understanding. And with God's aid, I have ever since tried to walk close in the way prescribed by him; and I trust that my dear father's dying prayer will indeed be answered, and that we shall all meet in heaven.

JACK. Well, Tom, I congratulate you, for although I make no pretensions to religion myself, I sincerely respect it in others—that is, where it is genuine, as I am sure it is in your case; but I can't stand playing soldier in religion, Tom, as I have seen it done by some hypocrites.

TOM. So much the worse for them, Jack. But, my dear fellow, I advise you, as a friend, not to put off seeking religion another day. *This day* may be your last, Jack. Don't you remember the story of the rich man in Scripture, who said, "Soul, thou hast much goods laid up for many years; take thine ease, eat, drink, and be merry?" But God said unto him, "Thou fool, this night thy soul shall be required of thee." O Jack, don't put off this most important of all works to a dying bed, for you may not have one; you may be called into eternity at a moment's warning. You surely have not forgotten the awful death of swearing Joe Swifter, who was shaken off the yard into the boiling sea in that terrible night off the Canaries, when we were all aloft close reefing the Alert's maintopsail? And, Jack, can you ever forget his cry of agony as we shot ahead in the gale, forced to leave him to perish? I am sure it will haunt *me* to my dying hour. Poor Joe, thou wert called with all thy sins upon thy head into the presence of an offended God.

JACK. Poor Joe. I remember it as if it had occurred but yesterday, Tom. It was an awful warning; and I don't think there were three oaths sworn on board the Alert for three days after. To tell the truth, Tom, I have had some queer feelings about death and the judgment, lately; and although I tried hard to drown them in grog, they would come up in spite of me. But I'll tell you more about it when we reach your lodgings, where we will be quiet and uninterrupted. You got safely back, I hope?

TOM. Yes, Jack, thanks to a kind Providence. I made two more voyages with the same captain; and I expect to go with him next trip as mate. I have been able to send my sister a snug little sum to keep her comfortable; and I have something handsome in the seamen's savings bank, as I told you before; together with a clear head and a happy heart; trusting in my God, and loving all who bear his image. Now, Jack, what do you think of temperance?

JACK. Think of it? Why, Tom, I always *thought* well of it, though I can't say that I have latterly *practised* it much; but I like it now better than ever. I have ruminated a good deal upon its evils, both at sea and ashore. Don't you think, Tom, that rum is at the bottom of nine out of ten of the floggings that take place in the navy?

TOM. Yes, indeed, Jack, I am sure of it. And I think, moreover, that if it were discarded *entirely* from the government and merchant service, insubordination and floggings would be of rare occurrence in the one, and trouble and mutiny in the other. And there would be fewer vessels and lives lost in the merchant-service, in the bargain.

JACK. I have often thought, Tom, what a degrading thing that flogging is. It sinks a man below the level of a brute, both in his own and the eyes of others. It seems to me that if I had ever been triced up at the gratings, and had a stroke of the cat, it would have completely crushed my spirit, if it had not broken my heart outright.

TOM. I think it would have had the same effect on me too, Jack. I am sure I could not have stood it.

JACK. And, Tom, to show more of the bad effects of liquor, I remember that I was once in Port-au-Prince, in the island of St. Domingo, during the sickly season, when a fearful mortality raged among the shipping, so that every vessel lost some of her men; most of them bringing on the yellow-fever by their intemperance. There were three ships that were left without a man; all were swept off, from the captain to the cook.

TOM. Awful, Jack, awful. I have also seen many a stout and noble-hearted tar, in those yellow-fever countries, stowed away under a foot of earth for the landcrabs to feed upon, just from drinking rum, or the strong brandy of the country. I'll tell you what it is, Jack, when the coppers are scalded by rum, physic can't get a hold—it is just like casting anchor on a rocky bottom—and so the grip of the grim monster Death is sure. The only safe man there, as well as everywhere else, indeed, is the teetotaler.

JACK. What is a teetotaler, Tom? I have often heard the term, without fully knowing what it meant.

TOM. A teetotaler, Jack, is one who conscientiously abstains from every description of intoxicating drink: rum, whiskey, brandy, gin, cordials, wine, cider, ale, and even beer.

JACK. What, Tom, you don't mean to say that you give such a wide berth to *beer?* Tell that to the marines, for old sailors won't believe it.

TOM. I do say it, Jack. I give even beer a wide berth. Don't you know that it contains alcohol? And what is perhaps worse, there is but little beer and ale made for sale that does not contain many hurtful ingredients—poisonous drugs. No, no; nothing for me that can in the slightest degree affect my noble reason, that great gift of Almighty God. Pure cold water—Adam's sparkling, life-invigorating ale—and coffee and tea, are my beverages. Try them once, Jack, and the word of an honest sailor for it, you will never go back to alcohol, or any of its accursed family.

JACK. Well, Tom, I think I will. The fact is, you seem to be so well in body and happy in mind, so comfortable and respectable in worldly matters, and speak so cheeringly of another world—to which I know that the rapid current of time is hurrying us both—that I'll follow in your wake, and try to make a little headway in these things myself.

TOM. Well said, my hearty. Give me another shake of your honest fist. Now I begin to recognize my old true-hearted friend and messmate Jack Halyard in his early days, when we swore friendship to each other across the sea-chest, on board the Alert. You are the man for me, Jack; so come up with me at once to the Sailor's Home, and I'll rig you out a little more decently—make you look a little more shipshape—and to-night we will go to the great temperance-meeting at the seamen's bethel chapel, and you shall sign the pledge, which will be the wisest act of your life,

Jack, as I'll wager a barrel of pork against a mouldy biscuit: aye, I'll warrant me you will say so at some future day. There will be plenty of blue-jackets there that will lend a hand in so good a cause.

Jack. Well, heave ahead, old messmate. I did think of *tapering off*—quitting by degrees—but perhaps the safest and easiest plan will be, *to break off at once.*

Tom. That is the way, Jack, the only true way. Tapering off is not what it is cracked up to be. It is very hazardous; for it keeps up excitement, and the taste of the liquor hangs about the palate. Don't you remember Ben Hawser, one of the best maintopmen of the Alert—he who saved the first Luff from drowning at Port Mahon, when he fell overboard from the cutter?

Jack. Surely I do, Tom. Do you suppose I could forget such a noble-hearted fellow as Ben Hawser—as fine a fellow as ever laid out upon a yard, or stood at the wheel; and such a firstrate marlinespike seaman in the bargain? No, indeed.

Tom. You are right, Jack. He was a noble fellow, and a thorough seaman. There was nothing of the lubber about poor Ben: always the first man at his duty, and ready to share his last copper with a fellow-mortal in distress, whether seaman or landsman. Well, Ben once got into a great frolic ashore, and kicked up such a bobbery that the watchman clapped him in limbo for the night; and the justice next morning gave him such a clapper-clawing with his tongue, and bore down upon him so hard with his *reprimands*, as I think the lawyers call it, and raked him so severely fore and aft with his good advice, to wind up with, that Ben felt pretty sheepish; and, as he told us afterwards, didn't know whether he was on his head or his heels—on the truck, or on the keelson. He felt so sore about it, and so much ashamed of himself, that he did not touch a drop for six weeks. He then thought he would take it *moderately*—just enough to keep the steam up or, as some folks say, he thought he would be a *temperate drinker*. O, Jack, that *temperate drinking* is a famous net of old Satan's to catch fools in. Your temperate drinker treads on slippery ground; for as I verily believe that alcohol is one of the most active imps for the destruction of both body and soul, the temperate drinker is too often gradually led on by the fiend, until the habit becomes fixed and inveterate; and he drags a galling chain, each day riveted more strongly, and the poor wretch hourly becomes more callous to shame, until he sinks into the grave—*the drunkard's grave.*

Jack. But, Tom, you don't mean to say that poor Ben's reel has been run off in that style, do you?

Tom. Indeed, Jack, it is true, and sorry am I that it is so. Yes, I followed the worn-out hulk of Ben Hawser to the dark and silent grave a fortnight ago. He slipped his cable in the prime of life; and all along of *temperate drinking* at first. Ben, like many other men, thought he was strong-minded, and could stop at a certain point; but he found, to his cost, that king Alcohol was stronger, and that when once he had forged his chains around his victim, he was sure of him, unless the grace of a merciful God intervened, and plucked him as a brand from the burning. So I advise every one to beware of *temperate drinking*. Give it a wide berth, or it may wreck you for time and for eternity.

One thing more, Jack. I would like your temperate drinker to pause, and reflect upon the fact, that the quantity of brandy or rum that he took at a drink, when he commenced this downhill course, has been gradually increased;

so that in the second year, what had been quite sufficient to please his palate and produce all the desired effects in the first, was then insipidly small; and more so in the third year, if, mayhap, he could with any decency lay claim to the title of *temperate drinker* so long. Jack, this is a fearful reflection for one of this class of the slaves of alcohol; but let him think upon it when quite free from excitement, say after two or three days' abstinence—if he can abstain that long just to cool off for reflection—and I'll warrant he will tremble at the prospect.

Besides, Jack, the *influence* of your temperate drinker is ten times worse than that of the confirmed and notorious drunkard; for it is not likely that any one in his senses would desire to copy the confirmed sot in his beastliness. No, indeed; he would shrink with horror from the intoxicating bowl, if he felt sure that such would be the result to him, if he indulged. But he should remember, that no one ever became a sot *at once;* the degradation was by degrees. And it may be that your temperate drinker is a respectable and thriving man in the eyes of the world—say a great merchant, or lawyer, or master of a ship—and small folks do not imagine they are in any danger when they see such men stand fast, as they think: but they had all better remember the advice in Scripture, "Let him that thinketh he standeth, take heed lest he fall;" and so they follow in the wake, and perhaps nine out of ten go down to the grave *drunkards;* often, I am sure, in company with the very men whose example they thought so safe, but which led them to certain ruin. It is an awful thought, Jack, that we have been the means of misleading others, either by example or precept; and one that will weigh like lead upon the conscience of many a man on his death-bed. No, no; my motto is,

"TOUCH NOT, TASTE NOT, HANDLE NOT." The wise man of Scripture knew what he was about when he said, "Look not upon the wine when it is red, when it giveth his color in the cup; at the last it biteth like a serpent, and stingeth like an adder." The same wise man said also, that "the drunkard and the glutton shall come to poverty." But, Jack, what are poverty and shame, bad as they are, in comparison with the loss of the soul? Think of that—*the loss of the immortal soul*—for God says, that neither thieves, nor drunkards, nor any thing that defileth, shall enter heaven. And O, Jack, to think of being cast into hell for ever, with the devil and his angels; how awful! *but such must be the fate of the unrepentant drunkard.*

JACK. Awful, indeed, Tom. I am now fully persuaded that you are right; and so I'll follow your good example, and sign the teetotal pledge. And what is more, I'll try to be a Christian too, for I believe that religion is the best security against every kind of temptation.

TOM. I like that, Jack; it is truth itself. So we will shape our course for the Sailor's Home, under the direction of that noble institution, "The American Seamen's Friend Society;" there you will be out of the way of temptation, and there is a good deal in that—and to-night we will go to the Bethel. By the way, Jack, you can't think what excellent places these Homes are for the poor tempest-tossed mariner; and how snug and comfortable we all are there. The rules of the houses are excellent; neither swearing nor drinking is allowed; and every night and morning we unite with the families in worship; and on the Sabbath, and some of the evenings of the week, we are kindly invited to the Bethel chapel, where we have excellent preaching on the word of God; and in the family prayers, the good of us poor sailors, for time and eternity, is not forgotten, I can tell you. It reminds me of the days of my boyhood, when my dear father called us together, morning and evening, to praise God; and also of the happy time I have spent with my present good captain.

And then, Jack, when any of us are sick they are so kind and attentive—just like our own dear mothers and sisters. I saw how kindly poor Martin Gray was treated during his long illness, by the manager—a worthy old salt—and his excellent family; and how they smoothed his dying pillow, and did all they could to make his way easy towards the dark valley of the shadow of death. Oh, Jack, it is a great thing to fall in with real Christians at such a time. It makes one think of the poor man in Scripture who fell among thieves, and had his wounds dressed and care taken of him by the good Samaritan. Aye, aye, Jack; and I know, moreover, that the good example and excellent advice in these houses have been the means, in the Lord's hands, of saving both the body and soul of many a poor neglected, weather-beaten tar, who would otherwise have fallen into the jaws of the devouring sharks who are always on the watch, with open mouths, to prey upon the poor son of ocean, and to swallow him up without pity or remorse.

Jack. Well, heave ahead, my hearty; I'm the lad that won't flinch. So, three cheers for the glorious Temperance cause, for Sailor's Homes and Bethels, and for the mothers, wives, sisters, and sweethearts of all true-hearted seamen. And let every jolly tar who loves his family and domestic peace, and wants to do his duty and be respected in this world, and lay an anchor to windward of another and better world, toe the plank, and sign the pledge right off the reel. Huzza, huzza, huzza!

THE OX SERMON.

Among the laws given by the divine Lawgiver through Moses to the Jews, was the following: "If an ox gore a man or a woman that they die, then the ox shall be surely stoned; but the owner of the ox shall be quit. But if the ox *were wont to push* with his horn in time past, and it hath been testified to his owner, and he hath not kept him in, but he hath killed a man or a woman, the ox shall be stoned, and his owner also shall be put to death." Exod. 21 : 28, 29.

The principle of this law is a very plain one, and a very broad one—here applied in a specific case, but extending to ten thousand others. It is this. Every man is responsible to God for the evils which result from his selfishness, or his indifference to the welfare of others.

Ages before this law was given, God says to Noah, "Your blood of your lives will I require: at the hand of every beast will I require it, and at the hand of man." A stigma shall be fixed upon man or beast that shall destroy him who is made after the similitude of God. But why, in the case first supposed, is the owner quit, or guiltless? Simply because the death is not in any way the result of his carelessness or of his selfishness. From any thing within his knowledge, he had no reason to expect such a result. But if the ox hath been *wont to push* with his horns, and he knew it, he shall be responsible for the consequences, whatever they may be; for he had every reason to expect that mischief would be done, and took no measures to prevent it. And if the ox kill a man or woman, the owner hath done the murder, and he shall be put to death. Why? The death was the result of his selfishness, or his indifference to the lives of others. And according to the law of God, his life shall go for it. The principle of this law is a principle of common-sense.

You see a fellow-creature struggling in the water. You know that he can never deliver himself. And you know that a very little assistance, such as you can render, will rescue him from a watery grave. You look on and pass by. True, you did not thrust him in. But he dies by your neglect. His blood will be upon your head. At the bar of God, and at the bar of conscience, you are his murderer. Why? You did not kill him. Neither did the owner of the ox lift a hand. *But he shall surely be put to death.* You had no malice, neither had he. You did not intend his death—at the very worst, you did not care. This is just his crime. He did not care. He turned loose a wild, fiery, ungovernable animal, knowing him to be such; and what mischief that animal might do, or what suffering he might cause, *he did not care.* But God held him responsible.

Every man is responsible for evils which result from his own selfishness or indifference to the lives of men. In other words, to make a man responsible for results, it is not necessary to prove that he has malice, or that he intended the results. The highwayman has no malice against him he robs and murders, nor does he desire his death, but his money; and if he can get the money, he does not care. And he robs and murders because he loves himself and does not care for others; acting in a different way, but on the same selfish principle with the owner of the ox; and on the very same principle is he held responsible.

In the trial of the owner of the ox, the only questions to be asked were these two: Was the ox *wont to push* with his horn in time past? Did the owner *know it* when he let him loose? If both these questions were answered in the affirmative, the owner was responsible for all the consequences. This is a rule which God himself has established.

Is INTOXICATING LIQUOR wont to produce misery, and wretchedness, and death? Has this been testified to those who make and deal in it as a beverage? If these two things can be established, the inference is inevitable—they are responsible on a principle perfectly intelligible, a principle recognized and proclaimed, and acted upon by God himself.

Turn then your attention to these two facts. 1. Intoxicating liquor *is wont to produce misery.* 2. Those who make or traffic in it, *know* this.

1. Upon the first point it will be sufficient to remind you of the hopes which intoxicating liquor has blasted, and the tears it has caused to flow. Let any one of us count up the number of its victims which we have known—consider their character and standing in society—their once happy families and prospects, and what a fearful change has a few years' use of strong drink produced. Very few but remember twenty, thirty, fifty, or one hundred families ruined in this way. Some of them were once our intimate friends—and their story is soon told.

They drank occasionally, for the sake of company, or merely for exhilaration. The relish for stimulants was thus acquired, and habits of dissipation formed. They became idle, and of course uneasy. And they continued to drink, partly to gratify taste and partly to quiet conscience. They saw the ruin that was coming upon them, and they made some earnest but ineffectual struggles against it. But the resistance became weaker and weaker—by and by the struggle is ended—they float with the current, and where are they? One has been found by the temperance reformation, a mere wreck in property, character, body, and mind, and reclaimed. Another is dead: his constitution could not bear his continued dissipation. Another died in a fit; another was found by the road-side one cold morning, a stiffened corpse. Another was thrown from his horse, and is a cripple for life, but still can contrive means to pay a daily visit to the dram-shop. Another is a mere vagabond, unprincipled and shameless—wandering from shop to shop, a fit companion for the lowest company, a nuisance to society and a curse to his kindred. Another is in the penitentiary for a crime which he committed in a drunken frolic.

Go into the crowded court-house and you may see another; his countenance haggard and ghastly, and his eye wildly rolling in despair. What has he done? One night, after spending all his money for drink, and loitering about till all the shops were closed, he returned to his miserable habitation. He found a few coals on the hearth, and his wife and children sitting by them. He threw one child this way and another that, for he was cold. His wife remonstrated, and withal told him that what little fire there was was none of his providing. With many a horrid oath he declared he would not be scolded after that sort. He would let her know who should govern, and by way of supporting his authority, beat her brains out with the last remaining stick of wood. He did not mean to kill her. Her dying struggles brought him to his senses, and he stood horror-struck. He would give almost any thing that the deed were not done. If that could restore her to life, he would be almost ready to give a pledge never to taste intoxicating liquor again. Now look at the wretchedness of his family. For years he has made very little provision for them ; they have lived as they could, half naked and half starved, and not educated at all—with a most wretched example before their eyes. What encouragement had the wife or the children to attempt any thing—to make any exertion ? The children are abused and trampled on at home, and they grow up without self-respect, without shame, and without principle. Can any thing good be expected of them ? And if they do rise, it must be through a world of difficulty.

How many thousand families have been ruined in some such way as this. The father was a drunkard, and the mother—what could she do ? She endured, hoping against hope—and for the children's sake bore up against the current ; and many a time disguised a sad despairing heart under a joyful countenance, till at length she died of a broken heart, or died by the hands of him who had sworn to protect her.

These, and things like these, are the effects of intoxicating liquor—not casual, accidental, but common, natural effects, seen everywhere, in every town, in every neighborhood, and in every connection. Look which way we will, we see some of these effects. The greatest wretchedness which human nature in this world is called to endure, is connected with the use of inebriating drink. There is nothing else that degrades and debases man like it—nothing so mean that a drunkard will not stoop to it—nothing too base for him to do to obtain his favorite drink. Nothing else so sinks the whole man—so completely destroys not only all moral principle, but all self-respect, all regard to character, all shame, all human feeling. The drunkard can break out from every kind of endearing connection, and break over every kind of restraint; so completely extinct is human feeling, that he can be drunk at the funeral of his dearest relative, and call for drink in the last accents of expiring nature.

Now look at a human being, whom God has made for noble purposes, and endowed with noble faculties, degraded, disgraced, polluted, unfit for heaven, and a nuisance on earth. He is the centre of a circle—count up his influence in his family and his neighborhood—the wretchedness he endures, and the wretchedness he causes—count up the tears of a wretched wife who curses the day of her espousals, and of wretched children who curse the day of their birth. To all this positive evil which intoxicating liquor has caused, add the happiness which but for it this family might have enjoyed and communicated. Go through a neighborhood or a town in this way, count up all the misery which follows in the train of intoxicating liquor, and you will be ready to ask, Can the regions of eternal death send forth any thing more deadly? Wherever it goes, the same cry may be heard—lamentation, and mourning, and woe; and whatever things are pure, or lovely, or venerable, or of good report, fall before it. These are its effects. Can any man deny that "the ox is wont to push with his horn?"

2. *Has this been testified to the owner?* Are the makers and venders aware of its effects? The effects are manifest, and they have eyes, ears, and understandings, as well as others. They know that whatever profit they make is at the expense of human life or comfort; and that the tide which is swelled by their unhallowed merchandise sweeps ten thousand yearly to temporal and eternal ruin. But this is not all. The attention of the public has been strongly turned to this subject. The minds of men have been enlightened,

and their responsibility pressed home upon them. The subject has been presented to them in a new light, and men cannot but see the absurdity of reprobating the tempted, while the tempter is honored—of blaming drunkards, and holding in reputation those whose business it is to make drunkards.

But are the makers of intoxicating liquor aware of its effects? Look at the neighborhood of a distillery—an influence goes forth from that spot which reaches miles around—a kind of constraining influence, that brings in the poor, and wretched, and thirsty, and vicious. Those who have money bring it—those who have none, bring corn—those who have neither, bring household furniture—those who have nothing, bring themselves and pay in labor. Now the maker knows all these men, and knows their temperament, and probably knows their families. He can calculate effects, and he sends them off, one to die by the way, another to abuse his family, and another just ready for any deed of wickedness. Will he say that he is not responsible, and like Cain ask, "Am I my brother's keeper?" He knew what might be the result, and for a mere pittance of gain was willing to risk it. Whether this man should abuse his family, or that man die by the way, so his purpose was answered, he did not care. The ox was wont to push with his horn, and he knew it; and for a little paltry gain he let him loose, and God will support his law by holding him responsible for the consequences.

But a common excuse is, that "very little of our manufacture is used in the neighborhood; we send it off." And are its effects any less deadly? In this way you avoid *seeing* the effects, and poison strangers instead of neighbors. What would you say to a man who traded in clothes infected with the smallpox, and who would say by way of apology, that he sent them off—he did not sell any in the neighborhood? Good man! he is willing to send disease and death all abroad; but he is too kind-hearted to expose his neighbors. Would you not say to him, you may send them off, but you cannot send off the responsibility? The eye of God goes with them, and all the misery which they cause will be charged to you. So we say to the man who sends off his intoxicating liquor.

"But if I do not make it and traffic in it, somebody else will." What sin or crime cannot be excused in this way? I know of a plot to rob my neighbor; if I do not plunder him, somebody else will. Is it a privilege to bear the responsibility of sending abroad pestilence and misery and death? "Our cause is going down," thought Judas, "and a price is set upon the head of our Master, and if I do not betray him somebody else will. And why may not I as well pocket the money as another?" If you consider it a privilege to pocket the wages of unrighteousness, do so. But do not pretend to be the friend of God or man while you count it a privilege to insult the one and ruin the other?

Says another, "I wish it were banished from the earth. But then what can I do?" What can you do? You can keep one man clear; you can wash your own hands of this wretched business. And if you are not willing to do that, very little reliance can be placed on your good wishes. He that is unjust in the least, is unjust also in much. I can hardly conceive any thing more inconsistent with every generous feeling, every noble principle, than the traffic in intoxicating liquor at the present day. The days of ignorance on this subject have passed by; every man acts with his eyes open.

Look at the shop and company of the retailer. There he stands in the midst of dissipation, surrounded by the most degraded and filthy of human beings, in the last stages of earthly wretchedness. His business is to kindle strife, to encourage profanity, to excite every evil passion, to destroy all salutary fears, to remove every restraint, and to produce a recklessness that regards neither God nor man. And how often in the providence of God is he given over to drink his own poison, and to become the most wretched of this wretched company. Who can behold an instance of this kind without feeling that God is just. "He sunk down into the pit which he made; in the net which he hid is his own foot taken."

Another will say, "I neither make nor traffic in it." But you drink it occasionally, and your example goes to support the use of it. You see its tremendous effects, and yet you receive it into your house and bid it God speed. As far as your influence supports it and gives it currency, so far are you a partaker of its evil deeds. If you lend your influence to make the path of ruin respectable, or will not help to affix disgrace to that path, God will not hold you guiltless. You cannot innocently stand aside and do nothing.

A deadly poison is circulating over the land, carrying disease and desolation and death in its course. The alarm has been given. Its deadly effects have been described, seen, and felt. Its victims are of every class; and however wide the difference in fortune, education, intellect, it brings them to the same dead level. An effort has been made to stay the plague, and a success surpassing all expectation has crowned the effort. Still, the plague rages to an immense extent. What will every good citizen do? Will he not clear his house, his shop, his premises of it? Will he not take every precaution to defend himself against it, and use his influence and his exertions to diminish its circulation and thus diminish human misery? If he fears God or regards man, can he stop short of this? Can he, in his recklessness and selfishness say, "Let others take care of themselves—I'll make no promises—I'll not be bound—I am in no danger?" If he can speak and act thus, and stands aloof, and continues to drink, is he not guilty, and with the distiller and vender accountable to God for the perpetuation of these mighty evils, which but for his coöperation and agency must soon cease to exist? "I speak as unto wise men; judge ye what I say."

PUBLISHED BY THE AMERICAN TRACT SOCIETY.

www.ingramcontent.com/pod-product-compliance
Lightning Source LLC
LaVergne TN
LVHW010143110826
845151LV00002B/411

* 9 7 8 1 4 2 5 5 3 8 3 6 1 *